Teaching and Learning

Teaching and Learning

Philosophical, Psychological, Curricular Applications

DIANE LAPP
HILARY BENDER
STEPHAN ELLENWOOD
Boston University

MARTHA JOHN
Bowie State College

Macmillan Publishing Co., Inc.
NEW YORK

Collier Macmillan Publishers
LONDON

Dedicated to the learning of all children
but especially to the total human development of
Eric and Shannon
Paul and Marc
Heather
F. J., Bruce, and David

Macmillan Publishing Co., Inc.
866 Third Avenue, New York, New York 10022
Collier-Macmillan Canada, Ltd.

Library of Congress Cataloging in Publication Data
Main entry under title:

Teaching and learning.
Includes bibliographies and index.
1. Teaching. 2. Learning, Psychology of.
I. Lapp, Diane. [DNLM: 1. Learning. 2. Teaching.
LB1028 T253]
LB1025.2.T415   371.1'02   74-6633
ISBN 0-02-367600-0

Printing: 3 4 5 6 7 8   Year: 7 8 9 0

Preface

THE authors of *Teaching and Learning* welcome you to join in sharing our conversation. We view this text as a basic conversation about teaching and learning rather than as a new doctrine to solve all of your educational problems. Not recommending a particular style of teaching or learning, we will introduce you to the various aspects and opinions of this educational conversation as comprehensively as we can. Our purpose is to encourage and assist you as you formulate that particular teaching style which you can most comfortably and effectively call your own.

Teaching and learning are all-inclusive terms, each having innumerable definitions. This text explores both topics as they relate to *philosophy, psychology,* and *curriculum*.

In an attempt to enable you, the elementary or secondary teacher, to develop a sound educational framework, we have endeavored to review the interrelated areas of philosophy, psychology, and curriculum within the context of four teacher-learner styles practiced today.

Out of the multiplicity of existing teacher-learner styles we feel that the *classical, technological, personalized,* and *interactional* models validly and distinctively represent all the others. We readily admit that we have found no clear, airtight boundaries since the teacher of the interactional model may easily place some of Skinner's programmed texts on her interest tables. One may also find the teacher of the personalized model employing competency-based objectives and contracts in his program. Thus we readily encourage the realization that none of our students, and none of you, our readers, fit perfectly into any one of these four models.

Each model offers you an organized, valid presentation of a teaching-learning style. Your attempt to develop your own integrated style depends primarily on the power and success of your present and future teaching. Without such integration, you may well complete your eight-to-three o'clock time span each day, but its overall effect will appear fragmented to your students and will be less than personally satisfying to you, the teacher.

We have one suggestion to offer which, though not part of this book, involves an underlying presumption of our conversation. Theoretical reflection of classroom interactions will become much more understandable and practical to you if you can combine it and test it out in an actual classroom situation. If you are not presently teaching or your present program of study does not have a required practicum phase (field work in some local school), you can volunteer to help as a teacher aide in a local school for one or two days each week. You will not only find it a most satisfying experience, but one that will give you much more confidence in the results of your inter-action with these four styles of teaching and learning.

One by-product we have experienced in this conversation is worth mentioning. Educators avoid "talking shop" with colleagues who hold different theoretical positions: "You can't talk to her; she's a behaviorist!" Yet theoretical differences need not lead to conver-sational walls; in fact, such conversations can be rich and lead to your growth and development as a professional. Skinner has a lot to share with Rogers and vice versa; and both will be better thinkers for the exchange. So, too, the better you understand the contrast-ing views of other teachers and the more you converse with them, sharing and understanding without having to agree, the more pro-fessional and confident you will become as a teacher.

We welcome you to our conversation, which explores these four typical models of teaching and learning. We especially invite you to join us by evaluating each of the four models according to your own perceptions and classroom experiences. The results of this pursuit will then be the development of your own model of teaching that integrates *philosophy of teaching* with your own *theory of learning* and your *curriculum style*. This is a tall order, involving much reflection and even risk on your part, but the journey is exciting and, for you, personally very rewarding.

Because this is a journey teachers must periodically retake, *Teach-ing and Learning* is also intended for the experienced teacher. Teach-ers must often rethink their educational philosophy as it relates to how children learn or to determine the relationship of their teach-ing practices and educational philosophy. Thus continuous self-exploration receives high priority as an educational endeavor since we are part of an age when demands are being placed upon educa-tional institutions by our constituents. Thus, we must continually reassess these issues. While the task appears difficult, it is intended to be a personal human experience because we, as educators, have long realized the importance of the principles of accountability and have therefore been encouraged by its growing acceptance.

D. L. / H. B. / S. E. / M. J.

Contents

CHAPTER 1
Introduction

> Do you like to learn?
> Are you willing to work long hours?
> Do you enjoy working closely with other people?
> Does the candor of youth appeal to you?
> Does explaining an idea to someone else turn you on?

I F Y O U answer "Yes" to these questions, you should consider a career in teaching. Teaching requires all of the above factors and a dedication and enthusiasm that goes far beyond a 8:00 A.M. to 3:00 P.M., summer-free schedule. To be an effective teacher, you will need to search continually for new ways of communicating with young people. Sometimes at the end of an especially exhausting day you may find yourself having the following, or similar, thoughts: "I didn't realize that Ronnie was having so much trouble with social interaction. I must spend extra time with him tomorrow. When he discussed his problem with me today, his eyes and voice were filled with anxiety. He really needs acceptance from his peers. How can this be solved?" The sources of difficulty are very complex.

The elementary and secondary teacher's first task is to identify his/her most effective style of relating to students, thus encouraging comfortable student interaction and maximum learning. To determine one's most effective teaching style it is necessary to explore one's own self in order to answer:

How do I see the world and the purpose of education in it? Although students learn in many ways, how do I think they learn best? And what does 'to learn' and 'to teach' mean—again understanding that there isn't any one answer? What are the value priorities that I may be transmitting to my students, consciously or unconsciously? And, finally, am I encouraging my students to become a certain kind of person, and if so, what 'image of man' am I forming in them?

These are personal questions, the answers to which must be found within your personality; the answers will be given to you only bit by bit. Teaching is a personal experience, not a nine-to-five job. Therefore, your answers to these questions may be very different from those of other quite capable teachers since they will reflect your educational identity. Answering these questions will begin the development of that identity.

TEXT DESIGN

How are you to proceed in answering these questions? Every topic discussed, every reading, every class activity and assignment, assists you in responding. Each of these is designed to stimulate new thoughts and open new avenues of consideration. We have identified four separate models of teaching—classical, technological, personalized, and interactional. The general goal of this book is to encourage you to design your own philosophy and style of teaching. In order to carry out this design you can profit from experience in analyzing and evaluating the bases of the four selected models. Specifically, we have focused on:

—the philosophies and historical origins of each model.
—the learning theories embraced by each model.
—the curricular manifestation of each model.
—the teaching strategies most commonly associated with each model.

Importantly, too, we have explored educational issues that are common to all models, for example, evaluation, grouping, conditioning. Many of these issues are addressed, in detail, in only one of the four basic models. However, they are matters of concern to practitioners of all models. For example, grouping of students is discussed in depth with respect to the classical model; however, it is also a matter of concern to teachers in other models.

This text has also been designed to develop in teachers an immunity to educational fads and gimmicks. Most educational innovations, both broad and specific, can often improve the operations of the school. Frequently, however, the innovations are added to a school program without considering their philosophical and psychological assumptions. Frequently, also, they are regarded as a final salvation for educational difficulties. An illustration of this situation is the infatuation in many communities with performance contracting. It met the short-range and sudden goal of accountability, but in many instances had little effect on improving competency in a particular skill. Only a teacher who is fully informed of the wide range of alternative teaching styles and the rapidity of change in modern society can deal effectively with the problems generated by educational innovations.

We have endeavored to provide experience both in developing coherent models of teaching and in unifying these generalizations with the daily details of teaching. As long as the theory is not developed in a vacuum, we have found nothing so practical as a thoughtful theory. We are urging a continuing reflection on the part of teachers between their underlying theory and values and their method of teaching.

This book analyzes the various major teaching styles which are being practiced in the United States today. Each style reflects a different balance and different relationships among the teacher, student, and content. Each model includes the three variables shown in Figure 1–1.

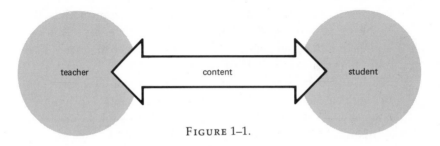

FIGURE 1–1.

Sometimes "content" will dominate; sometimes either "teacher" or "student" will dominate. Through variations and adjustments of this diagram, we will give you such a depiction-in-a-glance of each style.

It is a feature of American society to try to adapt and improve despite the apparent inclination to maintain the status quo. Even allegedly conservative educators have dabbled in educational innovations. Conversely, supposedly liberal, avant-garde educators attempt tactics that are fundamentally conservative. At times it becomes clear that the innovative technique and the basic philosophy are unalterably at odds. But often they congeal in a fashion not entirely recognizable to the teacher or the learners. We are not making the case that such bonding should be averted. That would ultimately result in a rigid fragmentation of the teaching models. Our aim is to sharpen the preceptions of teacher so that misunderstanding can be reduced and so that the full implications of a particular teaching strategy can be identified. It must be emphasized, too, however, that the ultimate aim of this explication is a respect for and ability to use techniques and ideas from each of the four basic models. Again there has been a tendency in American thought toward consensus —toward selecting the best of each component in our basically pluralistic society—for the purpose of building the best possible world. We are urging somewhat the reverse. It is possible for each model to operate poorly. We will be exploring both the inner assumptions and the external manifestations of each.

A vital larger question that lies beyond the scope of this book does help to put its aim in perspective. Imagine a school administrator and his board designing from scratch a new school and its program. They have a choice of:

1. Consciously selecting one of the four models and choosing only teachers and materials that adhere to that model.
2. Purposely selecting a balance from among the four models; that is, an equal number of teachers from each category. This presumes that the youngster will somehow balance his experiences and choose his own style of thought.
3. Selecting teachers and materials on the basis of their excellence of teaching, without regard to balancing the staff or to adherence to a single model of teaching. This presumes that an administrator can identify that higher criteria of excellent teaching—that is "it is open," that "the kids will get into college," "that it will be orderly," and so on.

The intent of this book is to inform educators, potential and practicing, of the panoply of implications revolving around each model. Having experienced a combination of theoretical and practical analysis in each model, you will be better equipped to respond to the value implications, the learning theory, and the teaching strategy in these or other curriculum models. Just as schools become ensnared in one model and rely on it exclusively, so can teachers. Some do so almost inadvertently; others have done so with the utmost zeal. The likelihood of a closed system producing shrewd graduates must be recognized.

To develop our idea, we approach each style from three different perspectives: curriculum, psychology, and philosophy.

CURRICULUM   describes both content and patterns of interaction between teacher and students

WHAT is the teaching style?

WHAT makes it distinct from others?

PSYCHOLOGY investigates the learning theory and method that underlies each model of teaching.

HOW does the teacher relate the content to the student?

HOW does the student learn?

HOW does the teacher relate personally to the student?

PHILOSOPHY searches for the background of each style, both in its historical-sociological context and in its basic purposes and values.

WHY does the teacher choose this style over others?

WHY does he find himself more at home in this style than in another?

Each model is often susceptible to oversimplified caricaturization. A more thorough characterization of each of the models communicates their inner natures.

Thus, the emphasis of this text includes not only the conventional history of education, philosophy of education, and psychology of education; but also explores the newer areas of sociology of education, anthropology of education, and the delicate matter of values in education. Exploration of these factions occur as the authors review the classical, technological, personalized, and interactional models.

Teaching models never came about by accident. They are generally the result of gradual reformations of a long-standing set of beliefs. They are the result, too, of a constant interaction between the school personnel and the demands of society. One of the several important barometers of any teaching model is the degree to which it intends "to preserve the spirit of the age" or to which it attempts "to prepare for and shape the future." These barometers do not fit convenient labels such as conservative and liberal. It is entirely possible, for example, for a teacher to "prepare for and shape the future," but to do so in an extremely dictatorial fashion both with respect to teaching style and to subject matter content. Similarly, it is possible that, in attempting to conserve the status quo, a teacher could seriously misunderstand the nuances of the very complicated status quo. The students would not be likely to develop a strong sense of stability. Future historians might well determine our age to have been confusing, paradoxical, and vexed. Yet, many teachers are instructing today as if there is a large body of accepted standards that must be maintained whatever the costs. With this limitation in mind a spectrum has been included in each model showing the degree of emphasis between preserving the present and preparing for the future.

This book, then, is not designed to advocate a new orthodoxy which bridges all four modes and models. We are chiefly interested in developing your ability to analyze any model of teaching and thus consciously establish your own model.

Education: Classical

The classical model seeks to conserve old ideas and transmit them from one generation to the next (Figure 1–2).

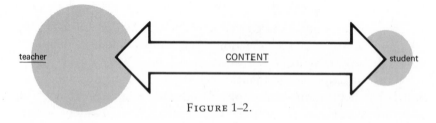

FIGURE 1–2.

CONTENT   Subject matter is first in importance. It consists mostly of information and ideas selected from the world the student knows. It is objective, clear, and logically organized. It is presented to the student in this orderly manner rather than according to his interest and involvement.

TEACHER   The teacher is the *expert* and *model*. Trained more in the *what* to teach than *how*, she brings the content to the student and helps him to absorb it.

STUDENT   The student is the passive recipient of this information and these ideas. For him, education is hard work, the fulfilling of assignments, and achieving in a competitive atmosphere. His intellectual training is the proper subject of the classroom, not his emotional growth or his social adjustment.

The following explanation by a classical teacher of his classroom procedure should help focus this most familiar of models.

In a junior high-school history lesson about Europe the teacher integrated dictionary skills with a social studies concept lesson. The teacher contended that the student needed to know the definition of several concepts in order to understand medieval Europe. A worksheet of terms such as feudalism, serfdom, nationalism was prepared from the dictionary. As the teacher explained each term and helped the students spell them phonetically the students thought about the approaching test on the material. In the minds of both the teacher and the students these several definitions were the building blocks which must precede any further understanding of the topic. It was fundamentally a memory process; the students had come to believe that they could not resolve problems until they had built up their storehouse of knowledge. After achieving some command of the terms appropriate to medieval Europe the class began to recount the chronology of events and broad developments from the fall of Rome to the Renaissance. Relying primarily on their textbook and the teacher's classroom explanation of the course of events, the class learned about the past as it really was. The justification, pedagogically, for such a survey of this time period is that the learner will be able to learn by example. According to this proposition, by observing an advanced learner (the historian and/or the classroom teacher) draw generalizations, conclusions, and inferences the student will be able to duplicate this process. The difficulty with this argument is that it depends upon accepting the notion that there is an interpretation of the medieval period. It further depends on the belief that schools must be efficient; that is, since there is such an enormous body of information to be assimilated as a foundation, the student cannot waste time in pursuit of his own interests or his own false hypotheses.

The subject matter in this project is inert emotionally. The student is supposed to try to pursue the objective truth independent of his biases, prejudices, inner emotions, and feelings. The information he learns gives him much needed experience and points of reference so that he can learn to think like an adult more quickly. The key to the kingdom of learning like an adult is a logical, rational thought process. As he sees each generalization verified by historical data the student comes to see clear thinking as a systematic procedure of drawing conclusions from a mass of data. What he does not see in this procedure is the material that is edited out and neglected by the particular historian who prepared his textbook.

Of major importance in this model is the predetermined subject matter which is transmitted by the teacher to a passive student.

Within this model, we discuss two different modes: perennial education and essential education. Perennial education sees content embodying and preserving the accepted truths of past culture. The past is its source of content, and the present and future, hopefully, will result in a continuation of these truths. The perennialist emphasizes the timeless truths of the past and ignores the demands of the present and the future (Figure 1–3).

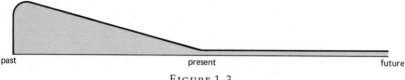

past   present   future

FIGURE 1–3.

Essentialists see education as the work of preparing today's student for today's world both by forming in him its values and by training him for a specific occupation. The essentialist is oriented toward the spirit of his own age. He is emphasizing the skills and attitudes essential to success in the status quo. It, too, is a largely conservative model (Figure 1–4).

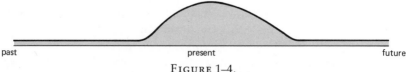

past   present   future

FIGURE 1–4.

Both the perennialist and the essentialist hold this view in common: Education is content taken by the teacher and transmitted to the student. Some would legitimately characterize this as "funnel" education (Figure 1–5).

Education: Technological

The technological model also regards education largely as the transmission of information. It emphasizes less the preservation of a culture. The technological model focuses on competencies of indi-

FIGURE 1–5.

vidual students and adjusts content to the levels of readiness exhibited by the student (Figure 1–6).

teacher CONTENT student

FIGURE 1–6.

CONTENT
The content is selected by experts in the particular
field. This content focuses on objective data and
behavioral skills that lead to vocational competencies.

STUDENT
The student absorbs vast amounts of complex
material and behavioral patterns efficiently and in
an unreflective manner. His new skills will be
immediately useful to the larger society.

TEACHER
The teacher steps into the background. Since the
machine has proven itself more efficient and accurate in this complex task, the human teacher is
"now free" to relate to the student's noncognitive
dimensions.

The following explanation by a modern technological advocate
should help bring into focus this recent educational model. For pur-

poses of comparison we will use the same lesson, a junior high-school history lesson about medieval Europe.

A large percentage of the youngsters' time in this model is spent at a sleek console that includes a television screen, head phones, a small keyboard on which student responses can be proffered to the machine. In large measure it is the traditional model gone modern. The key differences are that it is much more effective and efficient. And that it recasts the role of the teacher.

In terms of its effectiveness it might well represent improvement, if the underlying assumptions are accepted. It can make the same points the textbook makes but do so more vividly by using pictures of medieval scenes integrated with medieval music. This is not only an addition to the basic data of the original history lesson but comes closer to the McLuhan contention that the media is the message. The risk is considerable, of course, since the learner is conceived of as a passive observer who is supposed to be accumulating data so that he can more quickly become a fully functioning adult. During that passive waiting period he is also accumulating a large body of attitudes toward learning. These, of course, do not show up as readily on the standarized tests measuring achievement. If the content is good the students often do retain information more effectively.

The teacher can play at least three different roles with respect to this model. He can be seen as merely an adjunct reinforcing and buttressing the content created by experts. Many have accepted this role. Or he can pit himself against the content of the multimedia presentation by offering conflicting theories and interpretations of the material under examination. This represents a completely different philosophy and set of goals. In this same vein he can provide a critique of the media so that students become more analytical of the means by which they secure information. Few teachers have turned to this complicated alternative. A third choice involves leaving the entire content matter to the technological devices and devoting the teacher-student relationship to each individual youngster's general intellectual and personal development. This, too, requires a shift in philosophy away from the assumptions of the classical model. It is a more common alternative than the second, but teachers selecting it circumvent the key question of subject matter in the curriculum. In effect, they leave it in the hands of a distant committee of experts. This usually results in a topic that is seemingly irrelevant to students, medieval European history, becoming even more so.

Of major importance in this model is the content that can be transmitted in a multimedia fashion via technology. The student is still the recipient of information but in a much more persuasive manner. Importantly, the teacher can be freed from the task of merely transmitting information. However, the programmed material cannot respond to the specific and unique ways in which the student tried to identify a theme and a tone for medieval Europe.

The agricultural world is ancient history and the industrial world is steadily fading. The technological world is unfolding so rapidly that we are suffering from "future shock." We are not fully able to comprehend several of its prospects. Technological education is highly future-oriented, yet the future, in many cases, is already upon us (Figure 1–7).

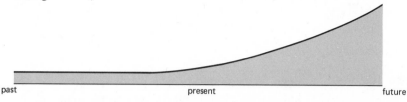

past   present   future

Technological education concerns itself, overwhelmingly, with the observable and measurable world. Its preoccupation with external behavior and the practical application of scientific discoveries allows it to be characterized as the idealized computer that programs other computers. It considers itself more efficient than the classical teacher-student model (Figure 1–8).

FIGURE 1–8.

Education: Personalized

Here the student becomes the center of the learning process. Teaching begins and builds around his interests, experiences, and psychological growth patterns. This model can only be described by reviewing the two options it is composed of.

PROGRESSIVE EDUCATION

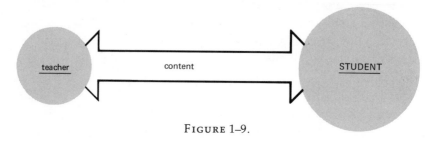

FIGURE 1–9.

STUDENT

Seen as a "whole person," his emotional growth and social adjustment are vital to his learning as is his intellectual development (Figure 1–9).

TEACHER

The teacher is second only to the student. He is an educational midwife, a psychologist, a methodology expert, a facilitator, and a resource person. He does not "transmit content," but leads and assists the student along his developmental path and through his experiences.

CONTENT

Content arises out of the student's experiences. These provide the basis on which the student reflects, comes to understand, and thereby acquires control over them for his future advantage.

ROMANTIC EDUCATION

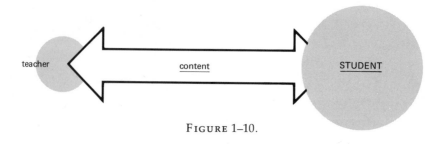

FIGURE 1–10.

STUDENT   All learning unfolds naturally from within the student as he interacts with his environment (Figure 1–10). He learns as a process of development in the same manner as he learns to walk and talk.

CONTENT   Experience is the natural teacher of the child. In a stimulating environment in which he is free to interact, follow his inner curiosities, and experience the consequences of his own actions, he retraces, according to an inner pattern, much of the learning of past generations.

TEACHER   The child cannot be taught; he can only be allowed to learn. The teacher provides an educational environment for his student, then gives him free run of it while protecting him from outside, disturbing interference. The teacher also serves as an environmental resource, should the student desire it.

The following explanation by a teacher subscribing to personalized education clarifies this model. Again, let us rely on the same general theme, medieval Europe.

The combined seventh- and eighth-grade teacher selected a topic from several choices in the school's kindergarten through twelfth grade curriculum guide. In an attempt to arouse their curiosity and to encourage students to express their feelings, the class was exposed to some of the issues and problems characteristic of medieval life. After a general experience with films, books, records, and a brief drama pertinent to the time period, the youngsters were invited to select a particular aspect of medieval life for further analysis. The youngsters were grouped according to the interests they expressed. The teacher placed a high value on keeping track of each student's activity and direction within the small groups. Each student was expected to follow his own particular interest to a full explanation of that activity. In effect the student was selecting what seemed to him to be the most cogent explanation of, for example, the role of the church in medieval society, or differences between French, German, and Italian medieval culture.

This kind of teaching presumes a wide collection of ancillary resources for students. Therein lies the heart of the difficulty with individualizing instruction too greatly. In order to have enough sources available for random and far-ranging student research the school must limit the number of topics that the youngster can pursue. As soon as this is done, of course, the instruction is no longer truly individualized. It means that the student is expected to sit himself on one of a few seats available, not to rearrange the chairs or to leave the room. This is nowhere near to being an interactional classroom, but it *is* a sincere effort to attend to individuality.

The epistemological and pedagogical assumptions of this teaching style differ substantially from the classical and the technological model. It first challenges the assumption that there is a fixed, identifiable body of knowledge that one must master as a sort of rite of passage into adulthood and more sophisticated thought processes. It also challenges the emphasis on the processes of learning and clarity of thought. In sum, it contends that the actual subject matter is of little consequence, but that the manner in which the learner integrates it with his own unique personality is vital. In actual practice this means, too, that the teacher winds up guiding 25–30 independent study projects. To those personalized educators of the progressive persuasion this can become a problem. Rather than a helter-skelter, everyone-does-his-own-thing motif, they argue that while there is not a standard body of subject matter content, there is, in fact, an ideal way of knowing. This means a modified version of the scientific method. It means, too, then, that each youngster individualizes his pace of learning and, to the extent of available resources, the content of his learning. It does not mean that he establishes his own process of coming to knowledge.

While the teacher is indeed the planner, the students are active participants. The content is secondary to the student's constant reevaluation of his own feelings, beliefs, and conclusions.

Both the progressive and the romantic are meliorists holding that the world is gradually improving with each generation standing on the shoulders of the previous and enjoying a broader, more accurate vision of reality. The present sums up the past and looks optimistically to the future (Figure 1–11). But, importantly, each generation learns by examining the evidence anew rather than by digesting uncritically the principles and conclusions of his forefathers.

The most common "characterization" of the progressive/romantic style of education is that of the "gardener" actively assisting nature

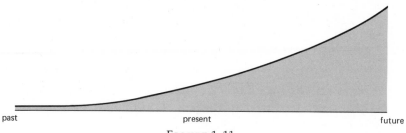

past   present   future

FIGURE 1–11.

by providing the optimum growing atmosphere for the student who, ultimately, matures out of his own inner nature (Figure 1–12).

FIGURE 1–12.

Education: Interactional

According to this school of thought, a permanent, unquestioned body of knowledge or set of values no longer exists in today's world. Education and schooling are not synonymous, so interactionalists bypass our present teaching techniques and operations. The educators search man's roots (Latin: *radice*, therefore sometimes called radical education) for new purposes and values by which men might better live together. This quest is the basis of the interactional model (Figure 1–13).

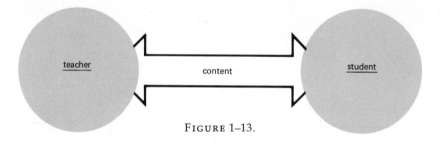

FIGURE 1–13.

TEACHER   Carries the responsibility of creating a "commu-
               nity" atmosphere of interdependence and trustful
               dialogue. Recognizing that his experiences are
               more mature, he shares and listens in the same
               manner as each of his students.

STUDENT   The student learns in his dialogic relationship
               with others; learning is an interdependent effort.
               He shares his perceptions of reality, listens in-
               tently to the perceptions of others, then revises his
               world view out of what he has learned.

CONTENT   After focusing on particular problems of our con-
               temporary sociocultural world, the student at-
               tempts to uncover inherent purposes and values.
               He critically evaluates and solves them in light of
               man's human dignity, then re-orders his life ac-
               cording to his new perceptions. His further ex-
               periences, then, will either confirm his new per-
               ception, or lead him to further re-evaluation. (For
               example, in respect to Women's Liberation, this
               educational style is called "Consciousness Rais-
               ing.")

One might characterize the interactionist educator as a person
whose "cultural home" has been demolished by the storm of time
and who now builds himself a new "cultural home" for his children
to live in (Figure 1–14).

The following explanation by a teacher in the interactional model
clarifies this most recent teaching-learning style. It is difficult to
maintain the same theme, medieval Europe, because the students are
concentrating more on their interrelationship with the present soci-

FIGURE 1–14.

ety and their vision of the changes they would like to make for the future society. Nonetheless, it is entirely possible that a learner would want to compare the lifestyle of a medieval village with that of a modern company town.

A clear illustration can be made of a learner examining the policy and regulations in a community dominated by a single company. As he searches for explanations of the present condition and for an alternative future policy, the teacher may suggest for him the exploration of a topic that seems, on the surface, to be extraneous, but which, in fact, could provide an excellent point of reference. The highest priority remains that he identify—and seek solutions to —contemporary public problems. However, he agrees to suspend such considerations in order to gain some perspective on the matter. To get outside the demands of the present problem and view, somewhat dispassionately, a similar conflict in a very different setting helps him to separate the light and transient features of the problem from the permanent and significant.

The interactional teacher forces a group responsibility much more than even a personalized educator would. The learner not only interacts by proposing and testing his ideas in a real world setting beyond the classroom, but he is expected to develop his ideas through interaction with his classmates. This posits a thoroughly different idea of the role of information and subject matter content in the activity of the school. In interactional settings students are not expected to defer their more mature thinking until adulthood, but are expected to pursue the solution of manageable problems. If, in so doing, it becomes evident that they need mastery of a particular set of facts, they will then stop and gain command of that material.

This model also raises the role of valuing process in the schools. If a youngster desiring to become a carpenter declares to himself that facile recall of the multiplication tables would ease his tasks, the result is essentially neutral learning. Clearly, the situation is not parallel with that of the youngster learning about the company town. The latter is going to take his own covert and overt values into the review of the medieval community. He will face difficult problems of selecting and neglecting information; and, he will have to be cautious that he does not suddenly find exactly what he was looking for to verify his beliefs about the contemporary town. Hopefully, when he is exploring a setting in which not much is at stake, he will be able to sharpen his own sensitivities toward contemporary problems and with respect to his own thinking processes and value system.

The interactionalist educator is appreciative of history and of man's past accomplishments. Nevertheless, he feels the impotence of man's past cultural "homes" and sees a critical need to search and build a new cultural "home" with new values and purposes of life (Figure 1–15). He sees education as the only reliable solution in this period of revolution.

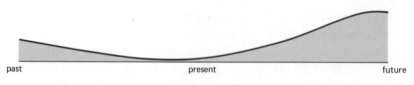

past   present   future

FIGURE 1–15.

In the classical model the learner's educational environment depends upon his elders' judgments. The environment of the technological model is determined by distant educational leaders. In the personalized model the environment is a function of the learner's own interests and attitudes. Finally, to the interactionist the environment is determined by the integration of interests in his educational community, that is, his peers, his teachers, and his social community.

As we explore in detail these four models of education we hope that you will be able to answer more specifically the probing questions about your individual goals as an educator. We also hope that you will generate more questions about the specific operations within these models. Only in this way will you become more than an uncritical perpetrator of an educational model. The distinctions we have made between the four models are nowhere as clear in the reality of dealing with children as they are on the pages of a textbook. Our aim is to enable you to reflect on the long train of assumptions and consequences of your teaching with a particular model. It is impossible to teach entirely in one model. It is not only possible, but essential, that when you are relying on the techniques of one model that you are alert to all its ramifications.

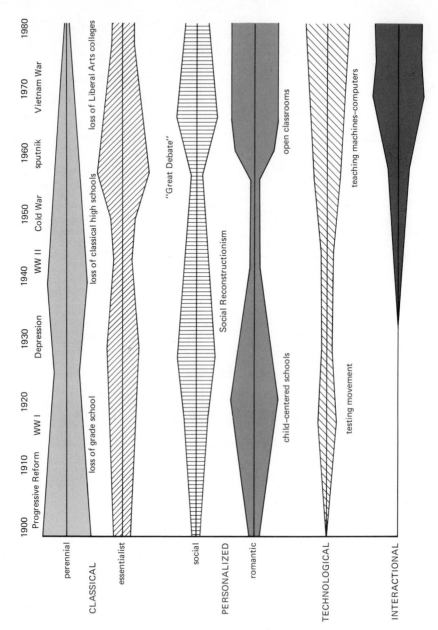

FIGURE 1–16. Time Line for Twentieth-Century American Education. This graph attempts to portray the comparative rises and falls in popularity of each of the four characteristic styles of teaching discussed in this text.

CHAPTER 2

Education: Classical

Philosophical/Social Commentary

THE CLASSICAL model of formal education has become a much maligned strawman in recent years. It seems endemic among many educational reformers to compare their vision of improved education with a sterile and oversimplified teaching model stigmatized as the "classical" or "traditional" way. Many succumb to the temptation to compare their model, functioning perfectly, with the classical one, functioning poorly. In one sense, then, one of the tasks of this chapter is to offer a more thorough understanding of the classical model by determining what happens when it works well. The misapplications of the classical model warrant treatment. They have been widely exposed and often exaggerated in the recent drives to improve our schools. These misapplications usually involve a complete failure to regard the individual learner's interests, goals, and experience. The learning content is determined before the learner is even identified, but misapplication occurs when all children are required to proceed in lockstep as groups of 30 through the unalterable content. Many other classical misadventures have emerged from the failure to modify academic disciplines in response to the knowledge explosion of the last three decades. A careful examination of the effective workings of the classical model is in order if prospective teachers are not to move capriciously from reform to reform without ever reflecting deeply about the original model on which they all are based. In our attempt to develop teachers who will become immune to these fads, we must shed light on the external fad of categorically debunking the classical model.

The classical model has been divided into two quite distinct categories, perennialism and essentialism. Basic characteristics common to both are discussed. Both, for instance, accept a static view of society. They contend that even though there may be frequent, popular changes in society, the real substance of the social fabric changes very slowly. Both agree that the proper subject matter for our schools can best be determined by a group of experts who place a high value on reason and a logical organization of the mate-

rial. Since this subject matter is of an unchanging quality, the teacher's role, essentially, is to transfer the material into the student's memory. The student's task is to passively absorb it without either challenging its validity or probing its implications. The result is a teacher-dominated classroom.

The classical model contends that an understanding of the subject matter "will take care of itself," that is, its relevance will become apparent to the student only after he has reached greater maturity and after the other categories of knowledge have been revealed to him. For the moment, he must accept the material without question and place a high priority on the values of patience and discipline. This is a function of the principle of "deferred gratification," a definitive quality of the classical model.

Classicists assume that youth can be uncritical acceptors of the traditions of the culture for a very long time and then shift to the role of evaluator. Many doubt that students can suspend their participation in life's affairs in order to assimilate the cultural traditions of which they are a part. More recent learning theories visualize an organic growth between the learner and his universe. To them the input from the learner's environment is vital to the learning process. How he relates to it, and attempts to influence it is the material of teaching. Importantly, his own conception of the input is the key —not someone else's conception of the environment that has been established *a priori*. This does not mean that the classical model is outdated and should be seen as a quaint and inert educational artifact. The classical model can serve to remind us that the "ivory tower" metaphor of the school is not without value. There is a risk in making education too much a part of the turmoil of daily life. As this happens in the more modern modes of teaching, the students often do not develop a sense of perspective and an ability to distinguish between the transient and the permanent events in their lives. This remains a fundamental advantage of the classical model. It should not be abandoned lightly.

These are general characteristics that require more specific classification. The term "classical" has become the favorite whipping boy (or idol) of many self-styled educational experts. In the process, it has become so nebulous that, when invoked, it manages only to confuse understanding. American classical education has developed two quite different models, each seeking to preserve a specific system. First, the older transmissive educational model is discussed and

second, essentialism, the American version of education as a process of transmitting learning to students is analyzed.

Perennial education stems out of our European heritage; essentialism is as American as apple pie. Despite their many commonly held beliefs, their differences are quite marked: The perennialist is centered in the humanities while the essentialist focuses on the sciences. The former originated in a predominantly agricultural society, while the latter is a child of the Industrial Revolution. The first is academic and seeks to develop the student's mind, while the second is utilitarian and prepares him for his future occupation. Perennialism is consciously philosophical and works from first principles and ideals, whereas essentialism is more pragmatic and is absorbed, in the immediate operation, with its success or failure. In some respects these two are often antithetical and cannot be lumped into the same "traditional" pigeonhole without inviting confusion.

The matter of values in a youngster's education is never directly addressed by a pure perennialist. In his vision, education is value free and culture free. The operations of the universe are independent of the mind of the learner. The timeless, immutable truths about the objective reality are to be the substance of schooling. The style of teaching is strictly expository and the style of learning is strictly assimilation. This theory of value corresponds to Philip Phenix's heteronomous value orientation. Heteronomists believe that values, like physical laws, are not made, but are discovered. As Phenix stresses, the heteronomist may be a staunch conservative, an orthodox communist, or a doctrinaire liberal. The definitive quality is always his ideological certainty. This manifests itself, pedagogically, in an uncritical transmission and inculcation of permanent and perennial values.

Within the classical model we find much greater diversity among the essentialists. To their thinking, the perennialists are too ethnocentric. Essentialists believe that certain essentials exist for the mature adulthood of everyone within each culture. They are much less confident than the perennialists that these essentials apply to all men for all time. Philip Phenix can be categorized as an essentialist here. He rejects what he identifies as anomic, nihilistic cynicism on the one hand and autonomic relativism on the other. He specifies his elusive value orientation as teleonomic. This means that he intends to develop a "persistent commitment of persons of conscience to the progressive discovery of what they ought to do." He later clarifies that "teleonomy interprets the moral enterprise as a venture of faith, not in the sense of a blind adherence to a set of precepts . . . but in a willingness to believe in a pursuit of right through the partial and imperfect embodiments" of human affairs. (Philip Phenix, *Realms of Meaning*, 1964, p. 44). This is important in establishing the essentialist classicists as something other than hard-core, law-and-order enthusiasts. Though we are talking about four distinct models of teaching in this text, it must be emphasized that Phenix's words could be spoken by a slightly modified modern existentialist. Many traditionalists would balk at being grouped with existentialists, but on important issues the boundaries between the four models are often blurred. We must remind ourselves of this factor in order to sharpen our sensitivities to the nuances of each group. We can say, however, that in general all classicalists are primarily concerned with accepting and conserving, not with any tendency to reform moral orders. From here, then, we will identify the origins and refinements on the perennial educational model. Subsequently, we will identify how the American essentialist movement evolved from this perennialist tradition.

SOCIAL-HISTORICAL SETTING FOR THE PERENNIAL MODEL

The perennial model of education is the oldest model to be found in American society today. It stems, relatively unchanged in its principles, back 2400 years to Athens. If we accept the notion that each teaching model is a specific manifestation of a larger culture, then we can profitably sketch and analyze the roots upon which we grew into a civilized people. In the words of Mortimer Adler and Milton Mayer,

> Anyone who undertakes to judge (the validity of perennial education) has to consider one stupendous historical fact: these are the principles upon which the men responsible for our culture were educated, generation after generation, century after century. They are the principles upon which Plato taught Aristotle in Athens and Mentor Graham taught Abraham Lincoln in Sangamon County, Illinois. For better or for worse, this is the outline of the education which (to whatever extent education civilizes) gave us our civilization. (Adler and Mayer, 1958, p. 24)

"Perennial" education is often described as being far more concerned with the past than with the present or future. In the view of those favoring perennial education, they are concerned with the *eternally present.* Their experience, confirmed over 24 centuries, is that the basics of life are permanent and unchanging. For all of the surface turmoil and transience, an eternal wisdom that all educated men should be aware of lies at the center. In fact, this awareness determines a man as being "educated." On this prime level of reality, there is no past, present, or future, but perennial truth, goodness, and beauty, as valid today and tomorrow as it was yesterday. It is the business of education to communicate this vision to each new generation.

We face a stark contradiction when, after describing this model as *the model* of Western civilization, we then note that, of the several discussed in this volume, this is the most criticized in the United States today. How and why did this massive transition occur?

Industrial and scientific developments of the past century have made the life experience in our present culture radically different from the one that gave rise to the perennial model. Until the nineteenth century, the Western world was largely agricultural. Men lived in rural communities, deeply attached to the land and to its perennial cycles, rooted in one location for several generations. This existence contrasts sharply with our present lifestyle in which the typical urbanite lives quite independent of nature's cycle and picks up roots on an average of every four years.

The perennial family lived in the home of grandparents, with three or four generations sharing the same household. In this "three-layered" family, traditions were strong and their basic lesson, although seldom expressed, was that life had remained unchanged as far back as anyone could remember, and would remain so into the indefinite future. This is as God had created and ordained the world. Even if there were wars or natural calamities to tear up the order of life, they too melded into the life-death, ever-recurring cycle of nature. "Nothing is new under the sun."

In the foundation of our country, the educational models established by the founding fathers were naturally copies of European models. There were varieties, from the professional schools of New England to the private tutors of the Southern plantation owners, yet all followed the same perennial model.

But from the start, new experiences required transformations. If our new nation was to be a *democracy*, with voting power in the hands of every citizen rather than in the hands of an aristocratic few, there was a need to formally educate the entire citizenry. Later, as the

Industrial Revolution replaced a rural populace with an urban, two-generation family, far more aware of immediate changing social conditions than of the perennial wisdom of the patriarchal grandfather, the interests and demands for new educational models increased. The institution called "schooling" was substituted for older familial and tutorial forms.

Finally, *science* gradually emerged from the status of an avocation of a few wealthy gentlemen to that of a serious, disciplined study—a discipline imposing enough to unseat the humanities as the central study of the new generation. All three, industrialism, democracy, and science created entirely new life experiences and radically challenged the older educational forms. Under the stress of this new mentality, perennial education gradually receded in the United States. Grade schools had no more imaginative task than to teach the basic communication skills—the 3 Rs—by means of memorization and rote repetition.

At the outset of the twentieth century, only 10 per cent of our students attended high school, largely perennialist institutions designed for the college bound. But with further economic adjustments and educational reforms of the next 40 years, the numbers increased to 90 per cent. The Compulsory Education Acts passed between 1870 and 1890 were a major factor contributing to the increase in public-school enrollments. The laws restricting child labor also led to increased enrollments in public schools. As the government attempted to assimilate a variety of immigrants into a homogenized American culture more students were forced into schools. Such vast numbers, including many immigrants and children of immigrants could never be confined to Latin, algebra, and the literature classics. Under this stress, the high schools began to reform educational models.

Many colleges began to give way to more diverse styles of education. The small, four-year liberal arts colleges, humanities oriented and predominately prescribed in curriculum, modified their programs and methods in order to compete with the vocationally oriented, professional schools found in state multiuniversities.

Perennial schools are declining, but they have not ceased to exist, and will not for many decades to come. The United States remains a culturally pluralistic nation and many of its citizens still identify with the perennial world. In cities as urban as Boston, one will find neighborhoods in which Italian is the language of the street and in which almost every vacant square foot of land is green with vegetable gardens. The men of the community might work in the mills by day, but they work—live—in their gardens in the evening. They are a people of the soil at heart. For them the local parochial school is "their" school. And even in a time when more community control is evident, they retain many of the qualities of the perennial model.

As long as America remains strongly pluralistic, with a variety of European ethnic communities desirous of retaining their pre-American heritage, a localized perennial education continues as a viable American model of education.

MIND-SET OF PERENNIALISM

To suspend our accustomed outlook on reality and enter into another, foreign outlook is a demanding task. Yet if one is to understand each of these various models of education, he must see not only their techniques and methods of teaching, but his basic perception of life as well. Only after this is understood can one discover the fundamental "why" behind each model.

The typical American, for example, looks at a method of teaching and asks: "Does it work or doesn't it?" If it does, he uses it; if it doesn't, he discards it and tries another. As Americans, we approach life very pragmatically—very much on the operational level.

The perennialist, by contrast, begins at the opposite pole. He examines a new method of teaching by asking: "What are you trying to achieve?" If you respond that you want the student to learn long division, he continues with his "why's" until you state your basic purposes and goals in educating this student. Only here can he decide if he is to use or discard your new method.

The perennialist is logical. He begins with a central goal of unquestioned validity, then searches for the appropriate means to achieve that goal. He works from principle down to details, not vice versa, and if he happens to be a bit sketchy on his particular method, he will be crystal clear on his purposes. This mind-set often opposes the scientifically oriented trial-and-error practitioner who might be vague about, or totally unaware of, his ultimate goals, but is quite articulate about his immediate methodology.

The world, as the perennialist sees it, is two-fold: spiritual and material. Both are real; both are aspects of the same real world. The material dimension is the more immediate, obvious component. Impressionable to our material senses, it is ever changing, very temporal, and riddled with conflict and chaos. That which is spiritual in us penetrates beneath this material surface and becomes aware of the heart of reality, the spiritual dimension. Here one discovers order, permanence, and the eternal. Here one finds those established principles that make the world an understandable whole, filling it with purpose and meaning, and revealing its essence. Everywhere the perennialist looks, he is aware of this dualism, and as an intelligent being, his attention and heart tend to penetrate beneath the chaotic material elements and seek the organizing principle.

This "two-story" world of the perennialist is dissimilar to the modern "one-story" material world. Adapting an interesting example from Max Weber illustrates this difference. Imagine a laborer who, after working for $20 a week, is given a raise to $25 a week. In response, the modern man would be encouraged to work that much harder, hoping for further increments. But the perennial man, in his two-story value system, would logically reduce his work week to four days. Since $20 is still sufficient for his needs, he is now that much more free to concentrate on the more fulfilling side of life: music, poetry, art, and philosophy. In fact, any other response would be irrational to his mind. (Weber, 1958, p. 59)

The perennialist also sees the world in a hierarchical schema, somewhat like a ladder, narrow at the top and broad at the bottom. Each element in the world is according to its essence, assigned to its rung on the ladder of creation: minerals, plants, animals, man, angels. He knows nothing of evolution, of a climbing up and down the ladder of reality. Each is permanently that which it was intended to be. This is as God has ordained the world.

So, too, has the social order been created. Some are created peasants, some nobles, and some kings. Those at the top of the ladder of society are privileged in dignity, yet bear the responsibility of providing order and means for those at the bottom. Thus the perennialist is authoritarian, not democratic in mentality, and trust and obedience are his central virtues, not creativity and innovation. Educationally, for example, he insists that, while there is value in all receiving the basics of learning, he believes that only a select few are capable of higher learning, and that they alone should receive an advanced education.

To contrast the European perennial value system with America's version, note that in Europe only an elite percentage receive doctorates, and the title, "Doctor," refers to a professor, a position of high esteem. In our country, the Ph.D is conferred at a continually increasing rate and the title, "Doctor," refers generally to the man who preserves material rather than spiritual life.

This belief in man's duality has other pedagogical consequences for a perennialist. Man, likewise, is two-fold: body and soul. The body includes his instincts and emotions, those elements he has in common with the rest of the animal world. The soul includes the intellect and the will, the rational side of man, that which distinguishes him from the rest of the animal world. This potentiality toward reason is what makes man human, and it is the task of education to "humanize" man—to put discipline and order into his emotions and to develop his ability to reason.

Human life, then, is seen very much from the viewpoint of the ancient Greeks, who portrayed man as perfect, never with the imperfections and limitations of this or that particular man. So the perennialist envisions the nature of man in its fulfilled, perfected state, and seeks to realize that perfect model in each student. When this belief is at odds with the social hierarchy, the hierarchy prevails and the education for perfectibility is only for the few.

Again, differing from many contemporary thinkers, the perennialist sees both truth and goodness as absolutes. Truth is unchanging, valid for all, and available to all who seek it through reason. While your perception or mine may differ because of our limitations, any thought of "relative truth" is inconceivable in his world. Equally so, moral actions are absolutely right or wrong and are to be observed or avoided as such. No matter what the circumstances, these values remain permanent and unchanging.

EDUCATIONAL THEORY OF PERENNIALISM

"If education is rightly understood, it will be understood as the cultivation of the intellect," wrote Hutchins (1936, p. 67). The purpose of a perennial education is to humanize the student, not in our modern psychological sense, but in the older sense of helping man become rational. "The mind itself desires to be free—from the animal within, from the enigma without . . . " instructs Van Doren (1959, p. 79). First the student is helped to discipline and subdue his emotions so that they are proper and can serve order. So freed, the student's mind is then capable of penetrating, through the skill of logic, into the hidden realities of the world. Once he has acquired this skill, he will be introduced into the "great conversation" of Western tradition, joining such minds as Aristotle, Shakespeare, and Freud. Through his education, the student will habitually see beyond surface confusion into the permanent order. Strengthened by this new insight, he then acquires confidence and poise, and can enjoy security in every situation and respond correctly to whatever challenge is offered. Education, then, is a search for the meaning of life; a journey to the center of reality from which all knowledge radiates.

The perennial educational task divides itself into three levels: the elementary, where the student must learn the elemental skills of communication, the three R's; the liberal, or general educational level (ideally the last two years of high school and first two of college) where each student is taught to reason and is introduced into this universally valid philosophy of life; and the university or professional training level where each student learns to apply this metaphysics to his particular vocation in life, such as law, medicine, or journalism.

The perennialists have little to say philosophically about the purposes of teaching at the elementary level. This tedious work may be made less painful and more interesting by a variety of devices and methodologies, but however it is done the task remains the same, that is, to teach the skills of reading, writing, and arithmetic. Discipline and memorization will always be central in educating students at the elementary level, even though materials and teaching strategies may vary somewhat.

Little more can be said of the professional level: it is not for the masses, but should be reserved for those few who are capable of attaining it. It should be academically oriented toward a study of the principles of a profession rather than engaged in specific applications.

But the heart of perennialist education lies in the liberal arts program. Under the pressures of a democratic era, perennialists insist that all men—whether destined to be lawyers or janitors—are potentially rational beings, capable of this "humanizing" experience and therefore rightfully entitled to it.

"More difference is made in a person by going to college than by anything else," insists a leading perennialist, Mark Van Doren (1959, p. 66) and of course he has in mind his liberal arts college. A four-year liberal arts curriculum concentrates on humanities, and literature of Western man as best exemplified by Hutchins in the *Great Books Program* sponsored by the *Encyclopedia Britannica* and the

University of Chicago. No electives are offered, since it is inconceivable that the student, yet uneducated, should prescribe what he does not know. Furthermore, Hutchins eschews any utilitarian or vocational orientation and anything that hints of what he broadly calls the apocalyptic four horsemen of education: presentism, skepticism, scientism, and antiintellectualism (Hutchins, 1943, p. 38).

Education is not life, but a preparation for life, insists Hutchins. It does not build on the student's experience, but rather communicates to him the wisdom and insight of the ages which, once received, can be applied to understand the experiences of his later life. Experiences bombard man from every side through life. What he so desperately needs is the key that will allow him to penetrate and determine their true meaning.

By way of example, Hutchins applies this point to teacher education. A teacher is best prepared for his profession not by special professional techniques, but by the liberal arts course itself. Teaching is an art, the art of communicating to others the skills of reason and logic, and of introducing them into the great conversation of Western man. Methodologies, "how to" courses, and the entire School of Education syndrome, so dedicated to practicum, could far better be labeled "training" rather than "education"; they have no place in the academic university.

> The education of teachers is an education in the liberal arts. When this education is good, and falls on the right ground, it produces persons with usable intellects and imaginations who know both what and why they are teaching. A teacher who can answer neither of those questions is no teacher, for thus he proves himself incapable of the one pleasure reserved to him among the pleasures possible to man: the pleasure of being intelligible." (Van Doren, 1959, p. 175–76)

SOCIAL-HISTORICAL SETTING FOR THE ESSENTIALIST MODEL

In essentialism, one finds a second model of transmissive, classical education. It has long been the predominant form of education practiced in America. Other models rise and fall, first capturing the public imagination, then fading away, but essentialism remains as a mainstay of American education. Why? Essentialism, as an educational form, reflects the American culture in ways that the others do not. Perennialism has ebbed over the last 100 years. By comparison, the personalized model and the technological model are recent educational developments. The essential model has been longer and more widely established so that it has created at least two generations who seldom question its assumptions or practices. This is reflected in its self-perpetuating feature. It must also be emphasized that essentialism has long reflected realistic values and purposes of American society. For example, essentialism is closely related to the work ethic and loyal patriotism that characterize our society.

At the outset of the twentieth century, perennial education was strongly attacked and replaced by the progressive education movement that reigned during the early decades of this century. Following World War II, progressivism came under a similarly sharp attack from the essentialists, who, in turn, have been recently challenged by the neoromantics. It is a back and forth pattern, very similar to the larger political patterns of America.

Nevertheless, underlying this undulation of ideas and experiments, there remains a solid basis of educational style that whether popular in our imagination or not, remains the basic pattern for our educational programs, that is, rote memorization of factual data.

Like perennial education, essentialism is conservative, seeking to maintain and pass on to the new generation the convictions of the older generation. But unlike perennialism, essentialism is nonreflective, nonphilosophical. It is far more prone to activity—to doing—than to "wasting time" on extensive philosophical speculation. Looking to the present rather than the past, and to science rather than to the humanities, it is primarily practical and pragmatic.

Essentialism gradually emerged as America broke from European traditions. Jefferson initiated the break by urging the separation of religion from public life, thereby severing theological foundations from education. Jacksonianism represents the second break that separated politics from education as well. Consequently, every man was eligible for political leadership, not merely the well-educated elite. Aside from the three R's, the basic rudiments to which every American is entitled, formal education was not to be a prerequisite or the necessary credential of the seeker of political office. Importantly, neither was education to be involved in political opinion or discussion. Thus, society saw their schools performing a practical function of delivering "just the essentials," the basic skills, free from politically and religiously tainted opinions and discussions, and free from academic subtleties and idea spinning. Schools were to teach only that practical information and skill training essential to leading a useful and productive life. Thus the rise of the term essentialism.

The nineteenth century was the age of the frontier, of the rugged individual who carved out his future with his own hands. It was also the age of religious evangelism in which, beyond the necessary skill to read the Bible, one's inspiration was far more to be trusted than the lengthy arguments of heady theologians. In the wave of this new spirit of America—sometimes described as antiintellectual by the academics—was born the public school, making each man's right to a basic education regardless of his material status a reality.

While characterized, basically, by the same system we know today, early public schools had two characteristics, different, in important respects, from those influenced by recent educational trends: *local orientation* and *social welfare*. They were almost totally local affairs, drawing personnel from within the same local community that financed the program through local taxes.

From 1820 to 1920 public education took seriously the goal of social reform. Socially concerned members of the upper classes, concerned about the needy children of the poor, rescued them from the throes of child labor and provided them with the rudiments of an education already enjoyed by the rich in their private schools. Since basic education was a key to employment, these schools inevitably tended to gear their curriculums toward practical vocational training rather than the classical subjects of the private schools. If, at this point, any remnant of perennialism remained, it was swept away during the immigration movement of the early twentieth century. Most of the immigrants had little use for Chaucer and Latin; they had a great need for practical, vocational subjects.

During periods of intensifying national stress, such as the Depression and World War II, essentialism rose to prominence. National moods of insecurity and conservativism were reflected in national concerns for practical, specific education. The clearest illustration of this trend was the demand for vocational education. During World War II, Isaac Kandel, in his popular *The Cult of Uncertainty* (1943), urged schools to give students the facts, clear and unclouded by debate and opinions. He believed there was enough uncertainty in the world without compounding it in the schools.

The most recent surge of essentialist education occurred during the late 1950s and 1960s. Although this nation was enjoying a time of material prosperity, it suffered under a cloud of tension produced by the Cold War and its threat of atomic warfare. Senator Joseph McCarthy intensified this climate by his innuendoes that America was infiltrated by communists, not only in our State Department and throughout other branches of government, but among our ministers, writers, and schoolteachers as well. This atmosphere was changed with the launching of the Russian satellite, Sputnik in 1957. The myth of Russian backwardness was destroyed and we were threatened by the military potential of Russia's advanced technology.

The most eligible scapegoat for our competitive failure was the American school system, flabby from decades of Progressive education and its student interested courses. In the atmosphere of an educational "Great Debate," schools were accused of being too permissive, too out of date, and even negligent of teaching basic skills and the hard-core subjects. It was time to return our schools to the rigor of the experts, to mathematics, science, and languages, to hard work. If America failed, it was because her schools failed. "Reform her schools and the national purpose will be restored!" was the cry heard from the revived essentialist educators.

There was more involved here than an antiprogressive polemic. The entire image of education was being altered in important respects. Schools, formerly locally oriented, were now set on a trend toward *nationalization,* national in control, in financial resources, and in public interest. Moreover, schools, formerly seen as public assistance for the less able individual, were suddenly recognized as our most valuable national resource: education equals strength for national security and industrial development. What banks were for the nineteenth-century merchants, observed John Galbraith, schools had become for the governmental-industrial complex: a source of power. (Galbraith, 1967, p. 382) And so education became the recipient of millions of dollars from the government and industrial foundations, investments to design and implement curriculum reforms to advance the physical sciences, mathematics, and languages. Later, in 1965, when race and poverty problems were recognized as national emergencies, the funding was expanded to the social sciences as well. The humanities, for obvious reasons, received none of these grants. This was now education for national purposes.

And if the corporate state saw education as a source of power, so did the individual citizen. Education was recognized as having the sole power of determining one's social status and future income: The more extensive the education the better the school attended, so the higher one's level of social advance in later life. This was education for personal power, as well.

The optimism and confidence of the Kennedy era enhanced this new educational attitude. We seemed convinced that, with sufficient government money, plus sufficient Harvard brains, plus the Kennedy spirit to believe it possible, any problem could be solved, be it putting a man on the moon, eliminating poverty, or finding a cure for cancer. And the beauty of it all, or so it seemed during those years, was that it all seemed to work!

In all this "revolution" the spirit of the schools embodied four components of essentialism: vocational education; the input and retention of factual information free of subjective impressions, opinions, and speculation; hard work and heavy competition; and an overall enculturation of the competitive, corporate life of the adult world. Only the disillusionments of the late 1960s—Vietnam, national strife, the flooding of employment markets, and a demonstrated "unworkability" of the American formula for success—have taken the latest bloom off the rose of essentialism. But, nevertheless, it remains our underlying national model. Its latest form, Career Education, currently proposed by the Office of Education is perhaps the 1970s version of essentialist education.

The fundamental concept of career education is that all educational experiences—curriculum, instruction and counseling—should be geared to preparation for economic independence and an appreciation for the dignity of work. (A 1972 publication of the Office of Education, published in an editorial, *The New York Times*, May 22, 1972.)

Essentialism, while often debated and challenged, remains the premier American form of education so long as our culture retains its present purposes and values.

MIND-SET OF ESSENTIALISM

What are the purposes and values that lie at the root of essentialism? These are far more difficult to describe than are those of perennialism. The perennialist dwells comfortably in his principles—principles he has thoroughly thought out and described. The essentialist does just the opposite—he dwells on the operational level of life, and has little or no time to waste in reflective speculation. Speculation is untrustworthy at best; counterproductive at worst! So to engage in a description of his purposes and values is, expectedly, seen as difficult and somewhat interpretive. Nevertheless, these points, at least, are generally agreed upon.

The essentialist is practical, a doer who has an optimistic conviction about the success of his procedure and goes about it quite pragmatically. Persistent effort works, and if it does not, another attempt in another direction will. Competition is a part of his world. The competition increases his motivation and eliminates the unworthy and unworkable. On the other hand, effort is combined—"incorporated" into a huge system in which each performs a specific task related only tangentially to the whole. The world is an institutional, corporate effort, and the individual's continuing task is to adapt his life to that corporate effort. Birth, the seeking of food, health, and shelter, even death and burial, have all become institutional processes, far more efficiently and conveniently handled in comparison than it was by our older, family-orientated society. The essentialist man, then, is a corporate man as well as a competitive man.

The individual, then, sees himself as a member of this larger operation, and one that must be sufficiently productive to satisfy the demands of the corporate process. He is identified, primarily, by his occupation, since this also signifies his social worth and dignity. Basically, social value is gaged economically.

Knowledge, to him, is largely a quantitative matter—receiving and retaining information and practical skills for use at a later time. Serious knowledge is located in the field of science and technology. The arts, classics, and other humanities are for personal enjoyment, but must be placed on the periphery of serious, workaday life. Knowledge, to the essentialist, is free of speculative opinion and value judgments and is well typified by detective Jack Webb of *Dragnet* fame, who, in staccato sentences, insists on " . . . the facts, Ma'am, just the facts!"

One can see more penetratingly into the essentialist's mind by examining his values. Interestingly, he proposes on the surface, an educational model free of values and religious intrusions. The latter he sees as opinions, not facts, a judgment itself that actually presents an enculturation that is deeply value laden. This superficial set of values is classically termed the "Protestant ethic." Max Weber, the famed sociologist, was the first to note this compatibility between the Reformation's religious values and modern industrial life, a compatibility quite parallel to that between Catholicism and the medieval agrarian life.

As proposed by Martin Luther and other reformers, man's salvation is achieved, not in a select area of "spiritual" activity, but in the immediate task given him by God—in his immediate material occupation. And God would judge each man by the wholeheartedness and dedication with which he entered into his given task. In modern terms, each man wins "salvation" by his conscientious endeavor in his occupation, and his effort is evaluated according to the success of his work, that is, his material growth. Hard work, thrift, honesty, competition, justice are the values by which a man lives his life. And little wonder that success and happiness are measured by two cars parked in the driveway of a $60,000 suburban home fronted by an expansive, green lawn. The work ethic has been the American ethic.

Another approach to essentialist values is presented by Robert Bellah, who observes America's values through our "civil religion" and its symbols. (Bellah and McLoughlin, 1968, p. 3) Americans see themselves as having been chosen selectively by the deity to make a noble experiment: to live as a free society by the democratic process. Americans bear this light of their freedom before a darkened world, upholding its way as enlightened and encouraging all others to form governments patterned after it. They believe in democracy, in the capitalistic system, in material life and the work ethic, much as peoples of the past believed in their religion. It is their culture, their vision of reality. Within the value of patriotism, Americans are committed to cooperate toward its ends, toward law and order, toward the enculturation of all diversity into this single value system.

It should be emphasized that our democracy has many ideals and values that are frequently applauded and about which Americans become highly enthusiastic, yet which have little bearing on their practical, daily lives. The values of the essentialists, on the other hand, receive little expression on the public forum, yet are lived intensely on the practical level of national life. Only in those moments when they are threatened by a divergent set of cultural values do they come to the surface to defend themselves.

EDUCATIONAL THEORY OF ESSENTIALISM

In a limited sense, essentialism is a form of vocational education that narrows its content to that basic information considered necessary for the student to lead a productive life—information free of speculation and debate, and especially free of the heavily biased areas of politics and religion. But in a broader sense, essentialism is a transmissive model of education, intending to fully enculturate the student into the adult corporate society of present day America, while it gives him the necessary know-how to perform his occupational role. In a 1972 poll taken by Gallup for the Kettering Foundation (reported by Fred Hechinger in *The New York Times*, Section 4, September 3, 1972) the major purposes of a "good education" are (1) to get better jobs, (2) to get along better with people of all levels of society, and (3) to make more money—achieve financial success.

The American public emphasizes the material goals of education, but often at the expense of intellectual and artistic development. Americans are practical people who believe firmly that education is the road to success in life and that success is measured by materialism. In the Hechinger report, parents expressed that their major concern with today's schools was neither integration nor public financing, but the lack of discipline.

A frequently unpleasant result has been a dehumanized atmosphere in the learning process. The classical model had little to protect itself against such excesses because it had conceived of the learner as a passive receiver of ideas. Unfortunately, in the rush to meet the demand for mass education, many classical educators lost one of the major advantages of their model, the emphasis on precision and rigor in their thinking.

Means to educate a mass population have been devised under the classical, technological, personalized, and interactional models. Yet, the problem of mass education is a vital matter that has not been solved successfully by use of any of the models. T. S. Eliot provides a solution echoed frequently among classicalists. Eliot believed in educating a minority in order to perpetuate a high culture. He felt that we "insist on educating too many people and heaven knows for what." He, of course, did not get into the difficult details of the criteria for selecting that minority. Unfortunately, our predictive abilities are nowhere nearly as accurate as we once thought, so we cannot find out who the high achievers are until we have thoroughly exposed everyone to formal education. As suggested earlier, the classicist also assumes that formal education is the dominant force in the development of the attitudes and knowledge of youth. While this may well have been the case with T. S. Eliot and Robert Hutchins, neither could deny that the composers of some of the very masterpieces they honor were unsuccessful in formal academic matters. Classicists could then, ironically, be supporting a system in which potentially creative people are either overly schooled or absolutely nonschooled. Thus arises a need to determine what specifically has been the curriculum of the classical model.

Curriculum Implementation

The curricular implementation of the classical model relies heavily on learner observation as the means of transmitting knowledge. The curriculum content is selected without the consultation of students. Often this content is selected by a panel of experts that does not include the teacher. The teacher is the agent responsible for transmitting knowledge. Figure 2-1 broadly illustrates the educational process for a classical educational process for a classical educator.

CONTENT – – – – – ➤ TEACHER – – – – – – ➤ STUDENT

FIGURE 2–1.

There are few outside interferences and limited cultural crosscurrents in this process. Teachers are unconcerned with student interests or cultural background or experiences. The characteristics of each component are:

CONTENT
Objective, tightly structured, logically organized, discipline centered, focusing on intellectual dimension of student, no planned social or psychological dimensions

TEACHER
Active, responsible, pace setter; dispenser of "good" knowledge; determining content, method, evaluation; responsible for all content area with a self-contained classroom.

STUDENT
Passive, docile, cognitively pliable, information recipient

Given this framework one visiting a classroom could very possibly view the following interaction:

As Mary leaned across the aisle to read the note from her friend Nancy, she felt a persistent tap on her shoulder. She looked up to see Miss Cunningham looking directly at her. "Where had she come from so quickly," thought Mary, who, only seconds earlier, had checked to see that Miss Cunningham was three rows over talking with another student named Linda.

"Mary, there is not time for fooling around in this classroom; you're here to work. Besides, work is good for you. When you grow up you will appreciate knowing how to multiply. Don't ask questions. Settle down and get to work," stated Miss Cunningham in a soft but very direct tone. "Yes, ma'am," Mary replied as she again began to work on the multiplication problems she had been assigned.

As Mary worked, her young mind couldn't help but wonder what the note from Nancy had said, or remember the fun she, Nancy, and Linda had had last evening. "Multiplication problems," she thought. "Why should I have to do 50 more of these; I got 100 per cent on yesterday's test." Mary sighed and continued, for she knew that if she didn't have her work completed she would have to stay in during recess.

Miss Cunningham continued walking up and down between the rows of children who were busily working on multiplication problems—especially when she was looking at them. While being very concerned about these children, Miss Cunningham believed that some were "smart," and some were "slow," and many were "average." Although she had never defined these labels or made provisions for the individual differences among the children of each label, she did attempt to work with them in three groups.

"Okay, children," said Miss Cunningham, "put your pencils down. The last one in the row collect the papers. Get your desks cleared off; it's time for recess. Seems we never have enough time for our work, with such interruptions as recess, art, and music. Brian, be quiet and keep your hands to yourself, or you'll be staying in while your friends, who are obedient, go outside. Okay, line up by the door row one and row two. I'm only going to call the rows with children sitting tall with their hands folded—row four, row six. Brian, you're ruining it for your row. Row five, row three. Let's walk quietly down the hall. No talking until you reach the playground."

"Miss Cunningham, may I be excused to go to the rest room?" asked Denny. "We don't have lavatory privileges until we come back from recess; try and wait," answered Miss Cunningham. Denny dropped his eyes as the group filed out of the classroom, down the quiet corridor, and out onto the playground.

Miss Cunningham stood watching them running, playing, laughing, and shouting. She hoped they would release all of their energy so that when they returned to class they would pay attention and work quietly until lunch. As she turned to walk away, she noticed Denny standing along the building. She shrugged her shoulders and thought, "A rule is a rule, and I'm only one teacher in the system. He'll just have to wait."

This example of a self-contained classroom is very much a derivation of the essentialist process. It was founded on the theory that man has a dual nature consisting of good and evil desires. Man is constantly in conflict between doing good or evil. His body and its impulses move toward evil while his soul yearns for the good life.

Since children are born in the state of sin, it was believed that they are easily tempted to commit evil acts. Therefore, their elders in church and school must discipline the body, structure the work of the mind through involvement with the classics, and thus nurture the soul. The will of the child must be broken. He must learn to respect authority, for such authority is composed of people realizing his weaknesses. This authority plans what is best for the child in order that he may obtain the "good" life.

The belief remains among classicists that the powers of reason deeply imbedded in the mind must be nurtured with a large supply of dependable knowledge. Robert Hutchins, a leading classicist, argues further that "reason is the proper process, no matter what subject matter is at hand." Thus classicists denigrate sensory experience and empirical knowledge in favor of pure reason. To the classicists, the mind as the locus of reason is severed from the intrusive animal-like tendencies of the human character.

The classicist model generates little sense of changing the status quo. The learner is, rather, encouraged to find a niche in the ongoing functions of the society. Theodore Brameld has suggested that the most common error of classicist thinking is its confusing some of a culture's achievements with a verification of the total culture. The classicist is rarely encouraged to create a new perspective about the human social condition because reason and logic are seen as so dependable.

The classical model, which has enveloped our heritage since the middle 1600s, involves hard work with little diversity.

Religion was the prime factor of the early classical classroom. Early classical educational pursuits were readily found in Puritan homes. Families taught their children proper Bible reading and devotional techniques. When it was felt that general literary standards were not being met by all, the church asked for the establishment of such requirements. Thus, the Massachusetts Law of 1642 was designed and passed by the Commonwealth. Based on this law all children were: to be taught to read; to be taught the principles of their religion; to be taught the laws of the country; and to be engaged in profitable work.

While requirements were stringent, provisions were not made for school development or teacher training. This misapplication of law was rectified in 1647 when the Massachusetts court appropriated legislation requiring the appointment of a reading/writing teacher by every town of 50 families or more. It was further stated that grammar schools were to be developed by any town of 100 families or more. Content curriculum of these early elementary classical schools centered on reading and writing Bible text. Secondary education consisted of the Latin grammar school, which focused primary attention on educating one for college. In 1751 the academy was instituted for the purpose of instructional training in noncollege vocations and trades.

ADMINISTRATION AND GROUPING

School authority was administered through town meeting governance. Decisions such as teacher employment, funding, and methods were undoubtedly within the realm of town meeting decision-making policies.

Early classrooms found children being organized into groups for classification purposes. While such classification was operationalized, children were taught as if they were individuals.

Classification of children into three groups was based on one's reading ability. The lowest class consisted of children with only a very basic reading readiness, children who lacked knowledge of basic reading skills: alphabet, syllabication, basic sight words. The middle group, while somewhat more proficient in language, spelling, and reading, was still unable to master Bible reading. The highest group consisted of those pupils who were proficient enough in reading to master the Bible text.

While grouping was certainly part of the early colonial schools, teachers were seldom found giving instruction to total groups. Numbers were small enough so that teachers could work individually with students. Thus, the teacher could often be found listening to student recitation.

While the instruction of the early colonial classroom was highly individualized it seldom centered on anything other than the cognitive development of the student. Although methods, hours, and discipline were stringent the result was often inefficient learning. Such results have been attributed to poor materials, and lack of educational motivation.

School hours were fixed as follows: From March 1 to September 30, from seven in the morning to five in the afternoon; for the remainder of the year, from eight o'clock to four. An intermission was provided for, from eleven to one every day . . . (Brown, p. 132)

Brown described the daily routine of school in colonial Massachusetts as:

The daily routine in this school began with a short prayer, after which "the Master shall Assigne to every of his Scholars theire places of sitting according to their degrees of learning." Then, "having theire Parts, or Lessons appointed them," the unfortunate youngsters were required to "Keepe theire Seats, and stir not out of Dores," except as the master might give leave to one or two at a time. (Brown, 1926, p. 137)

DECISION MAKING

Decision-making practices of early classical education were primarily developed and implemented by ministers at a local level.

The ministers granted the certificate to teach; They also kept a close supervision over the school to see to it that the teacher remained sound in the faith and of good conversation. The selectmen and committees of prominent citizens also paid periodic visits to the school to make sure that it was being satisfactorily conducted. (Edwards and Richey, 1963, p. 104)

Decisions regarding children and programs were made, primarily, by listening to their oral recitation. Children were assigned specific primer, hornbook, or Bible passages. When they had memorized the passages, they recited. Thus, the test of memory skill was one frequently encountered by children of early classical education.

Programs designed to encourage reading, writing, and memory skills were also developed and evaluated at the local level. The main criterion for success was well-dispensed time allocation. Was the teacher spending sufficient time with each sector of the educational program?

Thus, until early into the nineteenth century the process of decision making within the classical model certainly lacked systematic organization. Courses were added and deleted without considerations for the total curriculum. The primary focus of the curriculum tended to be dictated by the local evaluators and teacher rather than student needs. While decision-making rationale fluctuated, logic and orderly memorization remained constant in early classical education.

Though classicists have held quite consistently to the belief that logic and command of data are the definitive qualities of an educated man, there has been a shift in emphasis among traditional schoolmen. In the eighteenth and early nineteenth centuries such authority was composed of priests, church elders, and tutors. In modern America we call these same people school boards, civic action groups, school administrators, or concerned parents. Regardless of title, the role of the teacher is one of an active responsible pacesetter who is the dispenser of "good" knowledge which is objective, tightly structured, and logically organized. While this model is still in existence, a major reason for its continuation may be the teacher's lack of exposure to other models. This model can also be perpetuated by the work of the community values as expressed by school action groups.

Attempts were made to shift away from the classical model during the 1930s and 1940s when child-centered curricula were being suggested by many educators. However, the launching of Sputnik (1957), the first Russian satellite, redirected thinking toward the classical subject-centered curriculum, at least in the areas of mathematics and the physical sciences. This was directly related to the content of the classical model, which focused on the intellectual dimension of the child, and did not center directly on his social or psychological dimensions. Such dimensions, if developed, occur per chance.

During the post-Sputnik era the school curricula concentrated on the separate-subject approach. For example, a science student would be enrolled in a specific science class such as biology, chemistry, and physics rather than in a general science class that gave little acknowledgement of the specific processes. Social sciences replaced broad social studies courses as students worked in the particular social sciences; for example, anthropology, sociology, and so on. The language curricula was not affected immediately by the rapid changes in science, math, and social science curricula.

Classicists realized that "the knowledge explosion" precluded anyone ever knowing all the pertinent information even in a very specialized discipline. The emphasis shifted importantly to developing a student's comprehension of the logical order and structure of a discipline. This assumed that the student could pursue the details of a discipline in his own time. Being in command of the processes followed by a professional in a particular field, the student could duplicate the specialist's activities. This, of course, depends on the validity of premises like Jerome Bruner's "knowledge is a model we construct to give meaning and structure to regularities of experience." This represented a major and unavoidable shift away from defining knowledge as an accumulation of information, but it still presumes a systematic and orderly structure of the disciplines. It can very easily become a frozen *a priori* by which we reduce the likelihood of imaginative thinking.

Thus, an important doubt is raised about this position. Educators have more recently found that the structures of knowledge can never be more than a "pedagogically heuristic blueprint." The so-called structure of knowledge fails when it is seen as a hierarchical series of subdisciplines and achievements. More recently, many have argued that even the metaphor of a blueprint implies too much fixity. The structures should only be the general plans that precede a blueprint. It must be provocative and heuristic, but not as set as a blueprint. The details and nuances of the structure of a discipline clearly will tell the tale. It is a matter of great delicacy. Regrettably, the structure is often seen as something immutable.

One important philosophical source from which both perennialist and essentialist educators proceed is the groundwork of the logical positivists. The classical educational model that attempted to inculcate information and structure joined readily with the positivists' deemphasis of ultimate aims, personal beliefs and feelings, and speculation about nonquantifiable relationships. The certainty with which the positivists, at the close of the nineteenth century, made their case had very serious ramifications not only for educators, but for philosophy in general. As William Barrett has effectively argued, "the movement known as logical positivism in this country actually trafficked upon the guilt philosophers felt at not being scientists." The unmistakable dominance of science since the mid-nineteenth century has meant that educators gradually came to ignore vital educational factors that were not measureable. The most significant illustration of this factor is the role of individuality. The thrust toward mass education in this country was not the only force that diminished the emphasis on individuality.

While attempts were being made to integrate the curriculum, few realistic attempts were being made to individualize instruction. Students enrolled in school during the late 1950s and 1960s were introduced to a highly structured science and math curriculum and, like Mary, Nancy, Linda, Brian, and Denny, while deviating only slightly from teacher authority, were primarily cognitive information recipients. Learning content was dispensed through one method and evaluated through standardized and informal testing.

The essence of positivism stood against individuality. Science is interested in general principles, not in individual exceptions. Karl Jaspers has summarized succinctly " . . . being is objectified, for positivism would be violated if individuality remained conspicuous." (Jaspers, 1957, p. 49) Not only did this mean that educators ignored nonmeasureable educational factors but it meant that they also tried to measure those aspects of teaching that may not be measureable. Grades and tests as indicators of learning are the most obvious examples of this phenomena. Many are now doubtful as to whether the formal learning of a classroom is much more important than the informal collateral learning. A less obvious, but perhaps just as important, illustration of this phenomena is the practice of basing teachers' salaries and employment on university credits achieved. Again, the correlation is nowhere near perfect between good teaching and amassed graduate credits. Such assumptions may have been a practical necessity in an age of rapidly expanding schools, but they are now being called into doubt. So the positivist emphasis on science and quantification merged with a need for more efficient schools.

Thus, the emphasis of classical education manifests itself in two important educational matters—creativity and the role of practice. The classical model suggests that mastery of basic information must precede one's creativity. It does not cultivate individual creativity because that is seen as an inherent quality.

As colonial America progressed so did the classical curriculum model.

Between the year 1800 and the breaking out of the Civil War, five new subjects found a place in the requirements for admission to the regular college course. These are given as follows, with the dates of their first appearance: Geography, 1807; English grammar, 1819; algebra, 1820; geometry, 1844; ancient history, 1847. Brown, 1926, p. 231 (summarizing Broome, 1903)

Thus, the Latin grammar school, while emphasizing Latin, Greek, and mathematics, began to direct attention toward classical literature and ancient history during the 1800s.

Progress within the classical model may also be seen as the academy became a dominant institution in secondary education. At its beginning the academy had not been instituted for college preparatory training alone, but was also to include a practical, vocational program as well.

One of the main purposes expressed in the endowment or creation of the academies was the establishment of courses which should cover a number of subjects having value aside from mere preparation for college, particularly subjects of a modern nature, useful in preparing youths for the changed conditions of society and government and businesss. The study of real things rather than words about things, and useful things rather than subjects merely preparatory to college became prominent features of the courses of study. Among the most commonly found new subjects were algebra, astronomy, botany, chemistry, general history, United States history, English literature, surveying, intellectual philosophy, declamation, and debating. (Cubberley, 1920, p. 697)

The curriculum of the academy was determined by teacher competency and student demand. As the core of the curriculum continued to be directed primarily toward college preparation, the majority of the students of the academy remained college bound. The classical model greatly emphasizes practice for mastery. It resembles training in that the student is incorporating the conclusions and beliefs of others. Classicists also believe that these important skills and information have a high transference.

The classical model can also be put in perspective by noting the similarity between it and the underlying presumptions of many recently popular street academies. Street academies emerged as a response to public school bureaucracies that became impossible to change. Often these academies focused on development of fundamental skills required for a permanent job—skills such as reading, writing, and arithmetic. Other street academies developed with different objectives, but a large percentage had a heavy emphasis on vocational competencies. The classicists and the street academy people often disagree strongly on the principle of deferred gratification. However, both groups contend frequently that the schools should focus only on basic education pertinent to life's operations. What many essentialists debunk as an educational frill, many modern reformers would also reject as covert moralizing and socializing. For example, many essentialists are suspect of art courses in school curricula. They do not want time wasted on free expression activities that might detract from more rigorous academic learning. Many reformers reject art courses as subtle means of shaping students' attitudes in a manner that encourages elitism. Surely it is true that some street academies are in the business of developing radical ideologies. But many others are only seeking economic independence for their graduates and want the schools to ignore other matters. This similarity is not always understood by reformers desiring to debunk, categorically, classicalism as an inert educational antique. Classicalism is very much alive with both the promise and the pitfalls we find in the other models.

SECONDARY AND JUNIOR HIGH SCHOOL

The American public high school originated during the period when the early classical model (1821) was in use with a very restrictive curriculum. The restrictiveness resulted from the demands of a primarily puritanical society interested in the development of a tightly disciplined person.

An 1824 sample of 28 Michigan cities and towns indicated that the 2748 pupils enrolled in the schools were distributed throughout the following curriculum: algebra; higher arithmetic; English; grammar; Latin; geometry; U.S. history; physiology; natural philosophy; physical geography; German; general history; rhetoric; bookkeeping; French; zoology; chemistry; English literature; geology; botany; astronomy; Greek; Greek history; geometrical drawing; mental philosophy; moral philosophy; trigonometry.

Consider that the philosophical intention of the public high school had initially been that of both preparing college bound students and also providing vocational education to others. If this was the intention, can we not surmise that theory and practice were not well-correlated within the classical model, since all of the above subjects, with the exception of bookkeeping are of a college preparatory nature.

Since the major proportion of students were not college bound they found little relevancy within the existing curriculum. Data provided by Alexander Inglis states that during the school year of 1914–1915, 41 per cent of the children finishing elementary school entered public high school, but only 14 per cent remained until their senior year. This data suggests that either the elementary schools were not equipping students with the basic skills needed to master high school, or, that since the curriculum of the secondary school was not highly related to the student's future plans, he was opting for nonparticipation.

Combining the felt concerns of this data classicists followed the suggestions of G. Stanley Hall and his apostles and developed the junior high school. It was hoped that the junior high school would not only provide provisions for vocational education, but would also design extracurricular dimensions that would encourage intellectual, emotional, social, and moral development.

The junior high school was composed of students from grades 7, 8, and 9 of the traditional elementary and secondary schools. Mandatory school attendance was crucial to the development of the junior high and secondary school development.

The junior high school provided special programs for adolescent age students. Laboratory facilities were designed to provide improved general, scientific, and physical offerings. The science curriculum began to include units discussing one's health. Language arts curriculums began to emphasize composition and literature. However, reading still remained the subject of primary focus. Social studies offerings included geography, world and American history, and civics. Mathematics curriculum expanded to include general mathematics as well as higher level offerings such as algebra and calculus. The content of the curriculum was expanding:

An idea of changes in the relative emphasis placed upon the needs of academic and non-academic pupils with the advance of years may be had from a computation of the percentages of courses in the fields making up the two groups which were offered at each period. In 1906–11, courses offered in English, social studies, mathematics, science, and foreign languages (considered as the academic studies) constituted 76% of the total number offered; in 1915–18, they constituted 61%; and in 1929–30, they constituted only 50% of the total for all fields. The diminution for this group of subjects is due to the relatively greater number of courses in the fine and practical arts, or non-academic group, offered in later years. (Loomis, 1933, p. 165)

At the senior high level American literature began to receive more attention than British literature. Speech and oral communication began to share curriculum space with grammar and composition. Courses combining social, economic, and political problems in America become as widespread as U.S. history, world history, and geography. While the curriculum of the classical curriculum has always been highly discipline centered, it has certainly expanded its offerings within the last 200 years.

During the early 1900s classical educators added the subjects of art, music, physical education, driver education, and safety education to the curriculum. Since their initiation all areas have become firmly established within American schools. While physical education was the most widely accepted of these and it grew more rapidly than the others, vocal music was rapidly accepted by both elementary and secondary schools also. Instrumental music was found predominantly at the secondary level. Unfortunately, art did not meet as favorable an acceptance as did physical education or music education. The personalized and interactional curriculum models are believed to encourage a greater degree of self-expression through the arts.

Driver education programs flourished after World War I because of the sharp increase of the numbers of automobiles on the nation's roadways. Although interest in driver education waned during the 1940's, it can still be found in many contemporary educational programs as a component of the secondary school program.

The chart below has been designed to help you to understand the content of curriculum existing throughout the classical model. While much of the content has remained similar throughout educational history, variation in implementation has occurred. Variation in implementation is highly related to one's educational philosophy and beliefs regarding children's learning styles. As you familiarize yourself with each curriculum model, the underlying rationale of each implementation variation will become more understandable.

Type of School	Course Offering	Approximate Time of Occurence
Latin Grammar School	Latin Greek Arithmetic Ancient History Classical Literature	1600–1880
Elementary	Reading Penmanship Spelling Arithmetic Geography U.S. History Catechism/Bible Manners Declamation Art Drawing Composition Language Arts Social Studies	1600–1976 +

Type of School	Course Offering	Approximate Time of Occurrence
Elementary (cont.)	Physical Education Health Music	
Academy	Reading Writing Greek Arithmetic English Grammar Geometry Geography Logic Latin French Declamation Oratory Composition Philosophy Trigonometry Navigation Astronomy Botany Chemistry History Literature Bookkeeping	1600–1880
Junior High School	World History Reading Arithmetic Language Arts Science Health Literature Algebra U.S. History Geography Civics Art Music Physical Education	1920–1976 +
Public High School	U.S. History Literature Home Economics	1880–1976 +

Type of School	Course Offering	Approximate Time of Occurrence
Public High School (cont.)	Physiology	
	Botany	
	Zoology	
	Biology	
	Music	
	Art	
	Foreign Language	
	Manual Training	
	Mathematics	
	Physical Sciences	
	Social Sciences	
	Ancient History	
	Physical Education	
	Agriculture	
	Bookkeeping	
	Distributive Education	
	Secretarial Training	
	Aeronautics	
	Electronics	
	Vocational Training	

SPECIAL EDUCATION

Education for emotionally or physically handicapped children originated during the early classical curriculum era. As early as 1876, eight eastern states had instituted 12 private institutions designed for mentally deficient children. These institutions were designed to offer the child emotional and educational, rather than custodial, care.

> The point of departure was the individual child as he was found by observation to be, with special attention to his individuality, specific limitations and talents. The aim was the comprehensive harmonious training of the whole child, physically, intellectually, and morally. (Doll, 1962, p. 26)

The mind set of humanity had not always been positively directed toward handicapped children. Review of the history of special education suggests that the following four broad categories have most often been used to refer to special education children: crippled or orthopedically handicapped; mentally retarded; blind; and deaf.

Crippled children were once in demand as jesters in the early European courts. Earlier generations found crippled children undesirous and, thus, allowed them to die. While classical America was definitely interested in the cure and prevention of crippling diseases, special education classes were not provided for orthopedically handicapped youngsters until the twentieth century.

The classicists of the 1890's were beginning to assume some responsibility for the educational needs of mentally retarded children. They looked toward the German special-class movement as a model. By 1875 Cleveland had initiated special education curriculum which was successfully imitated in Chicago, New York, Providence, Springfield, Philadelphia, Boston, and Portland by 1905. The special education curriculum model of the classical era included: self-care training; exercises in practical living; sensory, speech, and physical training; manual dexterity; and basic academic skills. Vocational training was also made possible if the individual showed future employment potential.

Chicago, in the early 1900s, was the first city to establish a class for blind children. Its example was quickly followed at the state level by Ohio in 1906, New York and Wisconsin in 1909. While the cost of educating blind children at the state level was more expensive than at the local level, the state curriculum was found to be more comprehensive. This comprehensive inequality may have existed because the local communities had neither the funds to buy needed instructional materials, nor sufficient blind populations to warrant the hiring of a special teacher.

The first school for deaf children was established in Connecticut in 1817 by The Reverend Thomas Hopkins Gallaudet. Since there was no obviously superior method of communicating with deaf children a great deal of controversy existed regarding the best method of instruction. Classical educators such as Gallaudet prescribed the manual method of communication which involves manual alphabet or finger spelling, natural signs, and bodily gestures. Others believed that the oral method base was needed so that deaf children could eventually learn to read, write, and speak.

While both methods were implemented within the classical era, compulsory education for deaf children did not exist until 1907 when Wisconsin enacted legislation requiring that all deaf children must have some type of school instruction. Schools for the deaf attempted to offer a wide diversity of programs that would eventually qualify participants for some type of vocational work.

ADULT EDUCATION

Education for the adult population of the United States began to receive some minor attention following the American Revolution. Interest in continuing education was apparent by the increase in town, country, and state lyceums. This form of study group first exhibited its powerful force as it moved to gain public acceptance for a tax-supported public school system.

Evening educational programs in public schools as well as an increase of museums, public libraries, books, poems, speeches, plays, and newspapers suggested that the desire for continued education was indeed realistic during the early twentieth century.

Four directions of change can be identified: (1) expansion of "Americani-zation" programs for immigrants; (2) expansion of vocational courses, especially in trade and commercial subjects; (3) extension into secondary and college level subjects with the opening of evening high schools, and (4) experimental sorties into informal adult education. (Knowles, 1962, p. 55)

While early adult education curriculums were primarily composed of vocational, academic, and Americanization courses, the 1920s and 1930s brought a change in focus with the addition of courses in the arts, public speaking, crafts, and creative writing. In 1944 the Servicemen's Readjustment Act, commonly referred to as the G.I. Bill of Rights, provided a rationale for expansion of the adult education curriculum.

. . . (1) they impelled the schools to place greater emphasis on counseling; (2) they increased enrollments in vocational and academic subjects (since many veterans wished to complete the requirements for a diploma); and (3) they influenced the schools toward greater flexibility in dealing with older students. (Knowles, 1962, p. 137)

Thus the proliferation of adult education programs during the period of the classical model's dominance continues to extend into contemporary education programs, as is evidenced by public school and university offerings. Education has truly become a continuous life process within the United States.

EVALUATION

The implementation of classical models of education often suggest that testing be implemented in an attempt to measure and predict success rather than to diagnose and plan curriculum accordingly.

Early forms of evaluation consisted of oral recitation since the major goal of educators was to train pupils to recite from memory. As written material became more readily available measures of evaluation began to include essay or problem-solving tests. Standardized testing became part of educational evaluation at the turn of the century when Alfred Binet and Therese Simon began (1905) developing standardized intelligence tests in an attempt to differentiate normal from retarded children. They eventually broadened their studies to include the measurement of intelligence of all children.

During the 1930s standardized testing began to be viewed as only one dimension of the process of evaluation that also required measurement through informal methods since many instructional outcomes are seldom incorporated within standardized test objectives. Thus testing was no longer viewed as an end in itself. Within the classical model, typically, the child is evaluated against his group. This is referred to as norm-referenced evaluation. An alternative to this is evaluating the child's behavior against some criterion. This is referred to as criterion-referenced evaluation.

CRITERION VERSUS NORM REFERENCED TESTING

Until fairly recently, the practice has been to evaluate students against some group, whether it is his own or an arbitrarily chosen one. This has the disadvantage of (a) making the same children the buzzards in every situation and (b) designing curriculum unrelated to the needs of the children.

The use of criterion-referenced tests are being encouraged by persons involved with personalized evaluation since many of the problems found in norm referenced standardized tests do not exist in criterion-referenced measures because the child is being evaluated only against himself. Criterion tests may be informally designed by the classroom teacher in an attempt to measure a specific behavior. For example, a criterion might be: Can Paula recite her ABC's? The criterion is clear and assessment is relatively simple. Here Paula is compared to an established criterion, that is, she can or she cannot recite her ABC's. Thus the test is criterion-referenced.

The criterion-referenced instrument may be designed to aid the classroom teacher in assessing individual competencies and designing alternate program planning based on individual need. The norm-referenced tests also look at the individual competency but as he/she relates to others in his/her group, that is, which pupils are college bound? Each measure looks at the same behaviors but with a different purpose. Therefore, in selecting or developing an instrument for classroom utilization, you need to state clearly your reasons for testing, as well as the criterion being tested.

Whether criterion- or norm-referenced evaluation is used, evaluation instruments must be chosen or designed.

A test that a classroom teacher devises we shall call an informal test. It can be either norm- or criterion-referenced. A standardized test can also be either norm- or criterion-referenced. The distinction between informal and standardized testing is that the latter has been tried out on many students and "standardized" before being used in an actual situation.

Whether you are using an informal or standardized test, it is essential that a test have the following characteristics:

Validity. The basic question to be answered here is: Does the test measure what you think it is measuring? For example, if a college instructor announces a test and says it will measure understanding and application and then asks five questions related to details on a footnote on page 47, is it measuring what he thinks (or says) it is? Obviously not. We say the test has no *content validity*. If, as a teacher, you want to measure problem-solving ability and give a page of 50 long-division examples, your test will have no content validity.

Where achievement tests are concerned, content validity must be established. First, decide what it is you intend to measure, then decide if your test (or the standardized test) gives a representative sample of the entire field you are interested in testing. If it does, your test is content valid.

There are two other kinds of validity: predictive validity and construct validity. Where achievement tests are concerned, neither of these is an extremely important issue.

Reliability. Another factor which must be determined is the stability with which your test (informal or standardized) measures. If you give a reading comprehension test on Monday and the same test to the same group again on Friday, and no one gets anywhere near the same mark on the two testings, the test is worthless, because it is not reliable. Tests must be constructed so that if the test is given only once (which most tests are), you know the grade is the same grade that the student would get if he took it again.

Ambiguous tests are not reliable because you are getting mostly guesses from the students. They would seldom guess twice in the same way. Long or very hard tests are not reliable; again, you get guessing but this time from fatigue. Very short tests are seldom reliable because the sample of work is so limited that you may or may not select just those items that the student happens to know.

A correlation coefficient indicates the reliability of a test. If $r_{tt} = .00$ (read: the correlation equals zero), the test is completely unreliable. If $r_{tt} = 1.00$ (read: the correlation equals 1) the test is completely reliable. Tests are never completely reliable, but what you want are coefficients that range in the neighborhood of .75 to .99.

If a test is both reliable and valid and you want to use it as a criterion-referenced test, you have no further concerns. However, if you want to use it as a norm-referenced test, you must investigate the norming procedures.

Norms. Norms are as important to the teacher as they are to the doctor. If you took a child to be weighed and measured and the doctor felt that the child was greatly overweight, you would question "Overweight compared to whom?" If you felt the comparison was inappropriate, you would not reject the weight but, rather, his comparison.

The same is true of achievement tests. The score the child receives may be accurate (depending on the validity and the reliability of the test) but the comparisons you make may be totally inappropriate. A child can *only* be compared to the group of which he is a member; that is a 10-year old, or an urban child, or a ghetto child, or a private school child. To make the wrong comparisons is totally misleading and certainly provides no helpful information. Actually it may provide very harmful information.

A test can be used if the appropriate norms are not supplied; just don't use the norms. Use the score in the context of the child's own classroom group, use it for diagnostic purposes, or establish a set of norms for that school. It really is not a difficult process.

The following is a list of other considerations to be made when choosing tests:

1. When was the test first published?
2. Has it been revised recently? Remember dialogue changes with each generation. Many children today have never heard of an "outhouse."
3. Is this an individual or group test?
4. Can the test be hand or machine scored? If it is scored by the testing company, remember to request that student answer sheets be returned. You can plan instruction if you know the consistency of errors made by the student. An IQ score of 103, or a reading score of 6.2 tells you nothing.

5. How many test forms are available? Perhaps you plan to post test after instruction.
6. How long does it take to administer the test? Be careful to measure the desired behavior rather than rate.
7. Does your budget afford the cost of this test?
8. What subtests are available? Perhaps one or two of the subtests measure the desired behavior. If this is the case, then why administer the entire test?
9. Are tables, maps, or graphs included? If so, be sure that they can be read easily.

Directions. The teacher must be careful to use the same directions in administering the test that were used in standardizing the test. Are the directions clear to all of the children? Lack of clarity in giving directions often measures one's ability to interpret directions as well as, or instead of, the previously desired behavior. Are the directions written in vocabulary appropriate to your grade level? Would it invalidate the test if you explained the directions to your children?

Some of this information will be found in the manual. However, keep in mind that the manual is written by the author or the publisher whose major intent is to sell the tests. A less biased review of most tests can be found in the *Mental Measurement Yearbook* edited by Oscar Buros. This reference should be consulted before investing time and money in a testing program.

To avoid misuse of facts it is very important that you state your reason for testing. What do I want to know about this child? How will this knowledge aid me in planning better activities for her? After answering these questions, carefully select your instrument, using the previously stated criteria. After scoring, diagnose and plan your curriculum accordingly. No one has to pass or fail if he is only competing with himself.

Go one step further and explain to your principal that the standardized tests being given to your class at the beginning of the year are really of little instructional value, if all that is returned is a list of scores. Be sure that you can fully persuade him to return the individual answer sheets so that *continued diagnosis* will be the primary function of testing in your curriculum.

Mary's teachers, who were told about tests but never taught test selection criteria, select tests and administer them for information about achievement, proper grade placement, and level of "native intelligence," but without any instructional purpose. They file the test results away, never to be seen again—unless, of course, the school begins a tracking program.

Standardized achievement test results, which may be used to diagnose and plan institution needs, can be correlated with informal test results in an attempt to acquire a more valid understanding of individual student skills. Correlation of standardized and informal tests, if correctly employed, provide a reliable and accurate assessment of student growth.

Informal measures, teacher checklists, textbook tests, interest and attitude inventories are easily constructed if the teacher is cognizant of the behavior she wishes to measure. Does she wish to know if the child has map skills, dictionary skills? Does she wish to gain some knowledge about his reading vocabulary? The behavior to be measured must be clearly stated so that materials designed to measure the behavior can be prepared. Too often teacher tests are not correlated with material that has been taught.

The need for accurate measurement cannot be overemphasized since student growth is the single most frequently used basis for evaluating teaching methods, teacher effectiveness, curriculum, instructional procedures and grouping practices.

Assessing the growth of the student is essential for making decisions related to the individualization of his program. Evaluation—or the comparing of a student's present performance with an earlier performance—must be continuous so that program changes may be made in accordance with the progression or lack of progression of the student. Correct utilization of test results aids the teacher in planning for both group and individual instruction.

GROUPING

Just as evaluation and testing have been misused by many classical educators, grouping has also, through misuse, retarded learning. The most common misuse of grouping is the three usual reading groups: redbirds, bluebirds, and yellowbirds. In actuality, they are treated as though they were stars, bluebirds, and buzzards. Effective grouping may aid the teacher who is interested in individualizing her curriculum based on the abilities of her students. Since most teachers are aware that from grades K–12 reading competence is a major factor in determining a student's academic success, this discussion is intended for persons interested in any area of education K–12.

Once instructional levels have been determined through informal and standardized testing, it is possible to group students for instruction according to their skill development needs, their achievement, their interests, purposes for reading, attitudes for reading, and so on. The practice of grouping is done primarily to allow for some individualization of instruction while at the same time providing for economy of teacher effort and increased student participation. It is more efficient for a teacher to instruct a group of children with similar need, interests, purposes, and so on than it would be to work with a total classroom of separate individuals. Grouping allows materials to be matched to the learner more effectively than would be possible if instruction were geared to a class. Grouping according to individual assessment is beneficial to the learner since the instruction is geared to his interests, needs, purposes, and skills.

Grouping has other results that are not necessarily tied to reading behaviors. These include developing independence in the learner, and helping individuals to work within their peer groups. These features of group-oriented learning are seldom pursued by classicists. Grouping remains little more than a convenience for the teacher organizing the subject matter.

Before effective grouping may begin, it is first necessary to define why grouping is to take place. This means that not only is it necessary to define what is to be taught, but how it is to be taught, and the eventual learning that should result from instruction. Thus, a teacher must first determine the instructional objectives.

Since most teachers plan programs involving reading, let's determine how to begin appropriate instructional groupings. Grouping should proceed on the basis of a preassessment of skills. This preassessment can be made through standardized reading tests, informal reading inventories, textbook testing, and teacher checklists, the uses of which have been described earlier. In addition to preassessment, grouping should also be determined by student interests, attitudes, and educational objectives.

Following this procedure, three different reading levels may emerge upon which groups may be based. First, some students —before beginning formal instruction—may be able to read at the level prescribed as the desired outcome of instruction. These students may be considered as functioning at the independent level of instruction. The teacher has two options for proceeding with the instructional program for these students: they may be allowed to advance on to a new and different program, or they may proceed with the original program independently, with minimal teacher guidance.

A second group of individuals may emerge; these students may be unable to handle the materials required in the instructional program because they lack the skills fundamental to dealing with the content. They would be totally incapable of benefiting from the instructional program as it is now planned. Such children would be considered as functioning at the frustration level. To make instruction meaningful to these children, the program would have to be revised to begin with the skills the student already possesses and develop and build from these the skills needed to master the original program.

Finally, a third major group of students may emerge, a group that can handle the materials and the instructional program, but still require teacher guidance and instruction. These students can be considered to be functioning at the instructional level and they may proceed with the program as originally devised.

While there are three types of groups based on three reading levels, the above should not be taken to indicate that there may *only* be three groups within any given class, or that there must be at least these three groups. Rather, it is to indicate that the three basic levels exist with varying options for instruction. There may be as many groups as are necessary to meet the needs of the learner while still efficiently utilizing teacher energies. It may be that in a given class there are no students at the frustration level, but at the same time students may be at various points within the instructional level. Thus, a teacher may form two, three, four, or five groups within the instructional level, each with different skills, interests, and purposes.

Since grouping is intended to increase participation for students, materials used for instruction are not necessarily uniform for all groups. For instance, the practice of grouping elementary school readers into "red," "blue," and "yellow" birds, has often been the extent of grouping within the classical classroom. Having each group use the same materials, purposes, and teaching methods, but at differing rates, is questionable since purpose, teaching methods, and materials should be modified, changed, and geared to meet the needs of the learners in a specific group.

It should be remembered that grouping must be based on students' interests whenever possible, and would therefore change throughout the different content areas. Groups are also modified according to specific instructional objectives. As a child progresses through the program and fulfills the objectives, the group for which that program has been formed may become unnecessary for all the learners within it or for some learners within it since each student does not necessarily progress at the same speed. If the objective has been met or determined to be unrealistic, the group may be dissolved. New ones, however, may be formed for different purposes and different instructional objectives. The same individuals may or may not be part of both groups. Also, children who progress faster than others may profit from working independently. Thus, for grouping to be effective, not only do specific instructional objectives need to be defined, but constant evaluation of student progress is necessary to maintain the validity of the group in terms of providing instruction geared to the needs of the individual members.

The fact that children's skills constantly develop as a result of instruction also underscores the need for continual evaluation, regrouping, and elimination of some groups and formation of new ones. Thus, groups should be viewed as temporary and changing. At the same time, it should be recognized that not all students need to be included in groups all the time. This is especially true of students capable of functioning at the independent levels.

The testing instruments that can be used in grouping are much the same as those that are used in determining reading levels: standardized tests, informal tests, textbook tests, and teacher observations. The standardized reading tests can be used to provide evaluations of reading levels to determine groups if the skills measured by the test are the same as those included in the instructional program and are tested in the same manner as the skills to be taught. Informal tests also provide reliable indications of reading levels on which groups can be based, especially since they are constructed from the actual materials used in the programs and contain questions related specifically to instructional goals. The validity of the informal test for grouping, as well as for determining reading levels, is dependent on the competence of the teacher devising it. Finally, teacher observations and textbook tests are especially useful in grouping. Such measures can provide a readily available means of charting, on a continuous basis under normal instructional conditions, student progress toward attaining the objectives of the program.

In sum, successful grouping practices, as with successful determination of reading levels, are contingent on the definition of what is to be taught, how it is to be taught, and the anticipated terminal behavior. It is also dependent on continuous assessments of student behavior, on flexibility of established groups, and on changing the instructional program to meet the needs of the students. In general the listed steps should be followed in using tests for grouping:

1. Define the objectives of the instructional program and how these objectives are to be taught.
2. Preassess student reading behaviors by either a standardized test (if it matches the objectives and definitions established for the instructional program), an informal test, a teacher checklist and/or any combination of the three.
3. Form groups according to preassessment (for example, reading levels, interests, purposes for reading, content of instructions, and student attitudes).
4. Evaluate continuously through informal tests, teacher checklists, or standardized tests (which match the instructional objectives), student progress with an eye toward moving students to independent activity if possible, or to regrouping on the basis of new instructional goals where the original ones have been met, or to eliminating groups when no longer necessary.

Many of the elements that determine levels of reading instruction contribute to effective bases for grouping, since a reading level indicates skill competence on a given task that is related to student interests, attitudes toward reading as well as toward self, intelligence, purpose for reading, and achievement. All of these factors are thus influenced by the students' socioeconomic background, peer group influence, and teacher attitudes. Therefore, much of what is said about using tests to determine instructional levels can also be said about using tests as a basis for instruction and grouping in any content area (social studies, science, math, arts), and grade level since a student's reading level is the one most important determinant of his success in any of these content areas.

Thus the curriculum content of the classical classroom is often carefully selected since those subscribing to the classical model of education usually develop one important quality of an effective educator—that is, an immunity to fads. The popular slogans of power—Black Power, White Power, Red Power, Poor Power, Rich Power, Student Power, Teacher Power, and Administration

Power—all underscore the danger of some of the nontraditional models. With his commitment to precision, logic, and reason, the classical educator does not easily succumb to the more aggressive and sometimes more short-sighted measures. These more myopic measures often end up as no more than a palace revolution. A reflexive, healthy skepticism of new ideas can prevent us from falling for a temporary solution when a long-range view is what is needed more. This skepticism cannot, of course, include an automatic rejection of new ideas. These sensibilities are cultivated in a successful, classical school. The emphasis on precision is not something that schools can abandon lightly.

Social/Psychological Ramifications

There are two broad concerns in psychology that deal with classicists' emphasis on preserving accumulated learning and social behavior. One of these concerns could be labeled observational learning and deals with imitative behavior and identification theory.

The individual is aware of a complicated task (for example, carpentry) that he wishes to accomplish, and then he observes a master craftsman at work. The novice, using a trial-and-error approach, is finally able to carry out the task set for himself. Practice teachers are actually doing this as they try to develop teaching skills. They are observing what works in the classroom and then trying to model these practical behaviors. This is perhaps the essentialist philosophy demonstrating itself in modeling behavior. The second concern deals with the student's ability to gain information from a body of defined materials, and could be labeled "mastery." Under this category the subtopics of motivation, remembering, and forgetting, and perhaps some elements from developmental theory need to be considered. If the society has a defined body of knowledge that must be learned, then it is important that the child be motivated to learn the information. Special techniques for stirring his interest in the selected topic may be needed if he is not curious about it. The student must remember the information he is exposed to. He must not forget the ideas that experts have given him to learn. This second psychological concern is central to the perennial philosophical point of view and can be seen in theories of motivation, forgetting, and retention. Separation of content here might imply that identification theory is unrelated to the mastery category. This is not the case. The subcategories that are specified under mastery are directly related to imitation, but they are being considered separately for purposes of clarity, not because the areas lack a common meeting ground.

Observational learning is generally labeled imitation in experimental psychology and 'identification' in theories of personality. Both concepts, however, encompass the same behavioral phenomenon, namely, the tendency for a person to reproduce the actions, attitudes or emotional responses exhibited by real-life or symbolized models (Bandura and Walters, 1964, p. 89).

If one is concerned with the preservation of society's ideals, then it is necessary that the young imitate—and thus acquire—the socially approved behaviors of the culture. How was Miss Cunningham providing for the maintenance of these ideals in her classroom?

IMITATION

In nearly all societies imitative behavior can be observed and is expected. In our culture, certain imitative behaviors are expected even among children and one who does not imitate socially acceptable behaviors may be referred to as an "oddball" or a "square". On the other hand, too much or too obvious copying is not approved. Children reprove one who engages in excessive copying as a "copycat" or a "mocking bird." The line between the two extremes is a tightrope on which one balances by using a sixth sense of what is socially acceptable.

Although imitation was recognized as an appropriate way of learning behavior at least as far back as the Greek Isocrates, it was not developed as a theory until Miller and Dollard (1941) provided a theoretical framework for the study. In *Social Learning and Imitation* they discuss three kinds of identical behavior. The first of these, "matched dependent behavior," occurs when a leader (model) recognizes the environmental cues, but a follower does not (he is producing this similar behavior at a subconscious level). The second kind of identical behavior occurs in "copying behavior." The copier will gradually alter his behavior to approximate that of the model. He must know " . . . that his act is an acceptable reproduction of the model act" (Miller and Dollard, 1941, p. 11). Skinner (1953), in his research on reinforcement, has used the term "successive approximation." Here, a reward is given for even a fraction of the learning that is desired as an end product. Successive approximation is the kind of behavior that we see in the "copying behavior" before it is an identical reproduction. The basic difference is that in "copying behavior" there are no interim external rewards, while interim rewards do exist in "successive approximation."

There is a basic difference in the process development of "matched-dependent behavior" and "copying behavior." The essential difference between the two is that " . . . in 'matched-dependent behavior' the imitator responds only to cues from the leader, while in 'copying behavior' he responds also to cues of sameness and difference produced by stimulation from his own and the model's responses" (Miller and Dollard, 1941, p. 159).

The third kind of observable identical behavior is referred to as "same behavior." This kind of behavior is very common and can best be described by an example: On a Saturday afternoon at a football game, everyone stands up and screams and waves his arms when his team makes a touchdown. No one is deliberately—or even subconsciously—trying to copy anyone else, yet all are doing the same thing. It is an accidental rather spontaneous, "same behavior."

Somewhat later, Rotter (1954) developed an elaborate theoretical system for explaining imitative behavior. According to him the probability of the occurrence of a given behavior in a particular situation is determined by two variables—the individual's expectancy that the behavior will be reinforced and the value of this reinforcement to him.

The concepts developed by Rotter remained largely speculative until Bandura began experimenting with the imitative behavior of young children. Several of Bandura's studies analyzed the variables influencing imitation of aggression. The main hypothesis of one experiment was "Nursery schoolchildren, while learning a two-choice discrimination problem, also learn to imitate certain of the experimenter's behaviors which are totally irrelevant to the successful performance of the orienting task" (Bandura and Huston, 1961, p. 311). The results of the study generally supported this hypothesis. Children did display a good deal of social learning of an incidental imitative sort. The incidental behavior they imitated most frequently was aggressive behavior.

Bandura carried out several experiments in which nursery school children were exposed to adult models who behaved in an aggressive manner (Bandura, Ross, and Ross, 1961). In some of the experiments the children were exposed to real-life human models, some to filmed human models, and some to cartoon models on film. The human model was rewarded for aggression whereas other human models who were aggressive were punished. The conclusions were these: (1) that children do imitate aggressive behavior, boys significantly more than girls; (2) that children imitate either the real life example or film-mediated models and that these did not differ significantly in stimulating total aggressiveness; (3) that children more readily imitate a rewarded aggressive model than they do a punished model.

Bandura and McDonald (1963) verbally described some social situations to children that would call for moral judgments. One group of children was exposed to a model who was reinforced for certain kinds of statements. The child was reinforced when he imitated the model. Another group of children observed adult models who were reinforced; however, they themselves were not reinforced for the same behavior. A third group of children had no exposure to the models, but each child was reinforced whenever he expressed moral judgments that ran counter to his "dominant evaluative tendencies." In this experiment the greatest change was observed in the group in which both the adult model and the child were reinforced.

Basically the research indicates that a child will imitate if he observes a model that has been reinforced. In this research the child was imitating an adult who was overtly reinforced. The adult was performing an act that the child could conceivably reproduce. The adult was reinforced immediately. In the young child-adult relationship, the adult is naturally a prestigious model. These variables would seem to be crucial for producing imitations: (1) the behavior being reproduced, (2) the kind of reinforcement, (3) the prestige of the model. These variables have been manipulated in various ways to investigate the effects of each. It might be helpful to look at the research on modeling in terms of the paradigm presented in Table 2–1.

TABLE 2–1
MODELING PARADIGM

Variable I		Range of Behaviors	
immediate acts	subtle behaviors	words	ideas
Variable II		Kinds of Reinforcement	
negative	none	positive	immediate positive	continuous immediate positive

Variable III		Types of Models (MODEL/IMITATOR)	
adult/adult	adult/child	child/adult	child/child
	(at various developmental stages)		

Variable I deals with the range of behaviors that one might conceivably imitate. The simplest of these is immediate acts, for example, swing the axe like this; and the most complex of these behaviors is the detection and imitation of ideas.

Variable II represents the various kinds of reinforcement that are possible in modeling. The imitator may receive negative reinforcement, none at all, or positive reinforcement, immediately following each response.

There are several model/imitator combinations possible as you can see under Variable III. It is possible for an adult to imitate another adult or for an adult to imitate a child although this is generally disapproved. For example, what is she trying to do, make everybody think she and her daughter are sisters? Why doesn't she act her age? A child may imitate an adult, and a child may imitate another child.

These variables can be combined in any number of ways. For example, one child may imitate another child's words with no reinforcement, or an adult may imitate another adult's ideas with immediate positive reinforcement.

SYMBOLIC MODELING

Symbolic modeling refers to the modeling of symbols such as words, language, and ideas. Mowrer (1950) describes the process of imitation in the acquisition of language. He is concerned with the relationship of reinforcement to the imitative symbol acquired. If we can take a big jump from the pure experimental findings of Mowrer (1950) with language acquisition in birds to language acquisition in human beings, we might suggest that individuals acquire language more readily when exposed to a positively reinforcing, affectionate model. "Language is essentially a matter of imitation of models" (Breckenridge and Vincent, 1943, p. 373).

However, symbolic modeling has sometimes restrained the students' language acquisition. If it is taught persistently as the only form of learning a language the student can only conclude that language is an inert, static phenomena. They do not become aware of the possibility that language is constantly evolving and influencing our perceptions. This is a departure from the classical model, which depends upon the learner internalizing a fixed set of extrinsic symbols as language. Classical educators are unsympathetic to the notion that language is organic and interactive.

Symbolic modeling has implication for use by schools. "Verbal instructions that describe the correct responses and their sequencing constitute one widely prevalent means of providing symbolic models" (Bandura and Walters, 1964, p. 49). It is a rapid, efficient way of communicating and reproducing information and ideas as long as the symbols are presented with care and in a context that has meaning for the child drawing on past experiences. For example, Sherif and Sherif (1956) report that:

One child, typically the one who most frequently initiates activity in a play situation, gave a name to the unnamed toy in his effort to coordinate group play around it. We see that groups standardize names for objects that are important to the activities of the group, thus making possible accurate communication among the members of a group (Kretch, Crutchfield, and Ballachey, 1962, p. 306).

The children were imitating each other symbolically. Those symbols may or may not have anything to do with the standard name for the objects.

In a recent study children were placed in small groups to discuss open-ended problem stories. All the children in the groups imitated other students' ideas, and the group that imitated ideas most also increased most in the quantity of ideas produced. Here is a small sample of one discussion (John, 1972, p. 32–45).

TEACHER. "What do you think will happen now?"
STEVE. "I don't think he'll return the *money. He'll keep it.*"
BRAD. "Yeah, *he'll keep the money* because he's having the time of his life and he won't want to return it."
MARY. "He should return the wallet to its owner."
JOHN. "The *check in* the wallet is *a big one,* the man must be rich."
STEVE. "*That's a big check* all right. I wish I was that rich."
ROSELLA. "Three hundred dollars is not that much money. He's not rich."

Note the italicized statements that show verbal imitation in this small group discussion.

Imitation is an accepted way of learning practical skills, even verbal behavior. Sometimes schools do not provide enough opportunity for children to imitate and learn from each other. The classical model depends heavily on the imitation process, but it is usually restricted to the child imitating the teacher.

MOTIVATION

Mastery of a fixed set of symbols and concepts remains a key pedestal of the classical model. It is easy to espouse learning based solely on the learner's individual interests. But a model that depends so heavily on extrinsic learning must be able to answer two questions: How does one get a child to want to learn? How does one know that the child did learn?

"A motive is any condition within the organism that affects its readiness to initiate and continue any activity or sequence of activities" (Klausmeier and Ripple, 1971, p. 314). "Motivation is an energy change which is characterized by affective arousel and anticipatory goal reactions" (McDonald, 1968, p. 112).

The energy change can be brought about by any one of several forces. Psychologists, Harlow, Maw, and Maw (1965) report that children exhibit curiosity and react positively to new, strange, incongruous, or mysterious elements in the environment. They will seek out new elements, approach and even try to manipulate new or strange objects. Maw and Maw (1965) indicate further that the child will actively scan his surroundings for new experiences and will persist in exploring and examining for extended periods of time. That curiosity is motivating, there can be little doubt. More curious, interesting uncertainties could be provided in the classroom to motivate the children. This is not a technique common in the classical classroom. Motivation there is dependent on more extrinsic and deferred rewards.

Drives and needs can be thought of as motivational forces. Maslow's (1943) hierarchy of needs is perhaps the best-known theory of motivation. It describes motivation as needs fulfillment. Maslow has proposed the following six basic needs: (1) physiological, (2) safety, (3) love and belonging, (4) esteem, (5) self-actualization, and (6) the need to know and understand.

These basic goals are related to each other, being arranged in a hierarchy of prepotency. This means that the most prepotent goal will monopolize consciousness and will lend itself to organize the recruitment of the various capacities of the organism. The less prepotent needs are minimized, even forgotten or denied. But when a need is fairly well satisfied, the next prepotent ("higher") need emerges, in turn to dominate the conscious life, and to serve as the center of organization of behavior, since gratified needs are not active motivators. (Maslow, 1943, p. 394)

One cannot be strongly motivated to know and understand when he is in physical danger or is cold and hungry. Thus, teachers often provide reinforcements of several kinds and develop a classroom climate where student needs are of prime concern. Classical educators seldom hold this hierarchy as their primary concern.

A study by Page (1958) entitled "Teacher Comment and Student

Performance" suggests that a personal approach to learning serves to motivate. In this study the teachers graded objective tests and randomly assigned each paper to one of three groups (1) no comment, (2) stereotyped comment, (3) personal extended comment. On the following objective test groups two and three outperformed group one. The greatest improvement was found in the group of students who did very poorly on the initial test. The personal interest and encouragement of the teacher was a positive influence.

It was said of Alcuin and Charlemagne that they had great respect for, and faith in, each other. Alcuin recognized great potential in his young student. Charlemagne loved and respected his learned master and was highly motivated to achieve and justify his teacher's belief in him. Nearly everyone can recall an instance in his own life illustrating how one individual reacted when another showed confidence in him. The students in your classroom have potential that cannot be measured by intelligence tests or achievement tests alone. This illustration is at odds with the classical model which places a high value on the subject matter as sufficient motive, and less emphasis on the personal interaction between student and teacher.

There are a number of procedures that a teacher can use to provide motivation for students. Sears and Hilgard (1964) stress three motives a teacher can capitalize on in the classroom:

1. social motive (warmth oriented).
2. ego-integrative (achievement oriented).
3. curiosity and cognitive (problem solving).

The classical classroom concentrates heavily on the ego-interpretive (achievement-oriented) motives. Though there is evidence of using the other two motives the activities primarily develop this concept. In other teaching models, of course, the emphasis shifts substantially, while the activities may appear similar. A few activity examples follow:

1. Take children on field trips
2. Have them discuss topics in small groups
3. Have children work in teams
4. Have classroom demonstrations and resource visitors
5. Develop the learning task as a self-competitive game in which the individual is responsible for setting goals for himself and is responsible for scoring his own tests

6. Provide frequent feedback on the accomplishments of subtasks
7. Focus students on a clearly defined objective and help them attain it
8. Plan for exploring new and unfamiliar topics

Teachers usually need to try several different approaches before finding the appropriate activity for each child. The spark that ignites Sally's curiosity into a flame may not be the same one that ignites Jane's interests. Motivation is personal and individual and requires some experimenting by the teacher who hopes to motivate *all* students to learn.

RETENTION AND TRANSFER

In attempting to answer questions regarding student motivation, Miss Cunningham and other classical educators examine students in one of several ways to determine if the information has been learned.

When a response is given once, the student is assumed to have acquired the material. If the student can repeat the performance at a later date, it is believed that he has retained the behavior; he has not forgotten it. If he can use the information he has learned in one situation in a new or different situation, then he has acquired the ability to transfer the behavioral skills he has acquired and retained.

Several theories have been advanced to explain why one cannot remember an event. One theory proposes that a response is lost from the repertoire of the individual due to lack of use. *Disuse* is responsible for deterioration or decay of connections in the brain that provide the desired response. Another theory holds that all learning is permanent unless it is interfered with by new learning. Forgetting is due to *interference* with the learning of a new response that replaces the old one. Still another theory contends that individuals forget, that the brain traces gradually disappear because they are a part of an *ill-structured field*. A high degree of logical organization would help the student remember the desired information. There is, of course, a more clinical theory of forgetting and this suggests that people forget or *repress* the unpleasant experiences they wish to forget. This theory contends that retention is at least partially a matter of will, and that we constantly decide what we will try to remember and what we will forget.

Since retention is pivotal to the classical definition of an educated person, that teacher must be sensitive to each of these theories about retention. Several activities follow that illustrate different ways of improving retention.

1. Apply the learning in a number of situations to increase retention.
   A. Have students engage in problem solving where the application of a learned skill must be applied to a new problem. Use a wide range of related problems to provide for flexibility in the learning situation.
   B. Provide construction projects and dramatizations that call on a renewal and reorganization of the learned behaviors.
   C. Have children keep charts of progress to provide reinforcement for the degree of retention they achieve.
2. Frequent use of what was learned will tend to reduce the degree of forgetting.
   A. Arrange contests, mutual sharing, and team discussions so that students will need to retain what they have learned.
   B. Provide for every pupil response sessions (that is, every child responds with a card that he holds up—a number or a word rather than one student answering aloud.) This provides for much practice and thorough mastery of the response. Team recitations and team exchange of information accomplishes the same objective.
3. A well-structured body of information and meaningful material is retained longer.
   A. Provide materials that are organized and follow through by making explicit the associations that are obvious to the teacher, but may not be so clear to the student.
   B. Emphasize principles and the main ideas in the information being considered. This will enhance transfer in the learning process.

Retention is closely tied to the transfer of learning. It is a common practice among classical teachers to separate retention and transfer of information. This difficulty is a heritage from medieval times, when it was possible to memorize virtually all known information about everything. At that time it was not necessary to consider the transfer of acquired information to completely unfamiliar settings, because there were no unfamiliar areas to the educated medievalist. Other models encourage teachers to draw from the acquired experiences of children both when trying to establish retention and when pursuing new learning. They place greater emphasis on transfer. Many classicists today recognize the importance of transfer in establishing retention, but it was not part of the early, long history of the model.

Once a number of techniques have been employed to enhance

retention of material teachers want to know whether the student remembers the data that has been presented. There are several ways to measure retention. The most commonly used techniques are:

1. Recall—determining a large number of responses having been given a few ideas. In school this usually takes the form of completion tests. Fill in the blanks is a modified form of the recall recognition test.
2. Recognition—determining information from a choice. The objective tests, sometimes referred to by the students as "multiple-guess" is one form, true-false is another form of recognition test.
3. Saving—determining the number of trials necessary for relearning. One might have a team of students review a set of multiplication flashcards until they could respond to all the facts they had learned. Then, after several days, see how many multiplication facts they know, and how many reviews they need to be able to recite all the facts again.

Retention of learning and educational practices involving rote learning have been widely accepted by educators espousing the classical model. Underwood, however, suggests that there are some educators who view rote learning with strong disregard:

Rote Learning: Let us imagine some free associations which these two words might elicit from people in psychological and educational circles, restricting the responses to those which meet standards of good taste. It is likely that the following would be among the most frequent responses: "dull", "Ebbinghaus", "narrow", "verbal learning", "sterile", "nonsense syllable", "memory drum", "serial list", and so on. Two notions might be culled from such associations. First is the notion that rote learning is closely associated with verbal learning, an association which is quite appropriate. The second notion is that rote learning is felt to be dull, narrow, sterile, and in a manner of speaking, deals with a form of learning that is almost intellectually demeaning. (Underwood, 1964, pp. 51–52)

Underwood is certainly not alone in his thinking, since for decades the importance of children learning to recite poetic passages and patriotic songs has been in considerable disrepute. One major often stated criticism is that, although children are able to parrot passages, they often do not understand them and even more often they soon forget them because they found them meaningless.

. . . The student would memorize the multiplication tables in rote fashion. He would be supposed to acquire this knowledge over a period of time and as a consequence of having to use multiplication in contrived situations, such as, say, play store. Undoubtedly no practice of this policy has been quite this extreme, but it seems clear that there has been a marked de-emphasis of rote acquisition. (Underwood, 1959, p. 112)

Thus the classical model of education might be described as "conservative" and "transmissive." "Conservative" because its major intent is to preserve a culture, that is, the values, purposes, and life customs that have given a society its identity and strength. "Transmissive" because it plans to accomplish this by instructing and forming each new generation into the culture through formal education. Many contend that all education, even the most liberal forms of our third model, are subtly transmissive. Whether or not this is true, we are concerned here with a model of education that is openly, intentionally, and on principle, transmissive in its design.

Beyond its intent to conserve a culture, there are other basic characteristics that describe this model. First in importance is its specific content; the set body of information or ideas, already well-established in the minds of the teachers and parents, and now methodically organized and presented to the students. What is to be taught is not based on the subjective interest of the student, but on the objective importance of the content, as determined by society.

Miss Cunningham, as the teacher, personifies the culture to be learned, and her presence in the classroom is its embodiment. She is a bridge between the present and coming generations. She is the *expert* who has absorbed all of the culture's important content and is prepared to present it piecemeal to her charges; she is the *model* who epitomizes the values her society holds high and who, thereby, educates her charges by teaching them to imitate her character.

Mary, Linda, and Nancy are students who play a rather passive role in this education model. Their task is to concentrate, absorb, and retain this content; to learn and imitate, to the point of identity, this set of social behaviors. They assimilate and conform.

While classical education is relying heavily on imitation for the transmission of learning it is becoming apparent in our media that information comes in many different formats. Often the message in the new media is based on an appeal to emotion. In such an environment there is considerable risk in setting forth a curriculum that is based very heavily on the learner behaving as an uncritical acceptor.

PERENNIAL EDUCATION IN AMERICA
A Capsule Summary of Its Background Philosophy

WORLD-VIEW — Continuing the Platonic-Aristotelian tradition, the world is dualistic: the immediate material side, apprehended by the senses, is temporal and changing, basically good yet transient and deceptive; the more basic spiritual side, apprehended by reason alone, is eternal, permanent, the key to the central meaning of reality.

IMAGE OF MAN — Man is a rational animal who seeks first to order and discipline his animal forces: physical and emotional, then to develop his rational potentiality, those which make him truly "human."

THEORY OF KNOWLEDGE — 1) Train the mind to reason logically; 2) introduce the student to the central, core wisdom of Western civilization; 3) teach him to apply these principles of truth to the various practical situations of his professional life.

VALUES — Respect and obedience before the authority of absolute truth and goodness and for those persons who are the representatives and spokesmen of that truth and goodness.

THEORY OF EDUCATION — Education is a humanizing discipline in which the rational potentiality of man is realized. By the power of his reason, the student is led to see the central meaning of reality from which all secondary sciences and phenomenon radiate. In this insight, the core of Western wisdom, the student is then able to understand and respond to any practical situation with confidence and ability.

MAN AND SOCIETY — There is an emphasis on individuality, but not on free choice. Man's fullfillment is defined very little in terms of his relationship to society. Society is only a small part of a larger universal order. Perennialists generally ignore cultural differences.

ESSENTIALIST EDUCATION IN AMERICA
A Capsule Summary of Its Background Philosophy

WORLD-VIEW	The operational world of American industry and business. The competitive, corporate organization that provides each citizen, not only with his financial means, but also with his status, style, and motivation of life.
IMAGE OF MAN	Man is a functioning, productive member of society, identified primarily by his particular occupation and evaluated by his material achievements. He is a worker, a "doer" more than a "thinker," a man of practical science more than a man of the arts and classics.
THEORY OF KNOWLEDGE	Knowledge is "know-how," factual and quantitative in content. Practical, it is oriented, ultimately, to the occupational skills and the financial success of the student's adult life. Education is primarily vocational.
VALUES	Primarily, his values are summed up under the "Protestant ethic": hardwork, competition, materials success. He is also deeply patriotic, seeing in America an almost religious purpose and mission to bring our democratic way of life to those still enslaved. Thirdly, he insists on organization, law and order, stability, and corporate unity.
THEORY OF EDUCATION	Education enculturates the student into the values and patterns of our American way of life. More immediately, it trains the student in his occupational skills and prepares him to be a working, productive member of our society.
MAN AND SOCIFTY	Man fulfills his life by successfully finding a niche in society. He does not ordinarily think in terms of

creating new perspectives for the society. The essential characteristics necessary for living in the society are determined by its elders, not by its younger generation. These essentials can change only very gradually.

REFERENCES

ADLER, MORTIMER AND MILTON MAYER. *The Revolution in Education*. Chicago: University of Chicago Press, 1958.

AUSUBEL, DAVID P. "Stages of Intellectual Development and Their Implications for Early Childhood Education." In *Reading in School Learning*, edited by D. P. Ausubel. New York: Holt, Rinehart & Winston, 1969.

BANDURA, ALBERT AND A. C. HUSTON. "Identification As Incidental Learning." *Journal of Abnormal and Social Psychology*, **63** (1961), 311.

BANDURA, ALBERT AND FREDERICK J. McDONALD. "Influences of Social Reinforcement and the Behavior of Models in Shaping Children's Moral Judgements." *Journal of Abnormal and Social Psychology* **67** (1963), pp. 274–281.

BANDURA, ALBERT, D. ROSS, AND S. ROSS. "Transmissions of Aggression Through Imitation of Aggressive Models." *Journal of Abnormal and Social Psychology*, **63** (1961), p. 25.

BANDURA, ALBERT AND RICHARD H. WALTERS. *Social Learning and Personality Development*. New York: Holt, Rinehart, & Winston, Inc., 1964.

BELLAH, ROBERT N. "Civil Religion in America." *Religion in America*, (ed.) William McLoughlin and Robert N. Bellah. Boston: Beacon Press, 1970, pp. 3–23.

BESTOR, ARTHUR. *Educational Wastelands*. Urbana, Ill.: University of Illinois Press, 1953.

BINET, ALFRED AND THERESE SIMON. *The Development of Intelligence in Children*. Baltimore: The Williams and Wilkins Co., 1916.

BRECKENDRIDGE, MARIAN EDGAR, AND LEE E. VINCENT. *Child Development: Physical and Psychological Growth Through the School Years*. Philadelphia: W. B. Saunders Co., 1943, p. 373.

BROOME, E. C. *A Historical and Critical Discussion of College Admissions Requirements*. New York: Columbia University Publication, 1903.

BROWN, ELMER E. *The Making of Our Middle School*. New York: Longmans, Green & Company, 1926.

BRUNER, JEROME. *The Process of Education*. New York: Vintage, 1960.

BUROS, OSCAR. *The Sixth Mental Measurement Yearbook*. Highland Park, New Jersey: Gryphon Press, 1965.

CONANT, JAMES. *The American School Today*. New York: McGraw-Hill Book Company, 1959.

COUNCIL FOR BASIC EDUCATION. *The Case for Basic Education*. Boston: Little, Brown, 1959.

CUBBERLY, ELLWOOD P. *The History of Education*. Boston: Houghton Mifflin Company, 1920.

DAVIS, ALLISON. *Social Class Influence Upon Learning*. Cambridge, Mass.: Harvard University Press, 1948.

DAWSON, CHRISTOPHER. *The Crisis of Western Education*. New York: Sheed and Ward, 1961.

DOLL, EUGENE. "A Historical Survey of Research and Management of Mental Retardation in the United States." In *Readings on the Exceptional Child: Research and Theory*, edited by E. Philip Trapp and Philip Himelstein. New York: Appleton-Century-Crofts, Inc., 1962.

EDWARDS, NEWTON AND HERMAN G. RICHEY. *The Schools In the American Social Order*. Boston: Houghton Mifflin Company, 1963.

FARR, ROGER. *Reading: What Can Be Measured*. Newark, Delaware: Eric/Crier, International Reading Association, 1969.

GALBRAITH, JOHN KENNETH. *The New Industrial State*. New York: Signet Books, 1967.

GARDENER, JOHN. *Excellence*. New York: Harper and Row, Publishers, 1961.

GOODLAD, JOHN. *The Changing School Curriculum*. New York: The Fund for the Advancement of Education, 1966.

HALL, G. STANLEY. *Aspects of Child Life and Education*. Boston: Ginn and Company, 1907.

HECHINGER, FRED. "Discipline Again Is the Main Concern." *The New York Times*, (September 3, 1972), Section IV, p. 9.

HIGHET, GILBERT. *The Art of Teaching*. New York: Alfred A. Knopf, Inc., 1963.

HUTCHINS, ROBERT. *Education for Freedom*. Baton Rouge, Louisiana: State University Press, 1943.

————. *The Higher Learning In America*. New Haven: Yale University Press, 1936.

INGLIS, ALEXANDER. *Principles of Secondary Education*. Boston: Houghton Mifflin Company, 1918.

JOHN, MARTHA. "The Relationships of Imitations to Children's Ideational Fluency." *The Journal of Education*, (Feb. 1972),Volume 154, Number 3.

JOHNSON, CLIFTON. *Old Time Schools and School Books*. New York: Macmillan Publishing Co., Inc., 1904.

KANDEL, ISAAC. *The Cult of Uncertainty*. New York: Macmillan Publishing Co., Inc., 1943.

KIMBALL, SOLON AND JAMES McCLELLAN, JR. *Education and the New America*. New York: Random House, Inc., 1962.

KLAUSMEIER, HERBERT S. AND RICHARD E. RIPPLE. *Learning and Human Abilities: Educational Psychology*, 3rd Ed. New York: Harper and Row, Publishers, 1971.

KNOWLES, MALCOLM S. *The Adult Education Movement In The United States*. New York: Holt, Rinehart & Winston, Inc., 1962.

KRECH, DAVID, RICHARD S. CRUTCHFIELD, AND EGERTON L. BALLACHEY. *Individual in Society*. San Francisco: McGraw-Hill Book Company, 1962.

LOOMIS, A. K., E. S. LIDE, AND L. B. JOHNSON. *The Program of Studies. National Survey of Secondary Education, Monograph No. 19*. Washington, D.C.: U.S. Office of Education Bulletin No. 17, 1933.

MARITAIN, JACQUES. *Education at the Crossroads*. New Haven, Conn.: Yale University Press, 1943.

MASLOW, ABRAHAM H. "A Theory of Human Motivation." *Psychology Review*, **50** (1943), 370–396.

MAW, WALLACE AND ETHEL W. H. "Differences in Preference for Investigating Activities in Schoolchildren Who Differ in Curiosity Level." *Psychology in the Schools*, **2** (1965), p. 263–266.

MCDONALD, FREDERICK J. *Educational Psychology*, 2nd Ed. Belmont, California: Wadsworth Publishing Company, Inc., 1968.

MCGUFFEY, WILLIAM. *McGuffey's Sixth Eclectic Reader*. New York: Signet, 1968.

MCLOUTHLIN, WILLIAM G. AND ROBERT BELLAH (eds.). *Religion In America*. Boston: Beacon Press, 1968.

MILLER, NEAL E. AND JOHN DOLLARD. *Social Learning and Imitation*. New Haven, Conn.: Yale University Press, 1941.

MORRISON, SAMUEL E. *The Intellectual Life of Colonial New England*. New York: New York University Press, 1956.

MOWRER, Q. H. *Learning Theory and Personality Dynamics*. New York: Ronald Press, 1950.

The New York Times, May 22, 1974. *Career Education*.

CHARTERS, W. W. JR. AND GEGE, N. L. (editors)

PAGE, ELLIS. "Teacher Comments and Student Performance." In *Readings in the Social Psychology of Education*. Boston: Allyn and Bacon, 1963.

PHENIX, PHILIP. *Realms of Meaning*. New York: McGraw-Hill, 1964.

RAFFERTY, MAX. *Rafferty on Education*. New York: Deven-Adair Company, 1968.

ROTTER, JULIAN B. *Social Learning and Clinical Psychology*. Englewood Cliffs, N.J.: Prentice-Hall, Inc., 1954.

SEARS, P. S., ERNEST R. HILGARD. "The Teacher's Role in the Motivation of the Learner." In *Theories of Learning and Instruction*, edited by Ernest R. Hilgard. Chicago: Sixty-Third Yearbook of the National Society for the Study of Education, 1964.

SHERIF, C. W. AND M. "The Standardization of Names. A Neglected Problem in the Study of Symbolic Behavior." An unpublished manuscript, 1949. Summarized in C. W. and M. SHERIF, *An Outline of Social Psychology*, Rev. Ed., New York: Harper and Row, Publishers, 1956.

SKINNER, B. F. *Science and Human Behavior*. New York: Macmillan Publishing Co., Inc., 1953.

UNDERWOOD, BENTON J. "The Representativeness of Rote Verbal Learning." In *Categories of Human Learning*, edited by Arthur W. Melton. New York: Academic Press, Inc., 1964, pp. 48–78.

UNDERWOOD, BENTON J. "Verbal Learning in the Educative Process," *Howard Educational Review,* **29** (1959), 107–17.

VAN DOREN, MARK. *Liberal Education.* Boston: Beacon Press, 1959.

WEBER, MAX. *The Protestant Ethic and the Spirit of Capitalism.* New York: Charles Scribner's Sons, 1958.

CHAPTER 3
Education: Technological

Philosophical/Social Commentary

TECHNOLOGICAL education, which bears some similarity to the classical model of education, maintains the thesis that a model of education is a particular construct of the larger society that engenders it. Thus it can be best understood in the context of this larger society; and it is therefore important to underline some of the dimensions and directions of the emerging technological society.

Following the European perennial society, with its emphasis on the past, and the American essentialist society with its emphasis on conserving the present, technological society is oriented toward the future. But it is a future arriving with such rapidity that it is already penetrating our present industrial culture beyond imagination. Toffler's *Future Shock* describes our consternation when we realize that yesterday's comic strip showing Buck Rogers rocketing to the moon became reality in 1969. Accelerated change, under the power of modern technology, sweeps the future into our laps. For example, moon flights fail to excite many children born in the space age. When asked by his first-grade teacher, "Did you see the rocket launch?", the child replied, "It's no big thing."

SOCIAL-HISTORICAL SETTING
FOR THE TECHNOLOGICAL MODEL

As industrial society once replaced the energy of man and animals with the mechanical energy of oil, steam, and electricity, so now technological society replaces the human mind with the mechanical mind of the computer. Its speed, accuracy, and capacity makes possible the solution of highly complex technical and organizational problems. As the medieval man struggled to coexist with nature and modern man rose to dominate it, so technological man now has the power to imitate and even recreate any facet of nature, including life itself. Through biology and medicine, he not only can decide how many children he will have and when, but he may soon be able to decide their sex, intelligence, physical features, and personalities. He can literally choose the next generation, and with this power of choice comes an awesome responsibility. For example, cloning, the possibility of exact replication of specific individuals, illustrates most clearly the complex choices that advanced technology has forced upon us.

The agricultural man, at home in rural society, was followed by the industrial man of an urban society. Now the technological man emerges into dominance in a "suburban" society of white collar workers—a middle class of technicians, organizational personnel, and "service" people of education, law, welfare, health, and similar professions. This is a new society of laborers who work with their minds.

This is not to say that we, today, exist in an era that is totally technological, but rather that our civilization is edging its nose into this new age. Civilizations do not march phalanx style out of one age and into another. Our present society remains overwhelmingly industrial, particularly in its economics, politics, and culture, as Victor Ferkiss so ably argues. In examining our present condition, one quickly sees people whose lifestyle is decidedly preindustrial and even some who have survived the centuries as preagricultural primitives.

The educator becomes particularly conscious of this curious overlap of time as he studies these teaching models. Educationally, our society is overwhelmingly essentialist, and the technological models described here are only beginning to develop. Moreover, who has not attended a "modern" university without seeing education conducted entirely in the lecture method—a style unchanged from the middle ages.

Technology in education originated in the 1940s from the needs of the military. The armed forces needed to train men quickly for very specific tasks. The inevitable conflict between the ineffable qualities of a broad education and the specific, precise qualities of skills training did not become evident during the wartime crisis.

The use of technology was, however, heightened during the late 1950s when two forces converged. First, the faith in science as a way of improving the quality of life was at its peak and virtually unchallenged. Second, the school population had grown rapidly and without interruption for nearly a generation. Teachers were in short supply, and the demand for inexpensive means of teaching students was widespread. With characteristic emphasis on hardware the American economy responded with a surfeit of technological aids designed to teach students more effectively and more economically. Few doubts were raised about any possible long-range ramifications of using technological devices extensively in classrooms.

During the decade of the 1970s, two important trends in American society profoundly affect this underlying argument on behalf of teaching technologically. First, a rather sudden decline in birth rates and a gradually declining school population has relieved some of the pressure for schooling more children with the same amount of money. Second, more people are interested in teaching as a career than there are teaching vacancies. It is entirely possible, then, that employing live teachers could prove far cheaper than purchasing technological hardware (for example, televisions, tape recorders, computer equipment) and developing the necessary software (for example, the actual content of a programmed learning biology unit or the lessons on a language laboratory tape). These trends may at least relieve some of the pressure for immediate adoption of educational technology. In fact, they enable us to take the time to assess carefully the hidden consequences of teaching with considerable technological assistance. No longer are the pressures so great that we must once again scurry onward with an important reform on an emergency basis. In such emergencies we seldom have time to foresee the future possible crises we may be creating. For example, it is entirely possible that while programmed learning imparts information readily or develops skills effectively, it narrows a student's conception of what constitutes learning.

In his book, *Self-Renewal*, John Gardner has restated a classic question of social reform. Instead of asking "How can we cure this specific ill?" we must ask "How can we design a system that will continuously reform and renew itself?" (1964, p. 5)

For educational technology, that revised question is not so grand but just as vital: "How can we be sure that we do not practice as teachers in ways that restrict or paralyze particular aspects of the human personality?" Such a risk is clearly present in the imprudent use of educational technology.

The technology is only beginning. Many of us are little aware of its power, but it decidedly exists in many forms, advances with amazing rapidity, and is inevitably reshaping our entire existence.

Specifically, then, what is the technological age? One part of the answer is the truth of Francis Bacon's axiom, "knowledge is power." The modern scientific "knowledge explosion," intensely accelerated

through the development of computers, is being applied to the material dimensions of our lives with such force and influence that it has become a primary force shaping the meaning of our lives. The "machine" is transforming our lives. "Machine" does not refer simply to the complex apparatus one sees in a Coca Cola factory or Charlie Chaplin's *Modern Times*, but to electronic devices, computers, psychological systems, biological and chemical methods, and, moreover, to man's "systematic, disciplined approach to objectives, using a calculus of precision and measurement and a concept of system." (Bell, 1968, p. 643)

Nor are we speaking just of man and the machine, as if it were a mere adjunct of his life. Technology is entering into every nook and cranny of contemporary man's life; it shapes his purposes and values to the point of becoming substantive of man himself. In the description of Emmanuel Mesthene, Director of Harvard's Program on Technology and Society,

Our technologies today are so powerful, so prevalent, so deliberately fostered, and so prominent in the awareness of people, that they not only bring about changes in the physical world—which technologies have always done—but also in our institutions, attitudes, and expectations, values, goals, and in our very conceptions of the meaning of existence. (Holtzman, 1970, p. 237)

This is an important point in the understanding of technological education. To illustrate it, let us look at the phenomenon of "rapidation." Man's picture of the world and of life's meaning is a synthesis of his basic experiences. But these basic experiences are being changed radically and will continue to change at an incredible pace over the coming years. Experiences which for centuries implied "permanence" and "always-the-same" now say "change" and "tomorrow-will-be-different-and-bigger-and-better."

Two examples: transportation and communication. In Figure 3–1 let each of the notches across the horizontal bar equal a life time, say 70 years, and each notch on the vertical bar equal a major change, a "revolution."

From the invention of the wheel up through the seventeenth and eighteenth centuries, man knew of no alternative modes of transportation beyond walking, riding an animal, or riding in a cart drawn by an animal. "It always was and always would be the same," was his primal experience of life. The nineteenth century saw a revolution in steam engines, and the beginning of the twentieth saw another one with the automobile. Then "revolutions" increased geometrically —airplane, jet, rocket, with speeds of from 15 mph to 18,000 mph and beyond—with several in each life time.

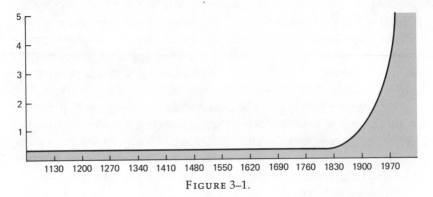

FIGURE 3–1.

Fifty years ago, a judge in a little western Pennsylvania county seat, owned a "winter" home across from the courthouse, and a "summer" home on the edge of town, twelve blocks away. Each summer he moved "to the country." Today, a typical businessman will commute by the "air shuttle" from Boston to New York, over 200 miles, and return each night.

Our experience is "I don't know what my transportation mode will be tomorrow, but it will be radically different from today's." Change is the primal experience of life, *a basic experience entirely new in the history of mankind*—not simply change, but change at a geometrically increasing rapidation!

A parallel example is man's mode of communication. The scale is duplicated. For centuries, the mode was verbal communication or written message. The nineteenth century introduced the telegraph. Then, in rapid succession, came the telephone, radio, television, and telstar, until we now watch men as they walk the surface of the moon. Shortly, we will be able to visually communicate instantly with any other person on earth—or in outer space.

Change! Geometrically accelerated rapidation! On the basis of this primal experience, technology's world view and its accompanying lifestyle will be in increasing discontinuity with the recent past. (Adolfs, 1967, p. 46)

What shall we think of this imminent environment? Shall it be the longed for messianic age . . . or rejected as a materialistic demon?

Both opinions fill our bookstores. Orwell's *1984*, Huxley's *Brave New World*, and Ellul's *Technological Society*, near classics condemning this new age, are now joined by a new series led by Burgess's *A Clockwork Orange*. Technological society, they say, will destroy man's privacy, individuality, personal life, and love. All society will be transformed into machines—cold robots.

The opposite theme, orchestrated by more heady although less literary men such as Herman Kahn, Marshall McLuhan, B. F. Skinner, and Alvin Toffler, accept the technological age as an enlightenment in which myths and superstitions are cast aside and man stands in full realistic possession of his powers. They urge us to put aside our fearful resistance and commit ourselves to technology's wonders—to technology's "progress" wherever it may carry us—to allow it to set its own pace and to discover its own goals. It is we who must adjust to this new age, not the age to us.

There is a third course including such European "humanists" as Fromm, Tillich, Teilhard de Chardin, Jaspers, and Buber, who concluded that man is entering a new level of human evolution. Technology itself is a tool, a neutral device in the hands of man. However, it can easily and subtly become a very powerful device. It is man alone who can and must infuse values and purposes into technology. He must assume responsibility and "humanize" technology, rather than allow it to "technologize" man. But, they further observe, man has yet to make his choice and, for the moment, we suffer an eclipse in human purposes and values.

Philosophically, there are three alternatives. For our purposes, however, it is the second path, that of the optimistic supporters of technology, which will be further investigated. Americans have a strong, unmitigated faith in technology as a value in itself. We trust progress, the scientific, and the near miraculous applications of modern technology. We are anxious that more Americans will openly trust this new era and enter into its wonders.

MIND-SET BEHIND TECHNOLOGICAL EDUCATION

By his very nature, the technologist is not the medieval metaphysician who broods on his basic principles and philosophy of life. He is an activist who finds ruminations of the mind impractical and who prefers to find his validity or fallacy in the immediate feedback of his experiments. Nevertheless, while he himself may not reflect upon and define his own thought patterns, they are there. They follow predictable patterns, and can be analyzed along the same lines followed when we examine other philosophies of education. The starting point of our inquiry is with the Logical Positivists of the 1920s.

Modern science is a recent phenomenon. In the European, perennial atmosphere, science was never taken seriously among the academics until the turn of the twentieth century. Even then, evaluated by traditional standards, it was hardly given the recognition which, in fact, it deserved. An understandable reaction developed among a group of European scientists and intellectuals who came to be referred to as "The Vienna Circle." In contradiction to the reigning metaphysical standards, they established their own principle of validity; only the empirical, that is, that which can be observed and measured, can give valid knowledge. If data under investigation can be proven empirically, we then know that it is valid and has meaning. But if our data is not of an empirical nature, we cannot test its validity. This is not to say that it is fallacious, but only that we can never know. It remains in the order of "nonsense" and is therefore meaningless. In this "unknowable" category must be placed almost all that was being taught in the European universities: all metaphysics, religion and theology, ethics, and all theoretical formulations of the social sciences.

Aligning themselves with this new principle, the social sciences, including education and especially psychology, have moved from their theoretical approach to the empirical. Their presentations are now based on hard data, objectively observed and statistically measured. The subjective is patiently disciplined out to present "value-free" conclusions. Rather than searching for an overarching theory, the social sciences now produce fact modules—bits of information which are stored, retrieved, and applied as needed. And since they are dealing with objective information, empirically validated, the work of the scientist is considered independent of its social ramifications and allowed to follow its own star, progress.

WORLD VIEW

How then does the technologist perceive the *world* in which he lives? First, he would describe it as a totally material world—an empirical world. That which cannot be observed or measured does not, for all intents and purposes, exist. The "spiritual" or similar dimensions are rather meaningless, more to be ignored than directly denied. He deals with quantitative reality, the type of things which can be scaled out on a table of distribution, the famous bell-shaped curve. In consequence, he tends to ignore the qualitative except to the extent that it too can be quantified and observed as overt behavior. Understandably, the technologist is far more at home as he places a man on the moon—a feat of precise engineering— than he is at attempting to eliminate poverty—a feat of human interaction.

The most interesting aspect of the American technologist's world is his faith in scientific progress. Science gives him a certainty, an indisputable rock in a highly fluid age, a certainty that replaces the reassuring "God" concept of the perennialist. The advance of research and its technological applications are unquestionably evaluated as progress—the "better"—and while this advance leads man into areas yet unknown, continually reshaping his life, he never questions that which *can* be done, *ought* to be done. There is something here of the spirit of Hilary, who, when asked why he climbed Everest, said simply, "Because it was there!" He has no doubt that what science will discover tomorrow and what kind of world technology will produce will be for the betterment of all mankind.

IMAGE OF MAN

What kind of *man* lives in America's technological world? Freed from much of the myth of prescientific ages, he is seen in his true light, a behavioral type.

G. DOLE

"The computer doesn't like me!"

Reprinted from *Sunday Parade* with the permission of George Dole.

Although more complex, he is not essentially different from any other animal who responds instinctively to the stimuli of his surrounding environment. One element especially ruled out of man's new image is the autonomous "inner man," the man who was said to have possessed a "free will."

B. F. Skinner's recent study, *Beyond Freedom and Dignity*, amplifies this point:

> What is abolished is autonomous man—the inner man, the homunculus, the possessing demon, the man defended by the literature of freedom and dignity.
>
> His abolition has long been overdue. Autonomous man is a device used to explain what we cannot explain in any other way. He has been constructed from our ignorance, and as our understanding increases, the very stuff of which he is composed vanishes. Science does not dehumanize man, it dehomunculizes him, and it must do so if it is to prevent the abolition of the human species. To man *qua* man, we readily say good riddance. Only then can we turn from the inferred to the observed, from the miraculous to the natural, from the inaccessible to the manipulable. (1972, p. 201)

Man is totally determined by his environment. Therefore, if we wish to relate to him (or better to educate him), we need only learn, scientifically, how to control his environment in such a way as to reshape his behavior. "What we need is a technology of behavior," Skinner advises us.

THEORY OF KNOWLEDGE

What does the technologist consider *knowledge*? Following the Positivists' lead, knowledge is that which can be verified empirically, the quantifiable. Purging out theoretical umbrellas and value judgments, he concentrates on hard data, collected in modules of statistically proven facts. Minute and more self-contained than interrelated, these facts are stored into knowledge bands and made available for retrieval when needed. Since he sees knowledge as content and as quantified, the technologist can well speak of a "knowledge industry" and a "knowledge explosion."

VALUES

Can the technologist have anything to say about values, since he urges for value-free studies? Pure technologists contend that one should not include the normative in this mode of education. To say "It is wrong to steal," is nonempirical and meaningless. One can say

"I am angered by stealing," since this is observable behavior on my part, or "Stealing is antisocial," since this can be researched and established or rejected empirically—but the simple values of good and evil are, in themselves, meaningless. Skinner does project the value that positive reinforcement is good and negative bad, but only on the empirical basis that the former is effective and the latter unpredictable and inefficient. What behavioral patterns we should reinforce is a mute question unless we decide on the basis of classroom efficiency or some other behavioral measure.

But there is a more basic point in this value question. Technological man, totally determined by his environment, cannot be held subjectively responsible for his actions. For example, advises Skinner:

We shall not solve the problems of alcoholism and juvenile delinquency by increasing a sense of responsibility. It is the environment which is "responsible" for the objectionable behavior, and it is the environment, not some attribute of the individual, which must be changed. (Skinner, 1972, p. 74)

There is no sense in praising some for heroic deeds or extraordinary service since they are as much conditioned to their behavior as the bank robber and murderer is to his. No one says "thank you" in Walden II. This need not open the gates to chaos; the people of Walden II are all pleasant, cooperative people. As a planned society, all hostility and antisocial behavior has been conditioned out and its citizens are happy and helpful to each other, not on the basis of an internal ethic, but on the basis of a conditioned social equanimity.

It must be stressed that we are considering the mind-set of "optimistic" American technological society, the mind-set informing most present technological educators. True, there are signs of a shift away from this kind of thinking and into the third, "humanized" technology, but if such a movement is afoot, it is a departure from most current technological education. How do "optimistic" technologists implement their ideas in the classroom? What is the theory of education that follows from this vision of reality? A discussion of these questions is our central task.

TECHNOLOGIST'S THEORY OF EDUCATION

Our schools face backward toward a dying system, rather than forward to the emerging new society. Their vast energies are applied to cranking out

Industrial Men—people tooled for survival in a system that will be dead before they are. (Toffler, 1971, p. 399)

Toffler has not spoken in vain; technological models are already emerging, both in fact and in theory. CAI (computer-assisted instruction), IPI (individually prescribed instruction), competency-based instruction, and the behavioral modification techniques of performance contracting form many educational programs across our country. To guide these programs, leading spokesmen, such as B. F. Skinner of Harvard, and Robert Glaser of Pittsburgh, have given a well-articulated theory of technological education.

As a first thesis, the theorists announce that education is now *a science* and no longer an art. Formerly, learning was a rather hit and miss, unpredictable affair, depending heavily on the "charisma" of the teacher. It was time consuming and wasteful. Technology now reevaluates education as a science, establishing the dynamics of learning and designing programs that yield 100 per cent efficiency. "Education is perhaps the most important branch of scientific technology. It deeply affects the lives of all of us." (Skinner, 1967, p. 17)

Technology establishes, as its working base, the *observable behavior* of the student. While quite popular, "personality" is an inadequate base. It is too general and inaccessible, too tied in with the prescientific "inner man" theory to serve as a practical basis for a design of instruction. Technological education sees man as a behavioral type and relates to him in terms of his external behavior. But with observable behavior as a basis such vague objectives as "education for democracy," "educating the whole child," "educating for life," and similar statements give way to specific behavioral objectives for which learning plans can be designed to accomplish their goals with measurable accuracy. Since the child is determined by his environment, the educator need only calculate how to manipulate his environment to effect the desired learning. And, as the psychology section will explain, this core process of learning through environmental control has been successfully researched in the reinforcement theory of Skinner. We have the technology of learning; we need only implement it in our schools.

This brings us to our third principle: the "machine" can be programmed as an effective teacher far beyond the limits of its human counterpart. "Teaching may be defined as an arrangement of contingencies of reinforcement under which behavior changes." (Skinner, 1968, p. 113) But a particular lesson, for example, how to solve a mathematical problem, may involve as many as 25,000 contingencies, a far greater number than could ever be mastered by an individual teacher, even if she were to concentrate on one student and to teach only this one lesson. Since these are clearly beyond the capacity of the human teacher and since effective mechanical and electronic devices are available, why should they not be substituted.

> The simple fact is that, as a mere reinforcing mechanism, the teacher is out of date. This would be true even if a single teacher devoted all her time to a single child, but her inadequacy is multiplied many fold when she must serve as a reinforcing device to many children at once. (Skinner, 1968, p. 22)

What, then, is the new role of the human teacher if not to teach in the traditional sense? Any variety of secondary roles. She is now free, say the theorists, for social concerns, to give guidance and counseling, or, in Buckminster Fuller's words, to return to her studies. But in any estimate, the teacher "is not the central element in the (technological) conception of the teaching process." (DeCecco, 1968, p. 12)

Through behavior modification techniques successfully developed and applied, disapproved behaviors are "extinguished," approved but weak behaviors "reinforced," and generally desirable behaviors of students are "shaped" into their optimum patterns. Programs, built on Skinner's model of positive reinforcement, effectively operate with simple tools such as the teacher's smile, a kind word, or a pat of approval. Utopian as it sounds, Walden II is actually being erected in many contemporary schools.

Our final inquiry involves the kind of student technological education envisions as its end product. And clearly, it is not everyman's student. When Charles Silberman vocalizes the critique of many, saying that the technological student cannot specify his own goals or reach them in his own way, that he cannot express a concept in his own words or construct his own application, he is in effect saying that the technological student is unique to this model. (1970, p. 201) He is a technological student, uniquely consistent with his own principles and to his own theory of education.

This education concentrates on data or information internalized and available for future retrieval and application, and behavioral skills necessary for present and future competencies. His tendency is to concentrate on the quantitative and the specific. As Glaser acknowledges, it is difficult in this model to teach an appreciation of Shakespeare, the value of patriotism, or to theorize on the meaning of history, but to the extent that these objectives can be quantified and translated into external behavioral performances, they can be programmed.

Technology allows the content to be internalized immediately. The university graduate student, studying statistics through a programmed text, is learning in essentially the same manner as a third grader learning to read through programmed materials, the autistic child learning to communicate via behavior modification, or the pigeon learning to walk in a figure eight through a simple reward system by responding to environmental stimuli and having that response reinforced. No complications arise from conflicting opinions or discussions; each step is simple and clear enough to require a minimum of reflection. In the end, the learning is based on instincts. As successful as this training might be, there is concern that it might become one-sided. Anthony Oettinger, a strong believer in technological education, comments that "without other forms of education, the student may mature under the dangerous illusion that there always exists a correct answer to every question." (1969, p. 148) As in all transmissive models, the student remains basically a receiver of information and a trainee of skills.

The vast resources of the computer allow technological education to escape the "lockstep" atmosphere of the classical classroom and meet the instructional needs of each student at every stage of his education. While atmosphere may be less "tailor made," progressivism, through a prescribed body of information, is "lockstepped." One must master a given set of information before being promoted to the next more advanced level.

The educational theory of the technologists is not simply theory. It is at work in hundreds of schools across the country. Further, it has every promise of expansion as the larger technological culture continues to replace our present industrial culture.

Nothing stands in the way but cultural inertia. But what is more characteristic of the modern temper than an unwillingness to accept the traditional as inevitable? We are on the threshold of an exciting and revolutionary period, on which the scientific study of man will be put to work in man's best interests. Education must play its part. It must accept the fact that a sweeping revision of educational practices is possible and inevitable. When it has done this, we may look forward with confidence to a school system which is aware of the nature of its tasks, secure in its methods, and generously supported by the informed and effective citizens whom education itself will create. (Skinner, 1968, p. 28)

Curriculum Implementation

CONTENT
METHOD $- - - - - \rightarrow$ STUDENT $- - - - - - \rightarrow$ TEACHER $- - - - - \rightarrow$ CONTENT
METHOD

FIGURE 3–2.

The generic characteristics of the technological curriculum are:

A. CONTENT   Governed by prescribed social competencies; electronically centered curriculum; student progression individualized; multisensory approach

B. TEACHER   Plans, aids, and supplements student learning

C. STUDENT   Passive recipient of knowledge.

Given this framework, which is based on the preceding philosophical view, one visiting a school espousing this philosophy could very possibly encounter the following interaction.

Eric Michaels entered his nongraded school and took his seat at a learning carrel. He keypunched his name onto the empty computer spaces.

Good morning................ The punching of his name alerted the computer to the fact that Eric was ready to begin study of the program his teachers had earlier prepared for him.

As the first frame appeared,

---

1. Programmed instruction is a learning experience in which a program replaces a tutor. The student is led through the program by a sequence of learning sets which are structured to teach the student a desired skill.

   _____ _____ is a learning experience that replaces a tutor.

Eric remembered that earlier in the week Ms. Roser, one of his instructors, had mentioned that since Eric was interested in computers he might enjoy learning about programmed instruction. With this recollection, Eric keypunched the words *programmed instruction* and smiled as frame two appeared.

2. Good work, please continue.

The program which may be presented to the student in the form of a teaching machine or a programmed textbook consists of statements, facts, and questions to which a student is asked to respond. The response may be made by filling in short answers or selecting an answer from multiple choices. Correct program responses are made available for the student to compare with his own. Frame one of this program asked you to respond by _____
A. filling in a short answer
B. selecting from multiple choices
C. leaving the space blank

Eric hesitated and then punched A. and B. Frame three appeared

3. Very good thinking, please continue.

In programmed instruction large subject areas are divided into smaller thought sequences called frames. Material presented in one frame is related to material presented in preceding frames. Material contained in a frame is brief, with generally one question being asked about the material. In many programs the ability of the student to answer the questions is a prerequisite for proceeding to the next frame.

The above discussion of a programmed instruction frame is in itself a _____.

While very interesting to Eric, this was somewhat difficult. He read the frame again and keypunched the word *frame*. Immediately frame four appeared.

4. Excellent, please continue.

B. F. Skinner's demonstration of a practical learning device based on reinforcement drew attention from academicians who began to discuss the educational possibilities of programmed instruction.

Programmed learning was early applauded by _____.

Easy, thought Eric as he punched *Skinner*. Frame five appeared

> 5. Well done, please continue.
>
> While the idea of programmed instruction may have originated with the Elder Sophists of Ancient Greece, Maria Montessori may have been the first to attempt to apply a mechanism to a psychological theory of child development.
>
> The first person to attempt to apply a theory to a mechanism was _____ _____.

Eric punched *Maria Montessori* and wondered who she was.

> 6. Good work, please continue.
>
> At the American Psychological Association Convention in 1926, Sidney Pressey, a psychologist from Ohio State, exhibited a teaching machine.
>
> Sidney Pressey presented a _____ in 1926.

Eric punched *teaching machine* and thought about those in his classroom: television; filmstrip projectors; slide projectors; record players and earphones; talking typewriters and books with recorded stories. He smiled and thought about the fun he had working with the teaching machines. Frame seven appeared.

> 7. Very well done, please continue.
>
> Industry has also adopted the programmed instruction for many on-the-job training situations. This occurred because programmed instruction could often accommodate daily scheduling better than could traditional lectures. Having two or three trainees using machines at one setting seems more practical in industry than stopping production to have the entire office attend one lecture.
>
> For job-training economy, _____ adopted programmed instruction.

As Eric keypunched the word *industry*, he wondered how many other people were learning through computer-assisted instruction at that exact moment. As frame eight appeared, Ms. Roser put her arm around Eric and asked if he needed any help. He told her of his thoughts. She smiled and reminded him that computers were involved in sending men to the moon, in developing new energy systems, and in eliminating disease and famine. She also explained to him that someday he wouldn't have to read to acquire information but that any knowledge he might desire could be obtained from an electronic bank where the information could be directly transmitted to his nervous system by means of coded electronic messages. These several uses of computers made Eric anxious to learn more about his nervous system. As he listened he thought of all the things he would like to learn without reading. Ms. Roser asked if she could listen to Eric read and answer frame eight. Eric began:

---

8. Well done, please continue.

While programmed instruction in many instances successfully supplements both business and educational programs, research suggests that success of this supplement is dependent on the acceptance level of both instructor and trainee. One weakness of programmed instruction seems to be that students are rewarded when their thinking positively correlates with the programmer.

In some instances programmed instruction is a _____ to both business and educational programs.

Eric keypunched *supplement*, and Ms. Roser smiled as frame nine appeared.

---

9. You are doing a fine job, please continue.

The program is the most important part of programmed instruction. One type of program which offers the student many answer clues is linear programming. In such a program the student is required to recall information presented to him in a frame by either filling in an answer or selecting one answer from a series of multiple choices. When the child obtains the correct answer, he is positively reinforced as he continues to the next frame. All students working the same program proceed through the frames in the same order.

This program on programmed instruction has thus far been a _____ program.

Eric keypunched *linear* and proceeded to frame ten.

10. You are doing very well, please continue.

The second major type of programmed instruction program is called intrinsic. Incorrect responses are corrected through a system known as branching. The sequence of frames which the student views is determined by his response to the questions. An incorrect response generally directs the student toward additional frames dealing with the subject with which the student experienced difficulty. A correct response directs the student to skip the additional frames.

If you think the above frame is linear, turn to frame 11. If you believe this frame is intrinsic or branching, turn to frame 13.

Although Eric realized the frame was intrinsic, he pushed number 11 to see exactly what happened with incorrect answers.

11. Frame ten is intrinsic because the direction which you took in your program depended on your response. The basis of the intrinsic or branching system is the computer's ability to record performance data and select sequential program frames on the results of previous performance. Branching provides for the individuality of the respondent by designing a program from his correct replies.
A program in which the direction of the program is determined by your responses is called an _____ or _____ program.

Eric keypunched *intrinsic* and *branching* and continued to frame 12.

12. Good work, please continue.

A linear program is one in which your response does not alter the frame sequence. All frames are viewed by all students.

A program in which all students follow the same frame sequence is called a _____ program.

Eric keypunched *linear* and frame thirteen automatically appeared.

13. Good, please continue.

A third type of program is the combination program. In the combination program, some of the frames are linear while others are intrinsic.

A _____ program combines aspects of both linear and intrinsic programs.

As Eric keypunched the word *combination*, Mr. Hill, his other instructor, approached and asked if he was enjoying the programmed instruction program. Mr. Hill and Ms. Roser were team instructors who believed that their major function was to work individually with their students. Mr Hill suggested that when Eric finished his program he might like to join with Mr. Hill and four other students to discuss how computers are programmed. Eric agreed, since he had been discussing this concept with Ms. Martin, the teacher aide, only yesterday. Mr. Hill watched as Eric began frame fourteen.

14. Well done, please continue.

A teaching machine is a device which presents a program. The basic function of all teaching machines is to teach a program frame by frame. Some programs, such as yours, are connected to a computer.

A teaching machine may serve as a _____ when it presents a program.

Eric hesitated. Mr. Hill reread the frame with Eric and suggested that the teaching machine is often the teacher. Eric laughed and keypunched *teacher*. Frame 15 appeared.

15. Good work, please continue.

A program must be reliable. To establish such reliability the program must be administered to students and revised according to their responses. Without this data one cannot be sure that the program teaches what it was designed to teach.

The _____ of the program is important to determine if it teaches what it was designed to teach.

As Eric keypunched *reliability*, he and Mr. Hill reviewed the term, since they had discussed it early that year. Mr. Hill moved to another student as Eric began frame 16.

16. Very good, please continue.

The final step in developing a good program is the development of a multiple choice or fill-in test which measures student knowledge of the presented material. Success on the test is determined by initial program objectives. If the main points of the program are not learned, the program may be revised through evaluation.

At this time you are to group with Mr. Hill, who will determine through discussion with you the degree of program competency. Thank you, you did very well.

This program, as well as others prepared by Ms. Roser and Mr. Hill, is being evaluated continuously and restructured in accord with stated program objectives. Some advantages of programmed instruction are (1) immediate positive feedback and reinforcement for the student, (2) release of the teacher from drill type teaching, and (3) individual student progressions. Among the disadvantages are (1) boredom with mediocre programs, (2) depersonalization and elimination of self-expression, (3) enormous initial outlay costs.

While several distinct educational applications of technology exist, this chapter deals primarily with classroom learning activities. However, one needs to remember that if the use of technological devices eventually reduces administrative efforts, it must be considered a school improvement. The time saved may well allow the principal to devote himself more to improving the human relationships within the school. Of course, there is a real danger that the principal will become fascinated with the improved technology and lose all human touch with his school.

Bergson's intuitionist theory of art contends that "Art catches us in our unawares." One of the aims of this chapter is to draw attention to similar subliminal influences of relying on technology as a teaching device. Because schools have traditionally operated as adjuncts of public policy, educators cannot afford to be cavalier and individualistic about the "unawares." A critique of the subtle consequences of technology will follow an explanation of the applications of technology and education.

Techniques, methods, devices, and media have been part of the educational process since man first endeavored to teach. Earliest attempts at teaching took the form of demonstration or personal exploration. Symbol illustrations conveyed messages on the walls of caves. These crude beginnings were followed by the blackboard and the printed page. For decades most information being taught was conveyed through these two fundamental teaching aids: textbook and chalk/blackboard.

Technologists have encouraged the emergence of many new teaching devices. Many of these devices appear with such rapidity that the classroom teacher is barely able to become familiar with one before another is introduced. Technology has become so much a part of contemporary man and his educational surroundings that it is difficult to imagine either teaching or learning without its aid. The classical educator did not have the same familiar experiences with technology.

The traditional methods of instruction were so wasteful that children would attend school for years and get only a smattering of reading and writing. One of the chief causes of this waste of time was lack of equipment. For instance, in the teaching of writing, engraved copy slides and steel pens practically revolutionized the method, leaving the teacher free to assist, suggest, and criticize. The introduction of slates in the early nineteenth century, although not hygienic, was an improvement from the standpoint of relieving the teacher of making pens. (Johnson, 1904, pp. 91–92)

Before 1800, few materials other than the blackboard, chalk, erasers, and globes could seldom if ever be found in classrooms.

The blackboard was not introduced into even the city schools earlier than from 1825 to 1830, and did not find its way into the best country schools till after 1840. Globes, imported from England, were found in a few of our colleges perhaps as early as 1800, but did not make their appearance in the public schools before 1850 . . . . The first school apparatus proper for illustrating geography, astronomy, geometry, and arithmetic, which came within the reach of public schools was that devised by Josiah Holbrook, and manufactured for him after 1835 by his sons . . . consisted at first of a five or six inch globe, a three inch globe in halves, a very simple tellurion, a few geometrical forms in wood, and a numeral frame or arithmeticon . . . . Competition presently brought several good 6, 8, 10, 12, 18, and 20 inch globes into the market, at reasonable prices, and spelling frames, large slates and frames with wooden panels, covered with liquid slating, slated walls, chalk-rubbers, crayons and crayon holders, drawing frames, chemical globes, geotellurions, celestial indicators, globe timepieces, microscopes, magic-lanterns, etc., followed in rapid succession. (Barnard, 1867, pp. 522–24)

Until the early 1900s teachers were not required to pursue training in educational technology. Because most teachers are not well trained in this area, many materials of the technological curriculum have never been fully utilized. Lack of understanding has also caused many teachers to feel fear when encouraged by the administration to surrender manual tasks to machines. This fear is described by Keppel.

Knocking at the door of the little red schoolhouse is the giant fist of American business—big business: International Business Machines, Xerox, General Learning Corporation, Radio Corporation of America, Raytheon, merchants of hardware, makers of electronic computers, copying machines that can make a million sheets of paper look exactly like the original, and above all, makers of money. On the other side of the door is the classroom teacher, facing something unknown, and frightening, and protecting children huddled in a corner. In seeming competition for the mind of the school child, America's tycoons appear pitted against a lonely, underequipped, underpaid classroom teacher. It is a modern picture of Goliath and David, and it is the result of far more fact than fear. (Keppel, 1967, p. 187)

Technological changes in education can be divided into three categories. First, we have witnessed a rapid, steady growth of the use of audio-visual aids in classrooms. These include films, tapes, television, records, filmstrips, slides, and still photographs. The aims of these diverse aids are two-fold: to impart information and to provoke thought. It is in these activities that we find the greatest amount of subliminal impact. A second category involves the programmed material. The principal aim of this activity is to train a skill or to impart a fixed body of knowledge for later use by the student. Again, in this category there are ancillary influences, but they are usually not subtle enough to be considered subliminal. A third category involves computer hook-ups to centralized data banks that permit a student to secure information about any larger question, however complex, that he is trying to solve. The aim here is to reduce the amount of tedious legwork so that the students can have more time for other explorations. It also serves to widen the horizons of students. Assuming that the data bank includes a universe of information and does no editing on its own, use of this kind of device results in a very limited amount of subliminal implications.

We will treat these categories separately, but one important issue underlies all of them. It is possible, except for the substantial subliminal effects in the audio-visual technology, to design the devices so that they are nothing other than helpers in the normal ways of doing things. Because such a large amount of money and energy is involved in developing and employing technological assistance, and because it is not easy to change the material, it is possible to wind up with a closed and immutable educational system. Any school system may assume that it has faults and contradictions in both its philosophy and its practices. Before engaging technological assistance in its program, a school must review its faults and inconsistencies. Too often schools either skip this step or expect the technology to cure the ills. Without such a review, there is some danger that using technological assistance will enable a school to continue perpetrating these faults and to do so more efficiently and more indelibly.

HARDWARE—SOFTWARE

The technologist views the hardware approach as important in stressing the origin and application of teaching machines to education and educational training systems. Controversy over this view dominates the literature of educational technology.

The software approach refers primarily to shaping behavior through programs associated with the technological model: programmed learning; task analysis; systematic evaluation; objectives.

Emphasis on both the hardware and software approach to technology flourished in 1958 when the National Defense Education Act was passed. This act provided selected school districts with funds to buy equipment for programs in science, mathematics, and foreign languages.

AUDIO AIDS

Audio equipment primarily includes record players, radios, language laboratories, telelectures, and tape recorders.

The portability and relatively low cost of the record player and radio increases their classroom utility. The tape recorder is another very versatile device because specialized sounds may be kept and replayed whenever the user wishes. The tape recorder may be used to highlight developmental language creativity by designing a sound collage.

Sound collage composition involves collecting environmental or commonplace sounds on tape; camouflaging these sounds through speed modification and tape loops; and then organizing and combining these sounds to form new combinations of sounds.

The result of the sound collage may be used in a variety of ways. These might include using it as a composition of its own, using it in a study of sound classification, or using it as a stimulus for creative writing. In addition to this the composition could be used as an introduction to twentieth-century art forms or as background sound effects for an original dramatic production.

The language laboratory is primarily used to offer students instruction in foreign languages. Students listen to a recording, and then verbally model the sounds they have heard. The teacher is able to moderate this experience through a mechanical device enabling her to listen to the conversation. The idea of the language laboratory has been incorporated within many technological reading programs for elementary schoolchildren.

The telecture enables groups of students to listen to prearranged conversations with renowned speakers. For example, a class studying child development might greatly desire to speak personally with famed psychologist Jean Piaget. Through the use of the telecture or amplified conference telephone connection technique this can be made possible.

Audio devices that basically pick up and transmit sounds supplement and enrich the curriculum. The listener may become involved with sounds existing outside of his environment. A supplement to the basic printed material, audio devices offer exposure unavailable by any other means.

Audio devices may be used in isolation or in conjunction with visual aids in an attempt to create the setting necessary for one to totally experience pictorial representations. For example, music by Palestrina would certainly enhance one's learning about the historical Renaissance period. A similar experience might involve one's listening to Debussy while studying Impressionism.

Audio devices not only offer the means of reaching large groups, but also provide for a great variety of individual student tutoring. The role of the teacher becomes less burdensome because she is freed from repeating lectures, and attempting to recreate situations for which she is unskilled.

VISUAL AIDS

Visual aids primarily include chalkboards, bulletin boards, opaque projectors, filmstrip, and overhead projectors, teaching machines, and textbooks.

Visual aids should be directed toward students who evidence a strong sight modality. Not all children learn equally well through the same sense. Unfortunately, without the aid of technology all children would be required to learn primarily through their auditory sense.

Of all visual aids the textbook is the one most frequently used. In many classes the textbook is the major information source, and teachers are viewed as extensions of textbooks. In other classrooms the teacher serves as the central factor synthesizing information from many textbook sources. The chalkboard is closely identified with this process since it has, for decades, been used in learning situations as a tool by which information may be transmitted.

Another long-time classroom tool utilized as a means of transmitting information has been the display or bulletin board. Two-dimensional demonstrations are often found on felt, bulletin, or display boards. Through these sources information may be either quickly conveyed, or reinforced.

The filmstrip projector is certainly the most commonly found projector in American schools. Filmstrips, made from 35mm film, may be used by individuals or groups of students. This instructional device also serves to free teacher time that may be greatly needed for working with individual children having difficulty with particular concepts.

Optical reflection is the principle on which the opaque projector operates. A darkened classroom is required for use because light is reflected off the projected material. This projector is widely used by students wishing to view photographs, drawings, documents, or other such materials. The opaque projector, like many other visual/audio aids may be used as a means of transmitting information without the total aid of the classroom teacher.

The overhead projector is another device found in the technological environment. It may be used as a means of transmitting information to both large and small groups. Tables, graphs, and lists are presented with considerable clarity through the use of an overhead projector.

Teaching machines that convey information on just about every subject may be found in many classrooms. While automated features may be characteristic of some teaching machines, this is not standard. Teaching machines differ primarily in their presentation of information and questioning.

Many educators look askance at programmed material and teaching machines because of their early use as review, drill, and testing measures. While today's programs do serve these objectives they are also being designed to individualize programs for independent study.

Educational programs completing and supplementing visual devices utilize the student's sense of sight. Visual aids may be employed in tutorial situations because they can be used to recreate the past, present abstract information, represent microscopic life, provide three-dimensional effects, and utilize natural color.

Technologists suggest that the role description of the "live" teacher must be redefined in light of instructional aids via technology. This redefinition must occur since the positive effect of technology upon the curriculum is dependent upon both extent of use and purpose.

Through audio as well as visual aids the following positive educational results are made available: individualized instruction becomes a reality; curriculum materials based on sequential development are made available; students are matched with materials according to their strongest learning modality; and, the classroom teacher is provided with planning time.

MULTISENSORY AIDS

Technological materials involving more than one sense in the learning experience are commonly referred to as multisensory aids. Motion pictures, television, sandtables, sandpaper cutouts, indented objects, and felt or velvet boards are the most common multisensory devices found in educational settings.

The use of motion pictures primarily involves the senses of hearing and sight as well as the extension of emotional and other human experiences. Simplicity of operation and a vast range of personal involvement have been two prime factors in encouraging motion picture adoption as a teacher aid. Students may explore their own world, and those of others, through film.

Television is a media that has advantages similar to those of film. While offering children the possibility of exploring the lives of others, television may also capitalize on the present, providing students with an opportunity for involvement in events as they happen.

Cognitive and psychomotor development are possible through the use of technological materials that involve the tactile and visual senses. Learning involving multisensory aids is strongly encouraged for young children in the process of developing reading readiness skills. Multisensory aids are inexpensive and adaptable to a variety of learning experiences. Staffs utilizing technology should continuously evaluate its effectiveness for a particular subject area or goal accomplishment.

COMPUTER-ASSISTED INSTRUCTION

Computers in their simplest form have been part of the educational scene since the 1950s. The first educational computer, the analog was limited in implementation accuracy because it arrived at answers by measuring. The analog was followed by the digital computer, which may be used for addition, subtraction, multiplication, and division, drawing pictures, and doing language translations. Presently being manufactured is the hybrid computer that combines the strengths of both of its predecessors.

Through the use of computer-assisted instruction the interests, motivation, and range of information provided to students can be greatly expanded.

The use of technology in an educational setting must be carefully implemented, and educators must be fully cognizant of the following concerns.

1. Who prepares the materials?
   A. goals
   B. programs
   C. in-service training
   D. research
   E. evaluation
   F. funding
2. Who is responsible for program control?
   A. administration
   B. faculty
   C. community
   D. materials
   E. funds
   F. values transmitted
3. What is the role of the teacher?
   A. developer
   B. diagnostician
   C. implementer
   D. evaluator
   E. in-service model

4. How are students affected?

5. What are the community reactions?

In implementing technology within the educational setting one must be careful to avoid direct application problems.

An experiment that might well carry these "direct application problems" was carried out in reading as taught by a computer at Stanford University. The results of this were reported in *Computer Assisted Instruction* (CAI) (Atkinson and Wilson, 1969). During a school year first-grade children, who through diagnosis were found to have potential reading problems, were instructed for 20 minutes per day before a color television terminal set that allowed for responses on a light pen. Correct responses could be pointed out easily by the small child. The computer had a number of options built in and if the student could not, or would not, respond to a given stimulus—"Place your pencil on the sound that 'blame' begins with," the same gentle voice simply repeated the instructions three times. If the child had not responded, he was branched to another alternative. The gently, charming voice suggested a story with a read-along response to the headset microphone. In observing the experiment, one could detect great interest, even fascination with the task on the part of the 17 children involved. Following a 20-minute instruction period, the results of each child's participation were analyzed and program adaptations were designed by a team of experts. The experimental results indicate rather outstanding success for the program. Indeed, the children did learn the well-presented phonic elements.

Two or three details about the experiment might be of interest. First, the program was carried out under federal funding of considerable proportion. Second, a highly trained team of experts was needed to analyze and provide program adaptations. Third, a manual for reading dealing with social interaction in the classroom was provided for the teachers. Plays, group discussion, and small-group interaction topics were suggested for the teacher. The experiment was carried out in "emergency" housing, not in the classroom. Certain problems of humidity, temperature, and dust had to be monitored carefully so that the computer would function.

Without it, there was no program. One day the computer was on the blink and instruction was carried out in the classroom. The children sent the computer a "get well" card.

You can see that nearly all the "direct application problems" apply here, and yet some questions might be raised. Should all learning take place in a classroom? Should not learning be the primary focus of all instruction, not time costs or equipment? You can undoubtedly raise any number of other questions regarding the Stanford CAI Program.

The Computer Assisted Instruction Program given as an example is only one kind of programmed instruction. There are several variations of computer-assisted instruction. Gaming, dialogue, drill and practice, problem solving, and tutoring are among the modes of instruction that a computer can provide. In all of these the student sits at a terminal and responds to the instruction, sometimes through microphone response, sometimes through multiple-choice buttons, and sometimes, as in the example, by touching a cathode-ray tube with a special light pen.

Besides the CAI programs, instructional television, programmed texts, or any system in which the student interacts with a machine, material, person, or any combination of these to attain specific behavioral objectives can be seen as an implementation of reinforcement theory. In all of these "individualization" is the standard, and "efficient use of time" the standard bearer. The rate of learning and degree of difficulty should be considered for each individual. A little third-grade boy was talking to a friend. He said, "Me and Roy are tied in math." "What do you mean, you're tied?" asked the friend. "Well, when it comes to solving problems, I'm better; but when it comes to figuring examples, he's faster." This youngster, at the age of eight, knew that speed and the degree of difficulty one can deal with are both important to achievement. Programs handle learning rate rather well since they allow the student to progress at his own rate and he can go as rapidly or as slowly as he wishes. To deal with degree of difficulty, branching programs have been developed. These programs provide the student with choices and seem to offer better opportunity for student learning than do linear programs. Branching programs require more room for storage and more initial development.

The principle for programmed instruction is this: Decide on a final behavioral objective and get the student to take a small step toward the goal. Reinforce the responses as the student goes through a sequence of steps toward the goal. This does not seem far from the goals and practices of education generally. This approach has gained wide attention since many states are studying possibilities for implementing competency-based institutions.

Producing the program for instruction in the classroom is a very difficult task. Persons who know computers do not necessarily have content expertise. It requires some group application of skills to develop and apply a program.

A good program is not developed out of the mechanics of program construction or out of familiarity with the psychology of learning; it is not developed out of subject-matter expertness, nor through the sheer artistry of an able teacher; it requires the collaborative effort contributed by the various expertnesses. (Hilgard, NSSE, 1964, p. 413).

Teachers are needed to help develop good programs. Teachers are also needed to provide balance in the student's program machine use and his need for interaction with others. What will you do with programmed instruction in your classroom? Can you think of innovative ways to use the essence of ideas from stimulus-response theory in your class?

Programmed instruction and the utilization of technology within the curriculum must be implemented systematically and continually evaluated for effectiveness. Such a process is most effective when program objectives are clearly delineated.

The utilization of management systems in educational planning is expanding. Through such a system the teacher is able to compare student growth with stated objectives and reschedule or recycle student programs according to exhibited competencies. An introductory step in implementing such a technical system is dependent upon the development of behavioral objectives.

MANAGEMENT SYSTEMS

The systems approach to education has become more widespread because of the increased use of technology during the 1950s and 1960s. Looking toward business management as a model, educational technologists designed curriculum strongly dependent on an interactional base. This interactional base involved the working together of parents, students, teachers, administrators, school boards, and community. The type of complimentary interaction desired is dependent on well-correlated goals and educational philosophy.

Two management systems that exemplify this complex interaction are the PPBS (Planning, Programming, Budgeting System) approach and the PERT (Program, Evaluation, Review Technique) networks. Both systems, while highly accountable, are being used by many school systems as an aid in identifying goals, programs, evaluative techniques, time allocations, sequential development, and cost effectiveness.

Technologists encouraging a systems or management approach to curriculum specify that one needs to begin planning by conducting a needs assessment. A thorough needs assessment can only be conducted if the program planner has a clear understanding of the general goals to be accomplished. For example, the general goal of a school may be to provide better reading instruction for all of its students, grades K–12. A needs assessment might include a review of existing programs, status of children within the program, definition of "better reading instruction," community and school support, and so on.

After determining and rank ordering needs, general objectives are designed to more precisely clarify the needs for measurement purposes. Participants are then preassessed to determine range of competency and individual needs. Based on this general assessment, specific behavioral objectives are designed. These behavioral objectives are closely related to the individual needs and learning modalities of participants.

Programs of instruction are then designed in an attempt to meet specified objectives. Teaching and learning strategies, materials, field or laboratory experiences are developed and sequenced in an attempt to fully develop the skills specified within the objectives.

Students movement through the management system curriculum is dependent on exhibited competency. A variety of activities and strategies, while available, are heavily dependent on original objectives. Such tight reliance on original objectives is closely related to the evaluation or program assessment of the systems approach.

After completing a segment of the instructional program, participants are again assessed to determine new mastery level. If the participant has met the intended goal, he begins a sequential program segment. If the participant has not mastered the concept, he is recycled throughout the program, and variations are made in instruction.

The technological educator is encouraged by the systems approach to curriculum because, while providing a clear outlining of the evaluative process, it also defines who is accountable for what. Thus, a systematic analysis and review of the educational program becomes an operative reality for the classroom manager (Figure 3–3).

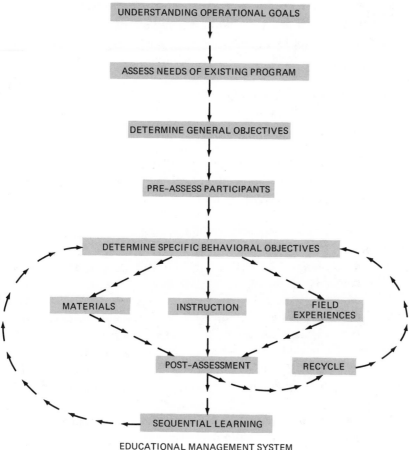

UNDERSTANDING OPERATIONAL GOALS

ASSESS NEEDS OF EXISTING PROGRAM

DETERMINE GENERAL OBJECTIVES

PRE-ASSESS PARTICIPANTS

DETERMINE SPECIFIC BEHAVIORAL OBJECTIVES

MATERIALS   INSTRUCTION   FIELD EXPERIENCES

POST-ASSESSMENT   RECYCLE

SEQUENTIAL LEARNING

EDUCATIONAL MANAGEMENT SYSTEM

FIGURE 3–3.

The role of the teacher manager becomes that of designing, developing, and evaluating the curriculum. The educational system becomes highly individualized because of the attention being directed toward each participant.

BEHAVIORAL OBJECTIVES*

While the relevancy of behavioral objectives to educational program planning continues to be debated, the current literature (Lapp, 1972) suggests that the acceptance or rejection is based on speculation that has often been a replacement for research.

* A behavioral objective is composed of three criteria: (1) the operational *conditions* existing when the behavior occurs, (2) the terminal *behavior* occurring as a result of planned instruction, and (3) the level of *performance* needed for mastery.

Unfortunately the training of prospective teachers, which includes instruction in writing behavioral objectives, often is not accompanied by training in the utilization of such objectives. Thus, the teacher is never sure of the value of behavioral objectives in curricular planning and evaluation. According to Gilpin, an adequately prepared teacher can develop instructional objectives more effectively if the following questions and procedures are followed:

1. What is it that we must teach?
2. How will we know when we have taught it?
3. What materials and procedures will work best to teach what we wish to teach? (Gilpin, 1962, p. viii)

Guidelines such as these may encourage teachers to define objectives before they begin to teach any lesson. Mager, for example, specified five steps to follow in the development and use of behavioral objectives:

1. A statement of instructional objectives is a collection of words or symbols describing one of your educational intents.
2. An objective will communicate your intent to the degree you have described what the learner will be doing when demonstrating his achievement, and how you will know when he is doing it.
3. To describe terminal behavior (what the learner will be doing):
   A. Identify and name the overall behavior act.
   B. Define the important conditions under which the behavior is to occur (given and/or restrictions and limitations).
   C. Define the criterion of acceptable performance.
4. Write a separate statement for each objective; the more you have, the better chance you have of making clear your intent.
5. If you give each learner a copy of your objectives, you may not have to do much else. (Mager, 1962, p. 52)

There are many instances when a general objective is contrived and then designed into a behavioral objective. For example, a classroom objective may be to introduce children to the community helpers. A behavioral objective derived from such a broad objective could be to enable the child to name at least one such community helper and describe his role in the community with complete competency. Why is an objective of this type needed or employed by the teacher? When the teacher is asked to state in specific behavioral terms what she wishes to accomplish by a specific lesson, she will be able to determine:

1. If the accomplishment of the stated objective is really of any value to the total development of the child.
2. If the child has accomplished the objective.
   A. If there are related objectives to be designed and utilized at this time.
   B. Methods of instruction and performance level needed for implementation of related objectives.
3. If the child has not accomplished the objective:
   A. Whether the objective can be accomplished by this child at this time.
   B. Whether the performance level of the objective was too difficult.
   C. What new methods of instruction are needed to better enable the child to accomplish the objective.

Curricular program evaluation is dependent upon clear explanation and explication of the behaviors one is attempting to measure. In 1962 Ammons reflected that educational objectives benefit the classroom teacher: (1) in selecting instructional activities appropriate to the achievement of the objective, and (2) in selecting evaluation techniques suitable for assessing both student progress toward the objective and the general quality of the program.

In order to facilitate the task of the teacher-evaluator, Hammond and a team of educators (1967) developed a model for evaluation that calls for the statement of objectives in behavioral terms. Closely related to this model is one proposed by Alkin (1968) consisting of five stages of evaluation: needs assessment, planning, program implementation, program improvement, and program certification. Alkin suggests the need for behavioral objectives at each stage of evaluation.

While the teacher may choose from a variety of evaluative models, she must be careful not to base her total evaluation on a few specified behaviors previously outlined in behavioral terms. We should never be so naive as to believe that measured behaviors are the only happenings of value within classroom settings. The teacher must be so aware of her children and their programs that she can intelligently estimate growth that has not been planned and/or objectively measured.

The classroom teacher, in designing a curriculum for students, must have as a primary goal *self-actualization* since Combs's self-actualizing persons are

1. well-informed,
2. possessed of positive self-concepts,
3. open to their experience, and
4. possessed of deep feelings of identification with others. (Combs, 1965, p. 23)

Given this goal the classroom teacher must design objectives that encourage cognitive, affective, psychomotor, and consequential pursuits. While immediate learning is often pursued through cognitive, affective, and psychomotor experiences, consequential objectives tend toward futuristic self-actualization since the learner is confronted with the synthesis of process. Thus teacher and student are exposed to the congruence of program objective and program output.

EXAMPLES

1. COGNITIVE OBJECTIVE — After having completed a unit of study dealing with European and American cultures, the student will be able to relate correctly two cultural similarities and differences.

2. AFFECTIVE OBJECTIVE — Following a survey of the existing cultures within the city, the student will display his interest and concern for persons in the lower socioeconomic groups by volunteering to offer assistance through one of the many ways she/he and her/his peers determine appropriate.

3. PSYCHO-MOTOR OBJECTIVE — After reading several stories discussing persons from other cultures, the student will pantomime the behavior of one of his/her favorite characters.

4. CONSE-QUENCE OBJECTIVE — Given a simulated experience dealing with a problematic situation occurring between children from two different cultures, the student will determine

a probable solution utilizing resources, experience, and self-exploration.

As you see, the learner is involved not only in accumulating knowledge but also in the processes or strategies of learning. Thus the end goals of the classroom teacher as she/he utilizes objectives in program planning and evaluation must concentrate on student learning, thinking, and problem solving. Proponents of behavioral objectives are often criticized for defining and measuring only observable behaviors. Unfortunately, this criticism is often unwarranted since the goals encouraged by the behavioral objective planner frequently cover all domains of learning: for example, the development of creative individuals. In an attempt to insure the development rather than the dream of such individuals, behaviorists encourage specification of behaviors that may result in such given ends.

As the classroom teacher becomes skilled at utilizing behavioral objectives an abbreviated system may be employed. Once the terminal behavior has been clarified the rest becomes relatively simple. Reluctance to employ objectives is quite similar to the reluctance of many educators to utilize instruction technology.

Many believe that if children are in a classroom setting that allows technology to dehumanize them, it is the fault of the person determining the objectives and the procedures for meeting the objectives. Television sets, radios, phonographs, programmed machines and other such technological hardware serve only as mechanical teacher aides. The planning does not come from the machine. The hardware is value-free. The teacher must distinguish between reality and fraud! If we consider textbooks and chalkboards as teacher aides, perhaps we could say that technology has always been part of the classroom. Materials should not dictate curricula. Teachers should plan the curriculum first and then select materials for implementation.

COMPETENCY BASED INSTRUCTION

As you viewed Ms. Roser's interaction with Eric and the other students in her classroom, it probably became obvious to you that many factors must be considered as one plans a curriculum. The role of the teacher planner is indeed complex since it involves diagnosing individual needs, prescribing a program to meet the determined needs, supervising the learning setting, advising, counseling, and evaluating. Thus a varied range of competencies are needed by the teacher as she/he both personalizes the curriculum and continually redesigns it to meet the changing needs of its participants.

While curriculum has often been developed to expose the learner to a variety of information thought to be relevant to effective growth and development, few programs have been designed to evaluate the learner's behavioral demonstration of such information or reteach areas where competency was not evident. Because of this lack of monitoring and personalized replanning, large numbers of illiterates have been processed through American public schools.

There are more than 3 million illiterates in our adult population. Thus, many states are calling for educational accountability. Such accountability encourages educators to reexamine the age-old questions, "What specific things must a student know before she/he may be thought competent?" and "What is the exact nature of the learning process?" These questions, and others, have been dealt with by Alvin C. Eurich (1962, p. 11) when he states:

1. Whatever a student learns, he must learn for himself—no one can learn for him.
2. Each student learns at his own rate, and, for any age group, the variations in rates of learning are considerable.
3. A student learns more when each step is immediately strengthened or reinforced.
4. Full, rather than partial, mastery of each step makes total learning more meaningful.
5. When given responsibility for his own learning, the student is more highly motivated; he learns and returns more.

The multiplicity of problems encountered by the classroom teacher attempting to implement a program based on these principles has often resulted in discouragement on the part of both the teacher and the learner. A possible solution may be found in competency based instruction since a program based on competencies is intended to suggest a multifaceted approach to learning rather than outcome. Therefore, in an attempt to foster total human development, learner performance must be broadly specified through cognitive, affective, psychomotor, and consequence objectives. Continual program evaluation insures the elimination of trivial, inappropriate behaviors and the inclusion of high-level behaviors that are often overlooked because they are difficult to put into operation. Thus, competency based instruction, often referred to as performance based instruction, may be defined as an educational process emphasizing delineation, learning, and demonstration of those behaviors relevant to the effective practicing of a given end.

As with most educational concepts, there exists a debate regarding the pedagogical value of competency based instruction. Thus, when implementing such a program, the following strengths and weaknesses of CBI should be considered:

1. Strengths
   A. Emphasis on exit requirements moves one toward a more open educational system.
   B. Time becomes a variable rather than a constraint.
   C. Responsibility for learning belongs to each individual.
   D. Dispenser of knowledge is no longer the primary role of the teacher.
   E. Assessment is no longer totally dependent upon cognition.
   F. Assessment and feedback are personalized.
   G. Multifaceted approaches to learning are available.
2. Weaknesses
   A. Trivial cognitive behaviors are easily put into operation.
   B. Performance criteria may neglect student creativity.
   C. Student success is measured only through observable skills.
   D. Destroys individuality since exit requirements are similar for all.

As the literary debate continues, the teacher-curriculum manager is encouraged to put this approach into operation and to engage in meaningful and continual follow-up analysis to ascertain the appropriateness of selected behavioral competencies and implementation procedures. The curriculum manager is encouraged to maintain the end goal as the development of a child intellectually, psychologically, and socially able to eventually function as a productive, responsible citizen, worker, and individual, that is, self-actualization.

PERFORMANCE CONTRACTING

Performance contracting, which began in Texarkana when business contracted with the public schools to raise the reading rates of their children, is a business venture, unique to the technological curriculum, and received with much skepticism by many educators.

Such contracts call for business to pretest students, implement a training program, and post-test the students. For each increase in student achievement the school pays a certain sum to business. In some contracts the amount of money paid is dependent on the amount of student gain. In many instances students are given gifts by the business firms if their scores increase on post-standardized test measures.

A study by Farr (1972) indicates that students' test-taking behaviors can be influenced by gifts. Farr and others contracted with a school district to raise the reading levels of their students.

For each student reading gain made, the following payments by the school would be made to Farr, et al.

Test Gains in Months*	Payment
one to three	$ 50
four to seven	75
eight to one year	100
one year one month to one year five months	150
one year five months +	200

*Test "losses" for contract students will result in a payment penalty according to this scale:

The population study consisted of three hundred forty-one junior high students in a small southern Indiana town. Students were randomly assigned to either the experimental or control group. All students were pretested with the *Nelson Reading Test*. No treatment was applied. After an interval of four weeks the control group was post-tested with the *Nelson Reading Test* and told that they were being tested to see if their reading abilities had improved. The experimental group was also post-tested with the *Nelson Reading Test*, however, they were told, "A few weeks ago you took a reading test and we have now scored your test. Now we would like to have you try to beat your first test score. We have some prizes for you if you can do better on this test than you did on the last test. We don't care who makes the highest score. We want to see who can make *more points* on this test than on the first test. All you need to do is *raise your own score* by as many points as you can. The students who raise their score the most will win prizes. *Remember*, it's not the student who scores the highest who wins; it's the student who *raises his score the most*.

If you are one of the top six students who gain the most points, you will win a transistor radio—not the six highest scores but the six who improve the most.

If you are one of the next nine students who raise their score the most points, you will win one of these Indiana University sweatshirts. And if you raise your score even as little as one point, you will get one of these candy bars. So everyone who gets even just one point higher will get a prize.

If you do not score any higher on this test than the first test there are no prizes."

The results of the testing were analyzed first according to the contract specifications outlined above. Forty-nine students in the contract group gained only as much as the average of the students in the control group; therefore there was no payment for them. Eighteen students in the experimental group gained less than the mean of the control group, resulting in a penalty of $1,125 for these students. However, 24 students gained more than the average gain of the control group; this resulted in a payment of $4,200. Hence, there was a gross profit for the contracting company of $3,075. It is too easy to regard this as the measure of success. On the average it may have meant an improvement, but that average is absolutely meaningless to the 18 students who performed more poorly as a result of the change. It must give educators pause then, about the criteria used to judge success of a change and the implications of using candy, Green Stamps, and cheap radios as extrinsic rewards.

Hopefully, this study will encourage school districts to consider *exactly what* it is they are paying for when they contract with business to provide academic student performance. Are children being mechanized and dehumanized through business, computers, teaching machines, and audio-visual devices? Or could we as educators be making implementation errors due to our fright of being replaced by machines?

While the Industrial Revolution era peaked years ago, we educators have been slow to adopt hardware in curriculum planning, implementation, and evaluation. Perhaps we need to better remember that while Huxley and Orwell are often overpowering we are the ones who program the machines. Thus, the development of curricula that will facilitate the needs of children is definitely the overwhelming challenge to the classroom teacher.

ACCOUNTABILITY

The decade of the 1970s has certainly witnessed a continuous debate regarding the controversial topic of educational accountability. Questions most often asked are: "Accountability, what does that mean?", "Accountable to whom, by whom?", "How will *it* be measured?" and "Who determines the goals?"

The most common descriptions of educational accountability include:

1. determining prescribed *goals.*
2. developing methods of *evaluating* the *achievement* of the goals.
3. *presenting* the information to the public.
4. *accepting* the results of the total process.

In a cost-analysis structure, accountability may be defined as an attempt to justify costs by reviewing the strengths resulting from expenditures.

Within the technological framework students will be accountable to teachers, and teachers will be accountable to society. As in all educational models the schools are asked to accept responsibility for society's ills, and also to remedy them. Sixty-seven per cent of the adults surveyed in a 1970 Gallup Poll agreed that educators should be held more tightly accountable for student progress.

Determining and monitoring accountability programs suggest many measurement problems, for example, validity, reliability, interpretation, generalizing. Since you will most probably be involved in designing, implementing, and evaluating curricula based on accountability, you must be cognizant of such measurement problems. Several enlightening references have been provided in the bibliography of this chapter.

As the great debate continues Gooler offers us some valuable insights into the strengths and weaknesses of accountability.

Accountability may force us to examine our goals, and our methods of achieving those goals. But accountability may force us to pursue goals most easily attained, or most easily stated. Accountability may force a kind of naive simplicity on a complex phenomenon.

Accountability may demand the best from all of us. We may need to clarify, to experiment, to work harder to make things work. Teachers and administrators may need to be more sensitive to the broader community of which they are a part. And the community may need to become less passive, less willing to take the general word of the educator that all is well.

Accountability may take the best from us. It may ask us to refrain from the creative, the spontaneous, the unexpected. We may need to become more mechanistic, more specific-goal oriented. The educator may find his direction provided by others, not by himself.

Accountability enables us to show our merit. We can do our job and assume our responsibility, because we know what it is. We can defend and justify our existence on the basis of our ability to enable learners to learn.

Accountability may make us uptight. Responsibility for gain and responsibility for failure is upon us, even though we may not be able, as individuals, to control many of the variables contingent upon student learning. We may be susceptible to political pressure; if we are different, if we espouse different values, we may be removed through some kind of misuse of accountability.

Accountability may enable us to show what we do with our dollars.

Accountability may force us to use our dollars in ways that we do not deem desirable.

Accountability may, for the first time, let us really see what we are doing.

Accountability may force us to depend only on those things we can now measure.

Accountability may work for us.

We may work for accountability. (Gooler, 1971, pp. 63–64)

Social/Psychological Ramifications

You took part in a programmed instruction sequence with Eric. A programmed sequence such as this is an educational application of one facet of a broad psychological theory. The stimulus-response theory has been developed by a number of psychologists who have elaborated on different elements of the theory. Thorndike, Watson, Hull, Spence, Guthrie and Skinner are among the prominent S-R theorists.

The stimulus-response theory focuses attention on observable, measurable events and on the objective environment. This emphasis is completely in keeping with the intent of the behavioral objective. An objective analysis of behavior is one of the commonalities of modern versions of S-R theory. It is also the goal of education, but measuring or analyzing classroom behavior in which perhaps 30 students are studying some seven or eight different content emphases is a gargantuan task.

Psychologists who have studied and developed stimulus-response theory have focused on different elements within the theory. Some of the theorists were most concerned with responses to a particular stimulus. Following a desired behavior, Guthrie might be inclined to ask, "What was the stimulus?" Other persons were more concerned with the reinforcement that followed the response. "Spence and Skinner agree that current behavior depends on the current reward contingencies" (Hill, 1964, p. 36). Skinner might ask, "What was the reinforcer?" Both the stimulus emphasis and the reward or reinforcement following the response are useful for consideration by the classroom teacher. What makes the child want to learn something; that is, what reward does he get for learning it?

The attempt of Eric's teachers to plan his curriculum through the aid of automation suggests an educational philosophy highlighted by learning theory tradition. Such theory places heavy emphasis on shaping or conditioning behavior through the environment.

Attempts to shape or condition behavioral responses are commonly referred to as behavior modification. Behavior modification has received much attention since the 1950s because it attempts to offer a comprehensive theory regarding the workings of the human mind. Its appeal has been primarily encouraged by technologists who applaud its simplicity of method, direct application, and action-oriented change for undesirable behavior problems.

In an attempt to effectively utilize behavior modification practices in an educational setting one must not only understand the underlying rationale but must also have clearly delimited the behavioral problem. Thus, the classroom planner has determined, " . . . when to do what, for which behavior, and with what resources, and knowing how to monitor and test treatment effectiveness continuously is the challenging aspect of behavior modification." (Kanfer, 1973, p. 4).

The two major antecedents of learning theory are classical and operant conditioning, both of which require the external factors of contiguity, practice, and reinforcement for occurrence.

CLASSICAL AND OPERANT CONDITIONING

There are as many learning theories as there are bristles on a brush. This is perhaps indicative of the fact that no one theory has provided sufficient empirical evidence to satisfactorily answer the question, "How do people learn?" However, some learning theories have been more valuable than others to the educator.

This section analyzes two theories that view learning as a form of conditioning. They are classical and operant conditioning. Before the value of these theories for the teacher can be discussed, it is important to be able to differentiate between them.

Classical conditioning is that form of conditioning first explored by Pavlov and his dogs. It is contingent on two stimuli presented simultaneously where the response elicited by one of the stimuli gradually comes to be elicited also by the other stimuli. As stated before, the most famous research done on classical conditioning was that done by the physiologist, Pavlov. He sounded a tuning fork and the dogs did not salivate; he showed them food, and they did salivate; so he paired the two stimuli, the tuning fork and the food. After several rounds of listening to the tuning fork and then immediately seeing the food, the dogs began to salivate at the sound of the tuning fork. Another example of classical conditioning is the experiment done with the eye blink reflex of humans. In this experiment the individual was asked to watch a light that became somewhat brighter. There was no response to the light growing brighter. However, being hit in the eye with a puff of air did cause the subject to blink. The classical conditioning procedure consists of presenting these two stimuli simultaneously, the light and the puff of air. Each time the person was confronted by the puff of air he blinked. After several times, the change in intensity of the light alone caused the person to blink, so that he was eventually blinking without the puff of air. Since the changing light was now causing the eye to blink, which it had not done before, learning occurred. In this case the puff of air that originally produced the blinking is called the unconditioned stimulus and the blinking in response to the puff of air is the unconditioned response. The light that increases in intensity is called the conditioned stimulus and the learned response of blinking to the light is called the conditioned response. This learning process is referred to as classical conditioning. Hilgard and Bower (1940) have most clearly distinguished between classical and operant conditioning by saying, "the essential element defining classical conditioning is that the reinforcement is independent of the occurrence of the conditioned response." In the case of Pavlov, we see that the food is independent of the dog's salivating and in the eye blink experiment we see that the eye blink occurred independently of the puff of air and, thus, was obviously learned. Pavlov used the terms unconditioned stimulus and reinforcement interchangeably.

	Pavlov	Eye blink
Unconditioned stimulus	food	puff of air
Unconditioned response	salivation	eye blink
Conditioned stimulus	tuning fork	light
Conditioned response	salivation	eye blink

Skinner's concept of operant conditioning differs from classical conditioning. This can be explained by looking at an experiment he did. He placed a white rat into a 12" square box that was soundproof.

At one end of the box was a lever that projected from the wall. This lever was connected to an automatic recording device and to a magazine filled with pellets of rat food. When the bar was depressed a pellet of food was released. If the rat was hungry when placed in the box he would explore, he would sniff the air and paw the sides of the box, eventually depressing the lever enough to release a pellet of food. Once the rat realized that depressing the bar provided food, he would press the bar at a rate of speed commensurate with his eating speed. Obviously the rat had learned something. Is this learning the same as that which took place in the Pavlov study or the eye blinking study? Can you identify an unconditioned stimulus and an unconditioned response? Can you identify a conditioned stimulus and a conditioned response? We see in Skinner's work that the response is contingent on the reinforcement and not independent of it.

In Skinner's study we cannot identify the unconditioned stimulus and we see that the unconditioned response happened quite accidentally. We again cannot define the conditioned stimulus but can observe that the conditioned response was conditioned by the presence of the reinforcement, in this case pellets of food. We can observe that the bar pressing becomes more frequent when the rat discovers the reward. Unlike classical conditioning where the unconditioned stimulus (reinforcement) is independent of the conditioned response, in operant conditioning the reinforcement is dependent upon the occurrence of the conditioned response.

Skinner explains the difference between the two types of learning by stating that we not only have two types of learning but also two types of responses: respondents and operants.

Respondents are acts of behaviors directly elicited by a stimulus, for example, the puff of air and the eye blink.

Operants are acts or behaviors for which there is no readily observable external stimulus, for example, bar pressing.

In the case of Skinner's white rat in the Skinner box study, we see that the response was what Skinner classifies as operant, and the conditioning instrumental. In the case of the eye blinking study, the response was respondent and the conditioning classical.

Once the difference between these two theories of conditioning is understood, one can readily see that instrumental operant conditioning is probably more useful to people in learning situations than classical conditioning. Operant conditioning is concerned with de-

veloping behavioral or desired responses by providing sensible reinforcements. In most cases an educator is not concerned with presenting two stimuli simultaneously because he/she hopes to teach the
student to respond to a conditioned stimulus as he originally did to
the unconditioned stimuli.

Operant conditioning is based on the belief that people will continue a behavior if it is properly reinforced and extinguish the behavior if inadequate or no reinforcement is provided. There have
been many studies proving that positive and negative reinforcement
do affect learning. It is with this practical application of operant
conditioning that every educator should be familiar. This application
was exemplified earlier with Eric and the programmed learning.

In order to experiment with schedules of reinforcement and effectively use reinforcement in the learning process, one should become
familiar with schedules of reinforcement and reinforcement theory.
A contingent reward must be given according to some schedule. In
the case of Skinner's rat pushing the lever, each time he pushed the
lever, he received a reward. This would be considered in laboratory
jargon as a fixed ratio schedule. There are two types of reward
schedules, ratio and interval. Each of these types has two categories,
fixed and variable.

Ratio schedules are divided into two classes, fixed ratio schedules
and variable ratio schedules. When a pellet is given regularly after
some predetermined number of presses, say three, the schedule is
known as a fixed ratio schedule (FRS). When the pellet is given after
different numbers of presses but on an average of once every fifth
time, it is on a variable ratio schedule (VR5).

Interval schedules differ in that the reward or pellet is given after
some predetermined amount of time has elapsed since the last reward. If the pellet is given every two minutes then the schedule is
called a fixed interval schedule (FI). If, however, the time element is
not constant but varies between pellets, the schedule is said to be a
variable interval schedule (VI). These schedules are those most commonly used in the laboratory; others are certainly possible, however.

It is clear that there are four variations based on the 2 × 2 matrix
shown in Figure 3–4. A *fixed ratio* reinforcement schedule means that
the reinforcement is given a specific number of times in a series of
nonreinforced behaviors. For example, John is practicing multiplication of fractions and the teacher tells him to come to her desk
whenever he completes ten examples. She checks these, tells him

that he is coming along fine, and sends him back to his seat to do more. This kind of reinforcement causes rapid responding for a brief period of time but vanishes rapidly when the reinforcers are removed.

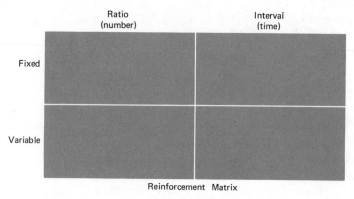

Reinforcement Matrix

FIGURE 3–4

A *fixed interval* reinforcement schedule means that a reinforcement is given once every specified number of seconds or minutes. Maria is exercising on the uneven parallel bars and the gym teacher checks on her every five minutes to see how she is doing with the exercise. Maria gets positive reinforcement and general suggestions from the teacher who returns again and again. This kind of reinforcement tends to improve performance just preceding the reinforcement. The behavior deteriorates immediately after the reinforcement and builds considerably before the interval reinforcer again occurs. Fixed interval reinforcement is not conducive to the best work habits of an individual. It is, however, a pattern used frequently in school—end of unit projects, term papers, and the like provide for fixed interval reinforcement. A reinforcement pattern that would establish better work habits is more to be desired.

A *variable ratio* reinforcement schedule provides reinforcement on an irregular number basis. For example:

	one R for x responses
THEN	one R for x + 3 responses
THEN	one R for x − 2 responses

The *number* varies between reinforcements. This kind of reinforcement tends to speed up responding. Janet has been working in a discussion group. These fifth graders are discussing the pollution of

Lake Erie and are trying to collect their research information and propose some solutions to this problem. Mike liked Janet's first suggestion and repeated it. Then Romona picked up her third comment and expanded it. For some time after this Janet's comments went unheeded. She began to wish very much to provide another suggestion that the group would think worthwhile. Peter liked the very next suggestion Janet made. It was her eleventh comment. This kind of reinforcement produces behavior that is resistant to extinction and is therefore desirable for classroom use. In the example given fellow students are the reinforcers and the pattern is $1 - 3 - 11$, or a variable ratio of reinforcement.

A *variable interval* reinforcement schedule provides variation in length of time between reinforcements. This tends to produce a rapid, stable rate of response. Bruce has made a contract with the art teacher to produce an India ink sketch, a design, and two variations of a still life for this quarter's assignment. Each period he comes into the art room and settles down to work on one of his projects. The teacher moves about the room informally helping students by suggesting where material can be found, or by raising questions about technique, balance, or composition. She comes by Bruce's drawing board just as the class begins and speaks with him about his design, and then stops by ten minutes later to say that she liked the angle he had used on the newest addition to his design. The class is just coming to a close as she comments on the work again (40 minutes later—schedule of comments is $0 - 10 - 50$). This is a variable interval schedule and again produces behavior of great permanence.

It is clear that variable ratio and variable ratio reinforcement may occur together. This is clearest in the example of Janet's discussion group where the number between reinforcement varies, but there is little doubt that the time between these reinforcements varies also.

One of the problems connected with variable reinforcements is that the reinforcement may not occur a sufficient number of times or with satisfactory frequency to be of value to a particular child. It would be difficult indeed to determine the best reinforcement schedule for every learning situation for every child in the classroom. Peer reinforcement and individualized instruction techniques that provide for self-directing, self-correcting materials tend to alleviate this problem.

As a classroom teacher you may certainly find reinforcers to be of value as behavior modification tools. Through the use of *social* reinforcers (voice, smiles, praise, pats) nondesirable behavior may be altered. The reinforcement pattern must be consistent. Reinforce with positive social recognition *only* those behaviors you wish to strengthen. Offer *no* attention to behaviors you wish to discourage.

Activity reinforcers may also be of value to the classroom teacher interested in modifying student behavior. This technique is employed simply by observing the activities students select during their free time. These activities (singing, talking with friends, playing games) may be used, with probable success, to reinforce a desired classroom behavior. "Watch what I am writing on the board, then you may play the game."

The study of operant conditioning principles has shown both that rewards can be very influential in developing or changing behavior and that reinforcements or rewards must be planned. Contingent rewards and punishments are usually distributed according to some system of rules. A father is unlikely to give his son a dime for each garbage can he empties if he has promised to give him a dime for emptying all four garbage cans. The reward is on a fixed ratio schedule (FR4), the boy gets a dime every time he empties the four garbage cans. A programmed text rewards you at each step/frame; this again is a fixed ratio schedule (FR1). Desired behaviors are rewarded and undesired behaviors punished or ignored. A teacher frowning at a student who answers incorrectly would be an example of variable ratio scheduling unless she frowned at every wrong answer, in which case it would be fixed ratio scheduling. Technological educators must always be aware that it is the variable ratio or interval that keeps up the work. If a child can anticipate the exact number of problems you will correct, or the exact day on which you will collect an assignment, he will work only on that day and relax in-between. But if you vary the interval and correct not every fifth example, but maybe the first, third, tenth, and so on, he will have to work hard all the time, never knowing when or where the teacher will check.

Reinforcements are stimuli that people seek or avoid. Positive reinforcement is related to praise and pleasure, whereas negative reinforcements are related to pain and displeasure. Reinforcements can take many forms; sometimes they are public and formal as in the case of medals of honor, certificates, imprisonment, scoldings, and so on, but they can also be subtle and private: a pat on the shoulder, a smile, a wink, a frown, a shake of the head, or whatever. The strength of the produced behavior is influenced by the following reinforcement factors:

Immediacy of the reinforcer affects the association that the learner makes between the stimulus and the response. How soon does the reinforcement follow the behavior?

Frequency of reinforcement must be consistent for the learner to draw a parallel between stimulus and response. How often does the reinforcement follow the behavior?

Number of reinforcers oftentimes determines the strength of the reinforcement. How many reinforcers follow a given behavior?

Reinforcements are usually received from other people or from official social institutions. A mother or teacher is certainly a good example of a pellet dispenser, and as suggested, the pellets may take many forms. We are all surrounded by socializing agents who are loaded with pellets ready for delivery.

CRITIQUE OF EDUCATIONAL TECHNOLOGY

Controversy over the use of technological aids in education has emerged in the areas of values, process, and expenditures. First, educational aids have been condemned as violations of humane values in education. The very basic assumptions about the nature of man and the nature of learning are seen as being at odds with a culture valuing individual creativity and personal freedom. This criticism deals with the actual claims made by the advocates of education technology. The second criticism deals with the subliminal effects of using technology in education. Recently, many educators have begun to argue that the process of, and the media used in, education are more important in changing the student's behavior than the actual content of the lessons. These educators fear the kinds of values implicit in educational technology. The third criticism deals with the practical matters of costs and benefits. Several doubters have come to believe that the expenditures are far too large regardless of whether one accepts the first two criticisms.

For many years B. F. Skinner has been in the vanguard of the movement to adopt educational technology. He has contended that his reforms in education should be pursued because they are based on the hard data of experimental findings and because they are effective in influencing the learning of children. In an important review essay of this position, Chris Argyris replies that both qualities do apply, but that we must consider other factors. Antibiotics and DDT both were based on rigorous science and both worked, but they also were found to have high-risk side effects that are not immediately evident. We must determine, for example, what schools are saying to students about the continuation of learning if they rely on machines to effect all the learning. Thus, media may be effective when appropriately utilized.

The most important weakness of Skinner's viewpoint stems from overextending his theory. He has applied a Newtonian conception of the universe to all of human behavior. To the physicist the unexplained phenomena of nature operate by invariant principles. By persistence man can uncover these principles and, therefore, predict events accurately. Though there may be conflicting theories intending to explain natural mysteries, eventually one theory will be proven correct. Three factors prevent this model from being adopted to human behavior. First, often the discovery of validity of a principle and disseminating knowledge about it changes behavior and thus changes the universe so that the principle no longer pertains. Second, codes of ethics throughout nearly all cultures disallow the use of humans in experiments. While this may be true, teachers realize that children are fascinated with new learning materials that may increase their rate of learning; however, little evidence exists to suggest that retention of learning is primarily dependent upon learning material. Since we cannot isolate every variable contributing to a behavior pattern, the best we can do with our theories is to establish levels of probability. This flies in the face of the value of individualizing instruction.

Third, values play a key role in the explanations of human affairs. Both Skinner and humanistic psychologists have claimed success with changing behavior of delinquents. Conflicting definitions of what constitutes success often account for this seeming discrepancy. Or, sometimes the behavior in the two groups is identical, but the motivations are very different. This may have an important effect once the reformed are one or two years removed from the sterility of the experiment. Also, we must be ever alert to the Hawthorne effect in areas of changed behavior. Students frequently perform differently merely because they are part of an experiment and any change would effect a change in behavior.

The Skinner model also proceeds from a narrow definition of creative thinking. He sounds strikingly like a classicist on this matter:

> The teaching of truly creative behavior is a contradiction in terms. Efforts to teach creativity have sacrificed the teaching of subject matter. Until we know more about creative thinking, we may need to confine ourselves to

making sure that the student is in full possession of the contributions of earlier thinkers. (Skinner, 1968, p. 89)

His desire to know more about the nature of creativity is understandable, but that does not lead to his conclusion that the students must be "confined."

A review of many famous creative thinkers would not show that they were always "in full possession of the contributions of earlier thinkers." Nor is it important that the student's act of creation be new to all of mankind, but that it be new to him. If a student independently determined the Second Law of Thermodynamics, he would be much better off than he would be waiting for the "full possession" of Newton's processes in identifying that law.

Similarly, Skinner argues that the student should not be asked to take a step he cannot take. Prerequisites to mastery of a skill must be taught first. The problem is how to identify what those prerequisites are. From one perspective this sounds very generous to the student in that it prevents him from failure. On the other hand, it is heavily teacher centered. The teacher is not always going to be available to sort out those experiences that have a high likelihood of success. The student must be assisted in developing criteria for determining which steps he can and cannot take. Only in this way will he become an authentically independent learner. It would also be prudent to develop an attitude that failure is not the same thing as incurable moral turpitude. Risk taking has been vital to many human successes. Herbert Spencer advised that "The ultimate result of shielding man from the effects of folly is to fill the world with fools."

At the same time that the student is expected to give full responsibility to the teacher for organizing his learning situations, we find the insertion of the spurious reinforcer. A young man going blind was unwilling to make the necessary efforts to prevent blindness. He was put on food deprivation so that he could be reinforced with food (spurious reinforcer). This enabled him to understand the advantages of better vision (natural reinforcer). In a crucial situation like this it is clearly a good practice, but to extend the practice of using spurious reinforcers in daily classroom activities can cause serious problems. Gradually, the student will begin to mistrust the teacher who holds out artificial rewards. This makes the whole learning activity extrinsic to the student and places most of the responsibility on the teacher.

Skinner attempts to answer the charge that his model involves far too much manipulation, indoctrination, and regimentation when he states:

> It has been said that teaching machines and programmed instruction will mean regimentation, but in principle nothing could be more regimented than education as it now stands. (Skinner, 1968, p. 29)

Undeniably, the recommendations Skinner has made do have a place in the growth of American education. But that place does have limitations. There are some psychological foundations of his model that must be better understood before his method can be fully implemented in schools. Subliminal consequences of technology are suggested by Skinner in *The Technology of Teaching* when he noted that,

> A technology of teaching will need to be much more powerful if the race with catastrophe is to be won, and it may then, like any powerful technology, need to be contained. (Skinner, 1968, p. 260).

CRITIQUE OF COMMUNICATION

Marshall McLuhan's controversial insights into modern communications have not been directed specifically at formal educational technology. However, it is not too difficult to extrapolate from his arguments and to derive some observations for schools. Importantly, too, his efforts have generated a whole new respect for the message within the media.

Though he is the most outspoken advocate of this point of view, there are many others who have contended for some time that our media shapes thinking on a problem in profound, yet ineffable, ways. Edward Hall's *Silent Language* affords rich illustrations of the ways in which word selection and syntax influence our thoughts. McLuhan also contends that each medium carries its own grammar and that grammar must be fully understood by the learner. These critics, then, are calling into doubt Ms. Roser's observation that the "hardware is value-free."

Though it is difficult to distill a central theory from a self-designated "explorer and prober," we can establish McLuhan's frequent argument that modern man has been trapped into linear thinking, which is that mode of thought associated with printed communication.

Great importance is assigned to the change from an oral culture to a written culture. The oral culture is epitomized by the wisdom of

Homer, "a specific operational wisdom for all contingencies of life, an Ann Landers in verse." Oral communication is more emotional and personal than written communication. Written communication is symbolized by the systematic classified wisdom of Aristotle. The heavy dependence upon the printed media, beginning with Gutenberg, locked this more orderly impersonal communication into the Western mind. Implied, then, is the notion that if educational technology takes the form of orderly programmed learning with workbooks and carefully sequenced behavioral objectives, students may be inadequately prepared to meet the multisensory communications of the Electronic Age.

Many of these critics are nonjudgmental in the conflict between linear communication and multisensory electronic communication. Some studies have shown that in terms of learning material more efficiently and more rapidly the differences in amounts learned through the different senses are very small (J. Trenaman, 1967, pp. 42–43). McLuhan contends that, instead of testing for comprehension and content, we should be trying to discover the subliminal effects of the medium itself. In the case of programmed learning those effects are fairly clear. If teachers will only realize that each mode of teaching carries with it its own ground rules for evaluation, then they will be able to see the importance of becoming alert to biases within their own thinking. For example, a teacher evaluating a role-playing lesson with a true/false examination will come up with an entirely inappropriate conclusion regardless of whether the response is positive or negative.

Similarly, each model evaluated only on its own terms can easily be judged coherent, successful, and influential. The teacher's task is to be precisely certain of what those terms are and to see that he is not asserting final conclusions about their mode without comparing it with others.

There are, then, those who urge the wholehearted endorsement of educational technology for very short-sighted reasons. They fail to see any long-range implications of relying heavily or exclusively on technological teaching devices. Correspondingly, those who categorically reject the use of educational technology as inhumane are behaving unrealistically. If the aim of education is to equip students with information skills and attitudes that will enable them to continue learning after they receive their diplomas, then the schools are obliged to come to grips with the fact that technology has invaded all of human life. The question is not whether we as teachers are going to indulge in this activity, but what will be the quality of our indulgence. It is insufficient for schools to study only "natural man" as many current romantic educators are urging, because after graduation the students will confront a real world greatly influenced by modern technology.

Criticisms of the technological model have been leveled at both its philosophical underpinnings and its unseen implications. These criticisms encourage the teacher to continue to question the technological model. Focus is directed on the discrepancies between lofty promises of technological advocates and actual enactment in the classroom.

For example, the critical dependence on artificial, or spurious reinforcers has been questioned on its ethical foundations. More practical critics would say that even if spurious reinforcers were ethical, and even if they effected a change in students' behavior, they would only do so once. To prompt a student to improve his reading rate by offering him a radio is risky. Soon the student will realize that in order to show rapid growth all he must do is score deliberately low on the diagnostic pretest.

Unbiased pretest data may be collected if the spurious reinforcers are not mentioned until after the pretest. This can be done once, but unfortunately for this system, students talk to each other and deliberately low scores during the second year would be assured.

A second practical effect involves the predisposition of the students. In an experimental setting we are seldom concerned with the students' earlier attitudes toward the medium used. Teachers who intend to rely on television must realize that students have had considerable experience with it. Television has had an isolating and narcotic effect on many young people. The nature of the medium and the substance of the programming eliminate face-to-face human dialogue. Television is frequently conceived on the commercial level as a diversion. Therefore, negative learning results may occur when a teacher attempts to employ a television set in an educational program since the previously set attitudes of the students regarding TV may not be changed.

A third practical problem involving the discrepancy between the intentions and the actuality of technological teaching stems from the misuse of slogans. Recently, "individualized instruction" has been one of the most popular educational styles. Of course, it has been cited as one of the virtues of using technology in schools. Unfortunately, this cliché has been confused with personalized learning, which means developing the content of the learning activities in response to the peculiar and specific interests and mode of learning of each student. Furthermore, each person's mode of learning can vary according to subject matter.

Since technical devices enable students to learn a preset body of information or skills at their own leisure, they are unable to respond to particular, eccentric student interests. These latter eccentricities are the essence of personalized learning. Confusion over these ideas results in discrepancies such as the following: Language Laboratories were sold to schools on the grounds that they individualized instruction. When they were installed in the schools, they were accompanied by a set of strict rules, one of which read, "No one is an individual in the laboratory. Do nothing and touch nothing until instructions are given."

A final practical consideration must also be rendered. It once was commonly believed that technological education would greatly reduce costs by releasing personnel. This has not worked out in actual practice. What has happened instead is that when a program is actually working and student population increases, the technological system provides more instruction at a lesser cost than would have been the cost of increasing the faculty. Thus, implementing a curriculum based on technology is no less expensive than implementing one devoid of mechanical aids. Realizing these limitations technology may be a benefit to the classroom teacher if correctly employed. *Wise* utilization is therefore the practical suggestion!

TECHNOLOGICAL EDUCATION IN AMERICA
A Capsule Summary of Its Background Philosophy

WORLD-VIEW   A material, cause and effect world we see before our eyes. Any possible "spiritual" realm is not knowable and therefore not considered. All reality is quantitative, environmentally determined, and, through science, progressively improves itself.

IMAGE OF MAN   Man is a behavioral animal, far more complex than, yet not essentially different from, any other animal. He is beyond the prescientific notions of a free will or self-responsibility for his actions and their effects. Rather, he is environmentally determined in all his behavior.

THEORY OF KNOWLEDGE
Knowledge is that empirical data which has been observed and measured and proven valid. It is that information or those behavioral skills which the individual has been programmed in through reinforced conditioning.

VALUES
Since man is environmentally determined and holds no personal responsibility, he has no values and does only what he has been conditioned to do. Technology itself strives to be scientifically objective and "value-free" (free of bias).

THEORY OF EDUCATION
Education is behavioral modification achieved through reinforced conditioning applied through technological devices. Content and methodology are determined by supporting technology. Essentially the teacher is the machine, replacing the human teacher, and the student is the trainee, learning those skills and data useful for his future technological occupation.

MAN AND SOCIETY
Man must rely on technological aids that enable him to comprehend an increasingly complex society. Society is generally accepted as an immutable given and each individual must establish ways of coping with it. Technology is regarded as a value-free instrument that can be used for welfare or for woe.

REFERENCES

ADOLFS, ROBERT. *The Grave of God.* London: Burns, Oates & Washburn, Ltd., 1967.

ALKIN, M. C. *The Use of Behavioral Objectives in Education: Relevant or Irrelevant.* Los Angeles: University of California, Los Angeles Center for the Study of Evaluations (May 9, 1968). 27 pp. EDO35067, Microfiche.

AMMONS, M. "The Definition, Function, and Use of Educational Objectives." *The Elementary School Journal,* 62 (May 1962), 432–36.

ARGYRIS, CHRIS. "Essay Review of B. F. Skinner's *Beyond Freedom and Dignity.*" *Harvard Educational Review* **41,** No. 1 (Nov. 1971), 550–567.

NATIONAL SOCIETY FOR THE STUDY OF EDUCATION. *Behavior Modification in Education:* The Seventy-second Yearbook of the National Society for the Study of Education. Chicago, Illinois: The University of Chicago Press, 1973.

BARNARD, HENRY. "Educational Developments in the United States," quoted in L. Stebbins, *Eighty Years of Progress of the United States,* Part II, "Education and Educational Institutions." Hartford, Conn., 1867.

BELL, DANIEL (ed.) *Toward the Year 2,000.* Boston: Houghton Mifflin Company, 1968.

BOLVIN, JOHN O. "Individual Prescribed Instruction." *Educational Screen and A-V Guide.* **47** (1968) 14–15.

BRUDNER, HARVEY J. "Computer Managed Instruction." *Science.* **162** (Nov. 29, 1968), 970–976.

COMBS, ARTHUR WRIGHT. *The Professional Education of Teachers.* Boston: Allyn & Bacon, 1965.

CRONBACH, LEE J. "What Research Says About Programmed Instruction," *NEA Journal,* **51** (Dec. 1962), 45–47.

DAVIES, IVOR K. *Competency Based Learning: Technology, Management, and Design.* New York: McGraw Hill Book Company, 1973.

DeCECCO, JOHN. *The Psychology of Learning and Instruction.* Englewood Cliffs, N. J.: Prentice-Hall, Inc., 1968.

ELLUL, JACQUES. *The Technological Society.* New York: Vintage, 1964.

EURICH, ALVIN and HERBERT A. CAROL. *Educational Society.* Boston: D. C. Heath and Company, 1935.

EURICH, ALVIN. "Technology in Education," *New Society,* **13** (December 1962), 11–16.

————. *Reforming American Education.* New York: Harper and Row, Publishers, 1969.

FARR, ROGER, et al. "How to Make a Pile in Performance Contracting." *Phi Delta Kappan,* **53** (Feb. 1972) 367–369.

FERKISS, VICTOR C. *Technological Man: The Myth and the Reality.* New York: George Braziller, Inc., 1969.

FROMM, ERICH. *The Revolution of Hope: Toward a Humanized Technology.* New York: Bantam Books, 1968.

FULLER, R. BUCKMINSTER. *Education Automation.* Carbondale, Ill.: Southern Illinois University Press, 1962.

GARDNER, JOHN W. *Self-Renewal: The Individual and the Innovative Society.* New York: Harper and Row, Publishers, 1964.

GILPIN, J. G. "Forward" in R. F. Moger. *Preparing Instructional Objectives.* Palo Alto, Calif.: Fearon Publishers, 1962.

GOOLER, DENIS D. "Some Uneasy Inquiries into Accountability." In *Accountability in Education,* edited by Leon M. Lessinger and Ralph W. Tyler. Worthington, Ohio: Charles H. Jones, 1971.

GLASER, ROBERT. *Adopting the Elementary School Curriculum to Individual Performance.* Report of the Learning Research and Development Center,

University of Pittsburgh, Reprint No. 26. Pittsburgh: University of Pittsburgh Press, 1967, p. 5.

————. "The Design of Instruction." In *The Changing American School: The Sixty-Fifth Yearbook of the National Society for the Study of Education, Part II.* Chicago: University of Chicago Press, 1966.

GUBA, EGON G. and DANIEL L. STUFFLEBEAM. *Evaluation: The Process of Stimulating, Aiding, and Abetting Insightful Action.* Monograph Series in Reading Education, No. 1. Bloomington, Ind.: Indiana University, 1970.

HAMMOND, R. L. *Evaluation at the Local Level.* Miller Committee for the National Study of ESEA Title III, US Office of Education, 1967. EDRS.

HILL, WINNIFRED F. "Contemporary Developments Within Stimulus Response Learning Theory." In *Theories of Learning and Instruction.* The Sixty-Third Yearbook of the National Society for the Study of Education. Chicago: University of Chicago Press, 1964.

HOLTZMAN, WAYNE (ed.) *Computer-Assisted Instruction, Testing and Guidance.* New York: Harper and Row, Publishers, 1970.

JOHNSON, CLIFTON. *Old Time Schools and School Books.* New York: Macmillan Publishing Co., Inc., 1904.

KANFER, FREDERICK H. "Behavior Modification—An Overview." In "Behavior Modification In Education," *The Seventy-Second Yearbook of the National Society for the Study of Education,* edited by Carl E. Thoresen. Chicago: University of Chicago Press, 1973. pp. 3–40.

KEPPEL, FRANCIS. "The Business Interest in Education." *Phi Delta Kappan,* **48** (1967), 186–190.

LAPP, DIANE. "Behavioral Objectives Writing Skills Test." *Journal of Education,* **154,** (Feb. 1972) 13–24.

————. *The Use of Behavioral Objectives in Education.* Newark, Delaware: International Reading Association, 1972.

LEONARD, GEORGE B. *Education and Ecstasy.* New York: Delta, 1968.

MAGER, R. F. *Preparing Instructional Objective Materials.* Palo Alto, Calif.: Fearon Publishers, 1962.

McLUHAN, MARSHALL. *Hot and Cool.* New York: Signet Books, 1969.

————. *Understanding Media.* New York: Signet Books, 1969.

MICHAEL, DONALD N. *Cybernation: The Silent Conquest.* Santa Barbara, California: Center for the Study of Democratic Institutions, 1962.

NELSON, M. J. *The Nelson Reading Test.* Boston: Houghton Mifflin Company, 1962.

OETTINGER, ANTHONY G. *Run, Computer, Run: The Mythology of Educational Innovation.* Cambridge, Mass.: Harvard University Press, 1969.

PITTS, CARL. *Operant Conditioning in the Classroom.* New York: Thomas Y. Crowell Company, 1971.

PRESSEY, SIDNEY L. "Auto-instruction: Perspective Problems, Potentials." *Theories of Learning and Instruction,* The Sixty-Third Yearbook of the National Society for the Study of Education. Chicago: University of Chicago Press, 1964.

RESNICK, LAUREN. "Programmed Instruction and the Teaching of Complex

Intellectual Skills: Problems and Prospects." *Harvard Educational Review*, **33,** No. 4 (Fall, 1963), 439–471.

SILBERMAN, CHARLES. *Crisis in the Classroom*. New York: Random House, 1970.

SKINNER, B. F. *Beyond Freedom and Dignity*. New York: Alfred A. Knopf, Inc., 1972.

_____. *Walden Two*. New York: Macmillan Publishing Co., Inc., 1948.

_____. "Science of Learning and the Art of Teaching." *Harvard Educational Review*, **24** (1954), 86–97.

_____. *The Technology of Teaching*. New York: Appleton-Century-Crofts, 1968.

Joint Economic Committee, U.S. Congress. *Technology in Education*. Hearings before the Subcommittee on Economic Progress of the Joint Economic Committee. U.S. Congress, Eighty-Ninth Congress. Washington, D.C.: 1966.

TOFFLER, ALVIN. *Future Shock*. New York: Bantam Books, 1971.

TRAVERS, ROBERT M. W. *Essentials of Learning*. New York: Macmillan Publishing Co., Inc., 1963.

TRENAMAN, J. *Communication and Comprehension*. New York: Longmans, Green & Company, 1967.

U.S. Office of Education Reading Seminars Pamphlet, May, 1971.

WEINER, NORBERT. *Cybernetics*. New York: John Wiley & Sons, Inc., 1948.

Chapter 4
Education: Personalized

Philosophical/Social Commentary

SHOULD our schools seek to conserve and transmit our social values, or should they critique and reform these values for a new generation and a better world? Should they serve as society's stabilizing agent, or as society's transforming agent? Regrettably, many teachers and many prospective teachers have seen these as the only options available. This Manichean outlook has prevented them even seeing a third alternative much less refining and developing other models. As a result pedagogical styles are often a function of whether the teacher is satisfied or unsatisfied with the operations of society. Importantly, then, the style fails to become a function of the expressed interests of the learners.

Essentialism has been one response to the limitations of the older, perennialist model. Supporters of this newer model of education emerged from the people who believed that the schools should help perpetuate the existing values of the society. Reconstructionism developed as a different response to the confines of the perennialist mode. Proponents of this point of view are unsatisfied with society's operations. They see the schools as a way of altering our beliefs about this society and developing agents to effect those changes.

One definitive quality of American life has never fit into this simple philosophy. Democratic codes embrace a deep respect for individuality. Schools have never been especially successful in meeting that obligation. This failure is, in large part, explained by the dramatic upheavals in American society since the common schools first became a feature of this society. In a state of constant flux since the 1850s, our population has paid only momentary heed to educational models that emphasize individuality. We must fully understand the sources of this trend and the conflicts that have preceded the current drive for individuality in schools.

The experience of democracy, industrialism, and science gave Americans a very different cultural pattern from that of our European ancestors. The need for an educated electorate created mass free schools; the rise of industry brought the majority of our citizenry into the city with its one generation family; the emergence of science totally reoriented our thought patterns and value system. The struggle between the drive for consensus in the mass schools and the democratic need for individuality was won in the nineteenth century by the needs of the mass school. However this tension exists in all societies and particularly in America where political persuasion is the basis of our system. The pendulum's momentum carries us first to the left . . . pauses . . . and then swings back to the right. Though this is the pattern of our national socioeconomic life, educators must be especially cautious of this to-and-fro activity. It can become a self-fulfilling prophecy to the extent that anticipating it precludes the emergence of other choices. Those who began to speak of individualized education broke new ground and directed attention away from the question of whether the schools should transmit or transmute society. This group eventually came to be known as the progressives.

The most important characteristic of the progressive model is its internal philosophical contradiction. All progressive educators are located somewhere on a spectrum. A spectrum *which exists more in textbooks than in actual classrooms.* At one end is the *romantic progressive* who emphasizes the individual and shuns institutional structure. Learning, he holds, comes out of the student, not the teacher. Provide a rich environment and place the child in it, and he will do his own learning according to his natural growth patterns.

At the other end is the social reconstructionist or *social progressive* who emphasizes the group and social cooperation. Man is a social animal who should join with his fellow citizens to reshape society into a better world. While oriented around the student and his growth, he retains a place for teacher direction, disciplined intelligence, and a planned educational structure.

If the reader bears in mind this inner paradox—and the continuing tension it generates—the mentality behind progress education may be better understood.

SOCIAL-HISTORICAL SETTING FOR THE PERSONALIZED MODEL

The publication of Darwin's *The Origin of Species* in 1859 ignited a cultural shock for Americans. For centuries prior to the publication of Darwin's book, the traditional "direct creation" thesis had been frequently assaulted and the scientific mode of thought had grown in strength, yet somehow Darwin was the breaking point that destroyed the religious thesis forever. Evolution, the continual pattern of change, evolving from one form to another, moving according to its own internal laws rather than according to an external providential God, revolutionized our basic concept of reality.

These new thought patterns were not limited to the physical sciences. Through the work of the English philosopher, Herbert Spencer, extraordinarily popular in the United States, evolution was carried over into economics, urging a theory of "natural selection." Naturalistic and deterministic at heart, this new model urged a laissez-faire economic system, that is, one in which government plays a minimal role and the capable can freely develop their financial empires. If this "natural process" of economic growth could unfold unhindered by legal restraints, they argued, the entire nation would benefit by a higher standard of living.

Americans quickly adopted this theory, particularly through the encouragement of Yale scholar, William Graham Sumner. These were the days of the empire builders, the Rockefellers, Carnegies, and the Morgans, who thrived on unrestricted individualism and saw Social Darwinism as a full justification of their policies. Reformers, on the other hand, were regarded as meddlers, engaged in the absurd effort of making the world over and violating natural laws.

Social Darwinism found an articulate critic in Lester Ward, a maverick in the world of scholarship. Ward accepted Darwin, but only within the sphere of biology. Man, he maintained, is not limited to the laws of the animal world. His mind enables him to rise above nature and control his destiny. The "genetic forces" of nature are counterbalanced by the "telic forces" of man. The science of medicine, for example, does not comply with nature, but seeks to control and redirect its patterns. Therefore, counseled Ward, the science of government should intervene into the affairs of business, regulating its processes and assuring an equal opportunity for all individuals. Material progress without social justice leads only to despotism.

In the time of Lester Ward, the extremes between the "haves" and "have nots" were dramatically obvious, and a generation of "muckraker" journalists exposed these extreme social inequities to the American conscience. This, in turn, set afoot the Progressive political movement, a reform movement that hoped to rebalance the scales of social justice through legislation and other political actions.

As a part of this movement, educators exposed the failures of essentialistic education and sought reform by developing new schools to demonstrate the educational effectiveness and good sense of the new designs. Francis Parker, the father of progressive education, imported European ideas and implemented them in Quincy, Massachusetts, and later in Chicago. At the turn of the century, John Dewey experimented with his Lab School in Chicago, then moved to New York and Columbia University. Out of Columbia Teachers College, the new mecca of progressive education, came such personalities as William Kilpatrick, Harold Rugg, George Counts, and John Childs, and here it was institutionalized into a formal movement with membership roles, magazines, and annual conventions. But as Cremin records in *The Transformation of the Schools*, progressivism began as many individuals across the nation experimented with this liberal approach to education. It was a grass roots application of the liberal mentality to the problems of education. Only halfway through its course did it become the formal Progressive Education Association.

Once established, why was it not able to sustain itself? Certainly not because it could not compete with the essentialist model. In the not too well-known *Eight Year Study*, published in 1942, students from progressive schools performed slightly better in academic areas than did students from essentialist and classical schools. However, they performed significantly better in leadership and social adjustment areas. The struggle between essentialist and progressive educators persisted; sometimes it was healthy conflict, sometimes it became counterproductive and wasteful war. Those favoring essentialist tendencies generally prevailed. The age of Sputnik proved the final coup de grace for progressive educators. It buttressed those who urged more rigor in the schools and, in so doing, it covered over a deep split within the progressive model.

The American creed promises *liberty* and *equality* for all. These are high sounding words that ring richly with the connotations of two centuries and more. And by this very fact, their precise meanings are not easily identified. Each is a relative term and the one compromises the other. Liberty appeals to the individual, to his freedom to achieve his own destiny without social intervention. Equality appeals to the social dimension of man, to society's ability to guarantee a world without social privilege and with an equal opportunity for all. To the degree that society equalizes through its regulations, it compromises each citizen's liberty; to the degree that individual freedom is protected, the social equanimity is compromised.

On the one hand, a break from the ritual of essentialism meant freedom for the child, an opportunity for him to express his individuality and creativity. These personalized child-centered schools, especially popular during the 1920s, were deeply imbedded in the educational philosophy of Rousseau and, in their less glamorous days, were often described as "permissive" schools. Discipline, order, structure, and pre-set objectives were all diminished in order to create an atmosphere in which individual creativity might develop unhampered.

Pressure to individualize teaching and learning developed as a response to the excesses of mass education and of classical education. The classical model greatly deemphasized individual interests and needs. It held that there is a fixed reality that the student must come to grips with through accepted ways of knowing. The discovery that people learned at differing rates led to one version of personalized instruction. This version left much of the classical model intact. In it the student remained generally a passive acceptor of the standard body of knowledge and standard ways of knowing. The fact that his learning might be rapid or slow broke down the groupism of education, but left all else unchallenged.

Many educators married this version of personalized instruction with the promising new technological devices of the early 1960s. This enabled schools to do exactly the same sorts of things they had been doing, but to do so more efficiently. Supporters of genuinely personalized learning were horrified.

A subsequent, fragmented and temporary, break from the social conformity patterns of essentialism meant the creation of schools in which students could develop a critical intelligence and objectively examine their society. Here we find emphasized the group, cooperative "team" efforts, and social concerns such as poverty, racial and ethnic discrimination, economic opportunity, and so on. Its philosophy set progressive education off in a different direction. Liberal education has never resolved this internal contradiction.

There is little doubt that many youngsters benefited from the progressive reforms. They were often relieved of the group pressures that accompanied their failures. Similarly, many youngsters were able to incorporate a great deal more classical learning without having to wait for the whole class to catch up with them. However, there is little doubt, too, that this version did not exhaust the possibilities of breaking the patterns of traditional education in groups.

But that was nearly 20 years ago and the pendulum continues to swing. As noted in Chapter 2, essentialism rose on a wave of national concern and optimism; it was believed that Conant-style education could restore power and dignity to our schools, and that, by virtue of these attributes we would be able to meet the challenges of the Communist threat. But then the Red threat faded and the Vietnam War became the intolerable situation. Thus, our attention has been forceably turned back to domestic social issues that can no longer be ignored and that cry out for social reform.

Indicative of this reversal are these two quotes from Harvard psychologist Jerome Bruner. In 1961, Bruner writes in a classical theme:

> We may take as perhaps the most general objective of education that it cultivates excellence; (i.e.) helping each student achieve his optimum intellectual development. (Bruner, 1961, p. 9)

But in 1971, another educational era, he writes:

> Education is a deeply political issue in which we guarantee a future for someone . . . Reform of curriculum is not enough. Reform of the school is probably not enough. The issue is one of man's capacity for creating a culture, society, and technology that not only feed him, but keep him caring and belonging. (Bruner, 1971, p. 21)

Education's present revival has once again embraced this same contradiction. On the one hand, educators of the late 1960s and early 1970s are concerned with the reconstruction of our social order, with the Coleman Report and the studies of Moynihan and Jencks, with the War on Poverty, and the Great Society fundings, with a variety of experiments aimed at redesigning our urban schools. Race, poverty, and equal opportunity have become our educational priorities.

But at the same time, another vital trend breaks away around the theme of the open classroom and free schools. A revival of the romantic philosophy of Rousseau recreates, in our own time, the individualistic, child-centered education of the 1920s. Freedom and creativity, spontaneity and openness become the new criteria of the educational discipline.

Enfolding these two polarities, American education has returned to the liberal mode of education, and, at least for the moment,

neoprogressivism is the popular, if not dominant, trend in education. In practice, these two themes are tightly intertwined. Each
contains at least the seeds of the other and most find themselves
somewhere on a continuum stretched between the two. But to give
you a clearer appraisal of the mentality and educational theory of
this movement, we must analyze the two polar mentalities separately,
rather than try to see the movement as one mind and one soul.
First, we shall discuss social progressivism, and then, Rousseauistic
romanticism.

MIND-SET OF PERSONALIZED EDUCATION

Three items illustrate the unique character of the social progressive: his preoccupation with *change*, his emphasis on *pragmatism*,
and his penchant for linking *science and democracy* into a singular
thought mode.

"Change" is the Copernican revolution of our era. Prior to
Darwin's introduction, the concept of an established world dominated, a world in which each species was thought to have been
created according to an inner, unchanging essence, and would,
therefore, conform to that essence for the length of its existence. This
is as God had ordained His world. But Darwin noted that, to the
contrary, the world is in continual flux and each creature is part of a
continuing process of growth and extinction, man included. Growth
and open-ended potentiality now displaced the discredited concept
of an established, goal-oriented universe.

But the optimistic American progressive saw an even further dimension to the Copernican revolution. If the evolutionary process is
not guided by some telic force, or a providential God, but develops
its own internal dynamics, then the destiny of the world must lay in
man's hands. He and he alone must assume total responsibility for
its direction—for his benefit or destruction. While his European
brother received this concept with an existential "fear and dread,"
the American progressive seized it with an optimistic spirit of challenge, thrilled by the power to shape his own destiny. Change,
reform, growth, development, became the key words in his new
vocabulary.

The spirit of Darwin not only opened up a new world for the
progressive, but it also inspired in him a new philosophy of life, a
philosophy that came to be called *pragmatism*. If the "established"
was now replaced by the "ever new," so established truths and abso-

lute values were no longer regarded as unassailable principles on which man was to base his life's activities, but, rather, as tentative hypotheses to be tested in the practical affairs of his life. Should they prove successful in helping him to achieve his particular goals, they would be held as working theories. Should they prove unworkable, they would be unhesitatingly set aside and new hypotheses would be devised in their place.

Man now constructs his own relative values and truths. And these are realized, not out of theory and by the force of logic, but out of the practical conduct of his life and by the results of trial and error.

This new philosophy involved several shifts of direction. No longer interested in first causes and ultimate truths, the progressive turned his attention to the immediate situation and specific practical courses of action. No longer thinking deductively from first principles, he began to "problem solve" by beginning inductively from his immediate concern and working upward. The progressive prizes the *practical intelligence* which means that when he sees his path hindered by some block, he searches all available alternatives and chooses that which effectively provides a successful escape route. This discovered route then becomes his "principle" as he continues into a new phase, advancing until he encounters the progressive's "scientific method" of investigation.

Science and *democracy* are continually linked together and raised for adulation by the progressive; he identifies his cause with theirs. Democracy has overthrown the tyranny of absolute authority and privileged position and, in its place, created a society of free men whose democratic processes are very similar to the processes of pragmatism. But more than a political process, democracy is honored as a saving force, almost as a religion.

In close parallel, science, too, has freed mankind from the dogmas and false absolutes of the traditional metaphysics that have bound our minds for centuries. Through discipline, mankind now begins to benefit from unbelievable advances of material progress. Through these two modes of modern thought, man has gathered the courage to resist the superstitions of the old ways, and has thereby entered into a golden age of free, progressive evolution.

Progressive education, cut from the same holy fabric and dedicated both to spreading the good news of democracy and science, and to converting our citizenry to its ways, is truly "American." One can hardly resist the euphoric atmosphere created by the social progressive as he tells of the wonders of this new trinity: progressive education, science, and democracy.

THE EDUCATIONAL THEORY OF THE
PERSONALIZED EDUCATOR

I assume that amid all uncertainties there is one permanent frame of reference: namely, the organic connection between education and personal experience. (Dewey, 1963, p. 25)

The child's experience is the essential footing on which his education is developed. If a topic of discussion has not been experienced by the child, and is pure theory to him, he can memorize the information presented, but it will remain largely meaningless to him. He will not have "learned" it. True education must center around the child and those experiences he is presently conscious of.

But the social progressive does not consider experience itself as educative. And here he develops his theory of a *reconstruction of experience*. Each of us has formed some unified perspective of reality, some mental picture in which we have organized all the data of our life experiences.

With each new experience, we stop and reflect, considering what meaning that experience has for us, how it fits into our present perception. If it relates well to our past experiences, we can immediately place it into proper perspective and thereby "understand" our experience. We know what it means. If this new experience is strikingly different from our past perception, then we must consider it carefully, readjust our mental organization, and thereby modify our previous perception. We say that we have learned something new and that our experience has "educated" us.

But this reflection on our experience is not undertaken for mental cultivation in itself, but rather for practical life. Once we have "understood" this new experience, we have also gained *control* over our future. We know how to respond to it, how to employ it for our purposes. We have gained power to shape our life and direct it to the fulfillment of the ends we choose.

Such reflection on experience to acquire meaning and control is, for Dewey, the heart of "education." The activity of schooling is merely an expansion of this activity. True, Dewey warns, all experience is not necessarily educative. For a particular individual, only those experiences that will help him build, step by step, a balanced, progressive mental "continuum" should be selected. Those that arrest or distort his perception are, for a particular student, noneducative.

On this basic theory, the social progressive sees the teaching situation as requiring a certain amount of discipline and direction. Some intelligent structure of experiences and planned-out goals are required. Furthermore, the teacher cannot stand back and allow the student to follow his own interests nor seek to satisfy only his felt needs. The child has real needs that must be fulfilled—needs he is not aware of. Therefore, the teacher in a social progressive classroom has a responsibility to guide and direct that is far more demanding than that of the essentialist teacher. While never a domineering authoritarian, he nevertheless has that far more difficult task of developing a "guided democracy" in his classroom.

The reconstruction pattern runs throughout Dewey's thinking, particularly in his description of the progressive school. In the agricultural society, Dewey explains, basic education for life was provided for within several institutions surrounding the family. But the new industrial society has weakened these institutions and left the educational function unfulfilled. Therefore, modern society has had to create "schooling" as a separate institution of its own.

Dewey's school is not a vocational preparation for life, a training center of skills and information. A classroom of students represents a simplified cross-section of the much larger society from which they have come. In this atmosphere, the students can recreate the basic social processes, the democratic way of life, found in the larger world. But they should not merely duplicate; here they have the opportunity to reflect and eliminate those qualities which they find least desirable in the present social order, and to develop those qualities that would improve their social order. For example, students can eliminate the heavy ethnic consciousness which, at the turn of the century, was so divisive to America, and develop in each student, a consciousness of his American identity. Or again, competitiveness could be played down and cooperation among students encouraged into a fully developed social pattern. In sum, the school, as a simplified model of society, can reconstruct within its four walls the future society of America.

An understanding of Dewey's model is crucial to the educator of the personalized model. Dewey never advocated merely indulging a student's expressed interests. He consistently resisted any pedagogy that imposed a way of thinking on a student without regard to the student's interests. However, he did not conclude that the teacher should condone any and all of a youngster's observations and conclusions. In order to develop a generation of self-sustaining, reflective thinkers, Dewey sought to get the student's instincts, interests, and conclusions out in the open where they could be honed, validated, modified, and connected to a value system. So the student's interests were only a point of departure. This met what Hunt and Metcalf were to later establish as one of the fundamental requirements of true learning; that it be near and dear to the learner. Having avoided the pitfall of externally imposed and irrelevant subject matter, what do individualized instructors of this persuasion do?

The answer to that important question best follows the explanation of another common misunderstanding of Dewey's model. To make Dewey responsible for the expression "we learn by doing" is to misread his beliefs entirely. This derives from Thorndike's connectionist theories of learning and more closely accords with the traditional model. It defines learning as a conditioning, repetitional procedure involved in memorizing and recapitulation. For Dewey it is not doing, which can actually be mindless and noneducational, but undergoing that makes an experience educative. He lucidly describes this as:

to learn from experience is to make a backward and forward connection between what we do to things and what we enjoy or suffer from things in consequence. (Dewey, 1916, p. 140)

This aids us considerably in understanding how Dewey responds to the important question above, "What does the teacher do after the learner's instinct is out in the open?" Dewey's thought matured in an age that had great faith in the promise and the methods of science. Though many of his other contributions tempered his emphasis on science, it is clear that his most highly valued mode of knowing follows the scientific methodology.

As this model gained favor among teachers trying to individualize instruction they began to zero in on the most easily managed phases of the scientific methodology—the stating of a problem, the establishing a hypothesis, the validation or rejection of the hypothesis. The more tenuous activities of a good scientist that Dewey considered, but that did not find their way into the public instruction, involved the imagination to perceive a problem and the larger and fluid perspective in which we can place the findings. He also challenged the accepted belief of his time that education in morality and education in facts are two distinct spheres. These are three important areas that anyone considering genuine personalized education must come to grips with.

MIND-SET OF ROMANTIC EDUCATION

The romantic mind is not easily defined. The romantics differ from both the perennialists, who state their theory with logic and order, and the essentialists, who focus on the practical consequences of education. Romantics "reflect" by the volume, but their reflections are highly idealistic, often polemical about what should be, and, as a result, they often fail to condense their thoughts into a logical system. In sum, just as the perennialists emit far more light than heat, romantics often emit more heat than light.

Jean-Jacques Rousseau is clearly the archetype of the present-day educational romantics. An examination of the views of this eighteenth-century French philosopher will give us the common ground needed to "pull together" our immediate romantics of the 1920s and 1970s. This is not by accident; Rousseau was a highly influential writer at the time of our American revolution and his thoughts are in our blood. Present-day romantics have a penchant for avoiding the complexities of our present, overinstitutionalized society, and a desire to return to the simplicity and idealism of the early days of this nation.

To properly understand Rousseau, we should place him into his own historic context. We have spoken of the cyclic pattern in American education; Rousseau exemplifies the basic cycle of Western thought, that which undulates between rationalism and emotionalism. Western man continually reaches out for the "clear and distinct" concept with which to understand his world. But dry, abstract ideas tend to become ends in themselves. They separate from the actual experiences of life, and gradually alienate man's "head" from his "heart."

Rousseau rebelled against intellectual gamesmanship and led France and the Western world back to each individual's inner conscience. Each man, Rousseau maintained, whether educated or not, has an inner consciousness. This inner truth he must discover, listen to, and follow.

In Rousseau's perception, there once existed, whether in the real order or the ideal, a primitive state in which man was free, good, and gentle. But as he increased and multiplied, he developed social institutions of greater complexity. These institutions squelch man's individuality and freedom, and teach him to be competitive, selfish, greedy, and violent. It is these corrupt social institutions which, in turn, have corrupted the individual.

Somehow, man must be restored to his original goodness. For Rousseau, there is no going back to the original primitive state. Man cannot escape society; but he can recreate it by recreating himself. Man must return to nature, not to the tooth and claw of the fields, but to that which is natural within himself at this level of evolution. He must free himself from the artificial man created by society and return to the natural, real man within. And this he can accomplish through a process of education.

If "all is good as it leaves the hand of God, and only degenerates in the hands of society," the art of education should be used to isolate the child from society. Place him in an environment protected from society's intrusions and allow him to mature as a free individual. For Rousseau, there is a need only for a "negative" teacher who will prevent any intrusion by social institutions and allow the child to freely experience his environment and the consequences of his actions in response to that environment.

Rousseau believed that each child repeats within himself the evolutionary growth of world history. From infancy to age five, the child develops, according to inner patterns, his motor and sense abilities. From ages five to 12 he develops basic skills of communication. From 12 to 15, his reasoning ability, an awareness of self, and an ability to submit to his own inner conscience is developed. From 15 to 21 he develops his social orientation, especially in regard to sex, religion, and his commitment to society. Each stage develops out of an inner growth; there is no need to teach it, nor is it possible to preadvance its development. As civilization has grown to its present level of advancement, so each man will grow without the necessity of outside intrusion.

In sum, Rousseau saw education as an individual process rather than a social process, fully unfolding as the child interacts with his environment. Moreover, he saw education as a lifelong personal growth process rather than an information and skill gathering process that exists only during the school years.

Having been so educated, Rousseau's mature man can now return to society and gather around himself other like-minded, free men.

Together they can plan a new social contract in which he and these other "best" men create a new "best government" that would not corrupt but would help free all men in the future.

Rousseau forces us to cope with the estrangement of doctrine from life experience. Not that he found a solution in his own life. This man, possibly the greatest writer of educational philosophy in the West, abandoned five children in foundling homes. But he recognized and struggled with the problem rather than fencing it out by simplistic statements. Out of respect for this commitment, we today must struggle to be fair to his thought. Rousseau recommended an extreme individualism in his educational method, disallowing not only the giving to the student the results of others' experience, but even the giving of the example of the teacher model. One learns only by pacing off the world for himself, not by free loading on the experience of others. But the purpose of this education was not for the individual as his own end, but for society, the end of education was the creation of a new society and a free people. Rousseau was not politically irresponsible.

Nor did he recommend license in the individual student. Quite to the contrary, the student was required to listen intently to the inner voice within him, follow it totally. Full responsibility to the 'ought' is far truer to Rousseau's thought than irresponsible license. These are important qualifications to keep before us as we see the romantic applications of this Frenchman's thought in our own times.

If Rousseau begins *Émile* with, "Everything is good as it comes from the hands of the Creator; everything degenerates in the hands of man," then John Holt can echo this thought with "Nobody starts off stupid . . . what happens is that [he] is destroyed by the process that we misname education, a process that goes on in most homes and schools." (Holt, 1964, p. 167) There is little movement from the theory of Rousseau to the theory of contemporary romantics, a theory which can be encapsulated under three principles:

A child learns through his experience. This has a different thrust from the "experience principle" of the social progressives. For them, learning came from the process of reconstructing experience through a student-teacher interaction. Here, the interaction is between the experience and the internal growth of the student. It is a natural growth process, as natural as physical development. Just as Yale psychologist, Dr. Arnold Gesell, has discovered that babies thrive when they determine their own feeding and sleeping schedules, and that children develop well-balanced diets when they are allowed to choose their own food in a cafeteria line, so romantics trust the organism's *felt needs* in education. The child learns according to a basic inner entelechy that leads him toward maturity and wholeness. Education, then, is a process of interaction between student and his environment, according to inner needs of his growth.

> Bill Hull once said, "If we taught children to speak, they'd never learn." I thought at first he was joking. By now I realize that it was a very important truth. (Holt, 1967, p. 53)

Personalized educators tend to believe that children learn through the experience of watching others speak and by responding to a need within themselves to communicate, not by having a "teacher" break down speaking skills into restricted, logical orders and working from A to Z. The romantic muses: If we learned so much before age six and schooling, how much more would we have learned without schooling's help?

Lest this natural process be disrupted, or even destroyed, the institution must not be allowed to interfere. Relating to groups, the institution tries to set learning according to group patterns or according to patterns of their own, certainly not according to the uniquely individual patterns of each child's own identity. Moreover, the institution strives to create group coordination via ritual and rules. Inner motivation is not trusted; it creates false motivation with grades and degrees. At best, it bores the students by its impotency; at worst, it destroys learning by creating fear of failure or selfish competition. Children are turned into "producers," striving to please the teacher.

> Schools give every encouragement to producers, the kids whose idea is to get "right answers" by any and all means. In a system that runs on "right answers," they can hardly help it. And these schools are often very discouraging places for thinkers. (Holt, 1964, p. 25)

After a few years of learning to be producers, children have great difficulty knowing how to be true to themselves about their own ideas.

To the romantic, learning is not only natural, but also intensely involving. Rogers reminds us of this when he says that learning must be personal to the student, never abstract, and should result in behavioral and lifestyle changes. "I have come to feel that the only learning which significantly influences behavior is self-discovered, self-appropriated learning." (Rogers, 1969, p. 153) No learner is ever passive. This touches on the romantic's second principle:

The teacher role remains outside the direct learning process. As the first principle's explanation indicates, the romantic is suspicious and uncomfortable with the institution and its use of power, authority, and roles. He agrees with Rogers that the teacher cannot teach in the traditional sense. He can only provide a rich environment for learning. All responsibility for learning must remain the student's. Herbert Kohl will advise his reader to find alternatives for the teacher role and avoid his "obsession with power and discipline everywhere," for the pathology of the classroom begins in this role. (Kohl, 1969, pp. 12, 14) He suggests that the teacher use his first name and make it a point to address each student by his first name.

The teacher can serve by protecting the student from the institutional press which imposes itself from outside the classroom. Kohl, again, offers lengthy advice on the strategies of dealing with the "establishment" of the school institution, everything from the use of double lesson plans to the use of countercharges and influential friends. All is legitimate to protect the learning process from being aborted by the institution.

In his relationship with the student, the teacher never imposes himself. His role is facilitator and resource person, providing a variety of educationally rich environments, confirming and encouraging each student by his positive regard, and responding to an invitation to offer guidance and suggestions. In any case, he is not the authoritarian figure who responsibly directs the class learning.

Fit the school to the child. Whether limited to his own classroom, or given responsibility in the entire school, the teacher strives to create learning environments oriented to the learning patterns of the children. Schools should be joyous, bright, and colorful. Moreover, an individual class should be allowed to "create" its own environment by initially designing its room, and then by continually moving desks, building models and displays, and rearranging them according to changing interests. "One of the most important things a teacher can do is explore the space of his classroom with and without his pupils and make it as comfortable and familiar a place as possible." (Kohl, 1969, p. 47)

This policy implicitly refutes the popular critique of romantic education, that it rejects structure and remains structureless. Romantic education does reject those structures that the institution imposes prior to a particular class. But structure is created and developed as the class forms; structure emerges from within the group and is formed democratically.

Within the above context, romantic education sees education as a natural growing process between the student and a stimulating environment. He dwells on the individual student and his unique individuality of learning style and learning needs. He always remains suspicious of, or even hostile to, any intervention by educational institutions that seek to take over the learning responsibility from the child. Continually criticized as being "permissive" and confused, he prefers to trust the designs of nature to those of man.

Curriculum Implementation

STUDENT — — — — — ► TEACHER — — — — — — ► CONTENT

FIGURE 4–1.

The general characteristics of the personalized educational model are:

1. STUDENT   Curricular focus is student centered. The intellectual, social, psychological dimensions of the student's development are equally weighted.

2. TEACHER   Facilitator of knowledge who develops the learning environment according to the student's needs and growth processes.

3. CONTENT   Organically related to the student subjectively, that is according to his needs rather than abstractly, or according to its own objective logic.

One visiting a school adhering to the philosophy and curricular implementation of this model might view the following interaction:

"José," said Mr. Hess, "the title of your book is *Emmanuel*; can you explain who Emmanuel is?"

"Sure," said José, "he's a guy who quits school because he needs money to buy things for his mother and sisters. But," he continued, "no one wants to give him a job because he didn't graduate from high school."

"Well, before his dad died he taught him to be a carpenter, and so Emmanuel wants a job as a carpenter. But everywhere he goes to apply for a job they ask why he isn't in school. He's getting really discouraged and starting to spend more and more time skipping school.''

''What do you think he'll do?'' Mr. Hess questioned.

''I'm not sure but I think it's unfair that he should have to go back to school to learn things that won't help him to be a better carpenter. Someone should give him a job. What's so great about a diploma?''

''A very good question; let's ask some of your friends who have also read this book what they think about your question,'' replied Mr. Hess.

Hess scanned his junior-high age class, beckoning Felicia, Ernestine, and Wong to join José and himself. As they approached, he told them of José's question and asked for their ideas.

What resulted was a decision by the students to survey their community to determine how many companies would have hired Emmanuel without a diploma. As Mr. Hess moved to another group of students working with the skeleton in the *Man: A Course of Study* series, he heard José suggesting that he and Wong might read to determine causes for students quitting school. Ernestine and Felicia decided to try to determine jobs not requiring high school diplomas.

''Perhaps,'' said Ernestine, ''we can make this information known to all the students here at school.''

''Yeah,'' said Wong, ''if they have to quit school they won't be in the same bind Emmanuel is in.''

''Okay,'' said José, ''let's have a meeting in three days to discuss what we've read and make further plans.''

Mr. Hess was eager to foster the interaction of the group. He thought that because of this wide range of ability, standardized test conformists would never have placed these four students together for group work. Although their test scores varied, Mr. Hess believed that learning must also be centered around the interest of the student. If a child is interested, he and his teacher will, through informal and formal measures, find his readiness level and he will begin pursuing his interest.

While Mr. Hess used the prescribed school syllabus, he developed divergent methods for meeting stated objectives. His methods were dependent on the individual attitudes and abilities of the children in his classroom. He believed that he must be the mediator between the individual and the prescribed curriculum. He continuously asked himself: What do I want for these children? He knew that he wanted them to have the realistic skills they needed to be effective individuals, workers, and citizens. As he further described what he meant by effective individuals, workers, and citizens, he knew that all of his children needed a basic functional literacy in reading, writing, math, social, scientific, and moral skills. Methods for developing these skills were dependent upon the interests, abilities, attitudes, and readiness levels of each child. While Mr. Hess does believe that there is a common subject matter for all children, he does not believe that each child learns through the same modality or by the same method. Although Mr. Hess is concerned about the future of these children, he is primarily concerned with their personal social/psychological development.

Children need to be themselves, to live with other children and with adults, to learn from their environment, to enjoy the present, to prepare for their future, to create and to love, and to learn to face adversity, to behave responsibly; in a word, to be human beings. (*Children and the Primacy: A Report to the Central School Advisory Council for Education,* London, 1967)

Although this and similar quotes gain acceptance from the public, many influential school policies—both noble and nefarious—have been perpetrated under the guise of individualizing instruction. Like each of our other three models of teaching, teaching for individual differences is beset with promises and pitfalls. The cliché, "individualized learning," is particularly alluring because of a long history of violations of individuality through the growth of mass education. As in many matters pertaining to school policies, John Dewey's counsel is especially valuable. He warned us against excessive use of the pendulum as a metaphor. The pendulum metaphor profitably advises us to avoid running to the other extreme in order to avoid the excesses of one policy. In this case, we should not formulate school policies that attend excessively to individual interests and needs in order to correct the overemphasis of group-oriented schools. However, the pendulum metaphor also intimates that the ideal is at the midpoint and that it is without motion. This sort of middle-of-the-road mentality of a perfectly compromised curriculum does not always fit the reality of young people. Our task here is to examine the sources of the tendency toward individualized instruction, the curricular manifestations of it, and the potential problems within this model. This should be determined without regard to a motionless and artificial midpoint.

The environment of Mr. Hess's classroom consists of continuous interaction between the teacher, the student, and the content. These

"All this education seems so silly when what I really want to be is a belly dancer."

Reprinted from *Phi Delta Kappan* with permission of Ford Button.

three variables, while dependent upon each other, vary in degree of dominance. The student is the center, with the content being redesigned for each student. The designer is the teacher who continuously interacts with each student in an attempt to supply to the student a series of activities that will motivate him to achieve a functional world literacy, as a citizen, worker, and autonomous individual.

The statement that individuals live in a world means, in the concrete, that they live in a series of situations. And when it is said that they live in these situations, the meaning of the word "in" is different from its meaning when it is said the pennies are "in" a can. It means, once more, that interaction is going on between an individual and objects and other persons. The conceptions of situation and of interaction are inseparable from each other. An experience is always what it is because of a transaction taking place between an individual and what, at the time, constitutes his environment, whether the latter consists of persons with whom he is talking about some topic or event, the talked-about being also a part of the situation; or the toys with which he is playing; the book he is reading (in which his environing conditions at the time may be England or ancient Greece or an imaginary region); or the materials of an experiment he is performing. The environment, in other words, is whatever conditions interact with the personal needs, desires, purposes, and capacities to create the experience which is had. Even when a person builds a castle in the air he is interacting with the objects which he constructs in fancy." (Dewey, 1938, pp. 43-44)

Mr. Hess realized that since the student explores his world environment both as a single individual and also as a member of a group, the environment of his classroom should be similar.

As early as 1600, educators were instructing individual children and since that time individualized instruction has been evidenced, in some form, in American educational institutions. While the topic of individualizing instruction has been continuous, it has involved various concepts and methods of implementation. For example, in the early 1600s children were taught individually by tutors, dames (scholarly women of the community), scribes, or priests. Where such individualization may have occurred because of the small numbers of learners involved, it is naive to infer that insight into the facets of the individual encouraged this practice. As populations grew, less and less individual attention was rendered by the teacher.

However, the advent of standardized tests in the early twentieth century suggested that there were differences among children. Unfortunately, this led to children being lock-stepped into groups that appeared to be teaching to the needs of separate individuals. In reality, however, one method of instruction was being exercised for several very different children. Philosophy and practice were incongruent.

During the 1920s the Dalton Plan and the Winnetka Plan were widely discussed methods of individualizing instruction. While such plans attempted to individualize instruction, their weakness was that they tended to value their long-term goal (development of successful adults) more highly than the everyday interactions of children.

WINNETKA PLAN

In evaluating the Winnetka plan, one finds several features to commend. It demonstrated a practical way of permitting children to progress at their own rate of learning in a public school situation, and it eliminated the undesirable practice of failing pupils. It also provided opportunities for group and creative work. On the other hand, the chief purpose of permitting children to progress individually seems to have been only that of enabling them to cover adult-prescribed increments of subject matter at their own particular rates. (Nila Banton Smith, 1963, p. 131)

DALTON PLAN

The essential error of the Dalton Plan, then, is, as with all external examination schemes, that it accepts childhood as a time of storing up learnings to be used when called for at a remote day, typically in adult life. It is on this assumed theory that it sets up a series of learning stints reaching upwards from the fourth grade. It assumes that a child can learn these successive stints and hold them stored up available for use when they shall later be called for. It further assumes that it does not hurt the child to be treated in this way. Both assumptions are here denied, at least to a degree to condemn the practice. But few things, comparatively speaking, can be so learned long in advance of use to stay with one till the distant use shall come. And the hurt, positive and negative, to the ordinary child when so treated is probably very great. (Kilpatrick, 1925, pp. 279–80)

During the 1930s, Dewey's individualized instruction, while being child-centered, was perhaps prescriptive in the sense that it primarily attempted to develop a successful social being.

. . . In this period [ages four to eight] the connection of the school life with that of the home and neighborhood is, of course, especially intimate. The children are largely occupied with direct social and outgoing modes of action, with doing and telling. There is relatively little attempt made at intellectual formulation, conscious reflection, or command of technical methods. As, however, there is continual growth in the complexity of work and in the responsibilities which the children are capable of assuming, distinct problems gradually emerge in such a way that the mastery of special methods is necessary.

Hence in the second period (from eight to ten), emphasis is put upon securing ability to read, write, handle numbers, etc., not in themselves, but as necessary helps and adjuncts in relation to the more direct modes of experience. Also in the various forms of handwork and of science, more and more conscious attention is paid to the proper ways of doing things, methods of reaching results, as distinct from the simple doing itself. This is the special period for securing knowledge of the rules and techniques of work.

In the third period, lasting until the thirteenth year, the skill thus acquired is utilized in application to definite problems of investigation and reflection, leading on to recognition of the significance and necessity of generalizations. When this latter point is reached, the period of distinctly secondary education may be said to have begun. This third period is also that of the distinctive differentiation of the various lines of work, history and science, the various forms of science, etc., from one another. So far as the methods and tools employed in each have been mastered, so far is the child able to take up the pursuit each by itself, making it, in some sense, really a study. If the first period has given the child a common and varied background, if the second has introduced him to control of reading, writing, numbering, manipulating materials, etc., as instruments of inquiry, he is now ready in the third for a certain amount of specialization without danger of isolation or artificiality (Mayhew and Edwards, 1936, pp. 53–54).

This emphasis on personalized instruction as suggested by the Dalton and Winnetka plans continues in current multiunit schools. One example is Klausmeier's model of Individually Guided Education. Two similar versions of individualized instruction have also occurred that depart more substantially from both the traditional and the technological models. The most radical departure holds that "groups cannot learn anything, only individuals can." Therefore, schools should only operate on the basis of tutorial arrangements based entirely upon the interests of the individual youngsters. Instead of attending to student progress toward preset ends, this version wholly individualizes learning so that each youngster creates his own perspective toward life and learning. In some forms this has meant that the teacher does little other than watch maturation. It often has meant that the teacher facilitates the student's learning whatever he wants to learn without any imposition of the teacher's beliefs. In this version truth is by no means fixed and the student can develop in myriad fashions. He can become highly specialized, following his interests in music, for instance, to the exclusion of the customary balance of other areas of study. The important presumption here is that the student does not necessarily need either mastery of, or even acquaintance with, all the conventional fields of study. Other educators holding to this model believe that the student's mastery of one field of study will enable him to better understand other fields of study whenever that becomes necessary. This is seen as preferable to the conventional procedure of having a student dabble in all fields and risk never understanding any one of them fully. Of course, too, since the students' pursuits are strictly voluntary it is presumed that many will choose a more conventional understanding of each of the disciplines and thereby satiate society's needs for a generally educated populace. At the root of all this is a faith in the student's ability to select profitable areas for investigation and a rejection of the customary fare of schooling as artificial and irrelevant to the individual growth of children.

A final, crucial presumption of this version of individualized instruction concerns the relationship between the individual and society. It assumes that each maturing member of the society following his own particular interest will eventually result in the common welfare. This seemingly radical pedagogical model ironically comes to a very conservative, laissez-faire socioeconomic model. It is no doubt, in part, a reaction to the mass education model that intervened too much in the interests of youngsters and excessively channeled their life options, but again, with respect to Dewey's aforementioned counsel we want to be chary of hopping onto the pendulum for a ride back to the other extreme without deep reflection on the implications of the other model. It does not mean educating the youngster to be devoid of any social responsibility or ignorant of any ways of knowing.

Most educators who have urged the schools to individualize instruction are aware of the pitfalls both of artificial individualization ("let them learn the same old stuff, but at their own rate") and of rampant and unrestrained individuality ("everybody do their own thing"). The ideal educated man to these moderate reformers is probably Hullfish and Smith's reflective thinker. Again, for this moderate group the impetus in large part has been negative, a reaction against sterile, expository, and anti-individual teaching. At the core of their thinking is John Goodlad's often repeated finding that the educator's fascination with numbering and categorizing students has come to the Kafkaesque conclusion that there are no more than three or four real fourth graders in the typical fourth-grade class. In our rush to make schooling more efficient and more systematic and without questioning the basic premise of a fixed body of knowledge we lost all sight of individual difference. Even if we grant that there is such a thing as a fourth-grade level of achievement in reading, in arithmetic, in composition, in analytical thinking and in a host of other areas we find that less than 20 per cent of the children are at a fourth-grade level in all these areas at the time that they are in the fourth grade.

One response to that fact has been that, since students learn at different rates in different areas, we should erase the demarcations and let the students move ahead at their own rates, but to the same immutable end. The response of those favoring the reflective model has been that those variations are not the function of biologically imprinted and, thus immutable, learning rates, but that they result from variations in students' interests, backgrounds, and value systems.

Let us examine some of the ways in which schools have proceeded to individualize instruction so that we can gain some perspective on the degree to which we as educators are really coming to grips with it.

NONGRADEDNESS

The most common form of effecting individualization is to break down grade levels. Only the nongraded schools can avert the damnable and artificial age stereotyping Goodlad found to be so antieducational. Since slower students no longer have the sword of nonpromotion dangling above them, they are supposed to gain emotional stability in a nongraded school. The brighter students presumably are no longer bored as they are in situations in which the teacher has to get everyone ready for the next grade. It was expected then that there would be a significant reduction in disorderly behavior. Many studies uncovered very enthusiastic support for this reform. One failed to find a negative response in 500 interviews! But one of the more sobering studies must also be considered. In a 1961 study a comparison was made on the basic skills, general achievement, and mental health of graded and nongraded students. It showed that the graded students performed better in achievement tests. It also showed that aside from one factor, social participation, there was no significant difference on the mental health scores. Goodlad contends that this study was made early in the trend toward nongraded schools. It revealed that many people were "claiming for nongrading what organization by itself cannot possibly achieve" (Goodlad, 1962, p. 234). This mistake means an overhaul in one's pedagogical thinking, lest it become a gimmick for doing the same old stuff more efficiently. The real intent was to enable learners to pursue their own interests with the aid of the teachers. This does not require that every student wander through an area without the assistance or judgment of the teacher. But more importantly, it does not mean a program of "continuous progress through a series of achievement levels." This becomes merely a cosmetic alteration of a much deeper problem. Individualized instruction means respecting the individual interests and personalities of both the teachers and the learners. This final notion has given rise to another model of individualizing school activities, matching teacher and learner personalities.

It seems to us that the scholastic aptitude admits of other things than intelligence; to succeed in his studies, one must have qualities which depend especially on attention, will, and character; for example a certain docility, a regularity of habits, and especially continuity of effort. A child, even if intelligent, will learn little in class if he never listens, if he spends his time playing tricks, giggling, in playing truant. . . . This explains to us that our examination of intelligence cannot take account of all these qualities, attention, will, regularity, continuity, docility, and courage which play so important a part in school work, and also in after-life; for life is not so much a conflict of intelligence as a combat of characters.

And we must expect in fact that the children whom we judge the most intelligent, will not always be those who are the most advanced in their studies. An intelligent student may be very lazy. We must also notice that the lack of intelligence of certain subnormal pupils does not account for their great retardation. We recall what we say when we followed the lesson for many hours in a subnormal class. It was surprising to see how restless they were, always ready to change their places, to laugh, to whisper, to pay no attention to the teacher. With such instability it would require double the intelligence of a normal pupil to profit from their lessons. (Binet and Simon, 1916, pp. 254, 256–257)

PERSONALITY MATCHING

This comparatively recent development has shown a great deal of promise. The "personality conflict" evident in many school situations has many mysterious implications, but it is clear that many unhappy relationships have blocked a great deal of learning. There is not a lot of data on this reform but we can identify a few of its features. Essentially it involves pairing of teacher styles and student style. Some youngsters learn best with a well-organized, systematic, mildly authoritarian teacher. Their personalities and their attitudes toward learning do not include widespread exploration of topics or a lot of uninhibited individual initiative. Without being judgmental in any way the school is geared toward getting those two philosophies together. Similarly, some teachers are more inclined to adopt classroom activities entirely to the expressed interest of the students. There is little preplanning in this arrangement. There are not many preset standards. There is not a direct path to a well-defined educational outcome. The teachers would be inclined to assist and guide without imposing material on the learner. This approach has considerable appeal in terms of the school respecting individuality.

There are two fundamental difficulties with personality matching. First, we cannot establish a list of personality variables that make a difference and that are acceptable to everyone. Even if we could come up with such a list we cannot measure it accurately enough to make it work. Oscar Buros' general reservations about testing are important here:

Unfortunately, the rank and file of test users do not appear to be particularly alarmed that so many tests are either severely criticized or described as having no validity. Although most test users would probably agree that many tests are either worthless or misused, they continue to have the utmost faith in their own particular choice and use of tests regardless of the absence of supporting research or even of the presence of negating research. When I initiated this test reviewing service in 1938, I was confident that frankly critical reviews by competent specialists representing a wide variety of viewpoints would make it unprofitable to publish tests of unknown or questionable validity. Now 27 years and five Mental Measurements Yearbooks later, I realize that I was too optimistic. At present, no matter how poor a test may be, if it is nicely packaged and if it promises to do all sorts of things which no test can do, the test will find gullible buyers. (Buros, Preface to the *Sixth Mental Measurements Yearbook*, 1965, p. xxiii)

A second difficulty arises if we continue to hold to the belief that education should be a little bit troubling and unsettling. There is a long pedagogical tradition holding that doubt and uncertainty are the first steps to learning. By only coming into direct contact with teachers of like mind the students could well get into a groove and emerge at the other end unaware of, and therefore unable to cope with, other people who think differently. It might well be that schools should begin to respect modalities of learning as urged here, but that learners should be obliged to experience some of the other modalities as well. This suggested reform does not imply that these modalities rate in any hierarchy or that one is more desirable than the others. Nor does it say that one is more rigorous than the others. Any one of the modalities can operate well and any one of them can operate poorly. The hazard remains that, though we must pay greater attention to various learning styles than ever before, we must be wary of customizing the education so much that there is no stress involved. It is possible for an educational act to be suitably disturbing without producing undue or counterproductive anxiety. This fine line the skilled teacher must find in each situation.

CONTRACT SYSTEM

A third manifestation of the trend toward individualizing has been the demise of according grades by means of a preset standard. The long tradition of evaluating students according to a predetermined standard pays little respect to students' individual differences. It has been an enormous force for conforming students to accepted ways of thinking. Genuine individualization of instruction cannot really abide this and the contract system became one of the basic reforms of the individualizing movement.

The contract system has assumed many forms, but two categories have become distinct. On the one hand it is merely affixed to a curriculum predicated on grades. In this way the student contracts with the teacher to do a set amount of work in a style that distinguishes him as superior (an 'A'). Another student could approach the same issue with less interest and define his desired learning as only average (a 'C'). Many such systems allow a student to contract for a substandard understanding (a 'D') of their topic. Though this may have some influence in terms of individualizing instruction, it is much more likely to be countenancing the same old stuff under a new name.

The second category of this contracting reform represents complete individualization. It places heavy emphasis on the professional expertise of the teacher. He must make the issue challenging to the student without overwhelming him. More significantly, he must allow the student to pursue his interest, however bizarre, to its own end. This implies, then, that the student can have his investigation turn out to be a failure. The emphasis here is on learning from the study and we can certainly learn from a colossal failure, particularly, if we have full control devising the study. This learning model can apply just as well to seven-year-olds as to 17-year-olds. The key to its success lies in drawing up the contract so that the student will learn either way. This is enormously different from a model that sets a quantity of information in contract form and then checks to see if he upheld his end of the deal. The latter urges a model that assures the student will learn about his topic as long as he pursues his examination to the end.

The former student begins to approximate what Dewey valued as his definition of the educated man. Here we have an individual not necessarily well-trained or well-informed of data, but capable of reflection and coming to grips with a problem. He talks about a man confident in his style of thought and able to generate and evaluate solutions. Perhaps Dewey emphasized too heavily the notion of this method eventually leading to the uncovering of truth. In doing so he underestimated the significance of creativity in the youngster's growth. If the modern teacher does not place all his faith in the scientific process and encourage the ability to feel problems and generate alternatives, then he will be well along the process of individualizing the learning.

BRITISH INFANT SCHOOL

Almost 400 years of attempts to develop the child-centered curriculum have been realized in the structure of the British Infant School where the open informal classroom concept suggests, once again, that the teacher must serve as the facilitator for the child who is, himself, the source of learning. The flexible curriculum that contains basic skill subjects is implemented according to the interests, modalities, and readiness levels of each student.

The philosophy of the British Infant school is that individualization must be the program rather than something to be built on the already existing program. The long-range goal of the curriculum must be to aid in the complete and individual growth of each child through his stages of development.

Piagetian concepts are given much attention in the British school model where the concept of teaching is geared to the development of the child in a relatively free atmosphere. The interests of the child are the basis for learning. For example, if a child shows interest in sand play, he may be encouraged to write his letters and numbers in the sand, just as the child who is interested in finger printing might be encouraged to pursue the same learning through paint. Skills are learned by various means, each of which is dependent on the individual's interests and development since, as Piaget suggests, intelligence is sequentially related to age. The British model, which has received much attention since 1967, again attempts to encourage the self-development of the individual.

Regardless of the philosophical beliefs of many who have supported the various curricular arrangements just discussed, Mr. Hess and the majority of educators agree that:

Children work hard and long when they choose their own jobs. They move ahead when they have opportunity to set their own goals. They read with greater enjoyment when they choose the material. In self-selection the teacher works with the individuals and knows their interests and needs more adequately than when a group works on a single book chosen by the teacher. (Jenkins, 1955, p. 125)

In Mr. Hess's classroom no one systematic method for student grouping is employed since "available research evidence seems to indicate that children supposedly grouped according to ability seem no more likely to make greater achievement gains than are their counterparts in heterogeneously grouped classrooms." (Morgenstern, 1966, p. 16)

DIFFERENTIATED STAFFING

The school administrators had realized that while many teachers are certified to teach several subjects within the curriculum, their areas of interest are usually closely correlated with their areas of competency. Thus, where differentiated staffing allows the teacher to focus her talents, superior performance may be the result. For example, differentiated staffing in high-school English classes might find one teacher who is expert as a classroom teacher. A colleague's expertise might be in preparing curriculum, and a third member might be expert in measuring and evaluating students. In an elementary school three sixth-grade teachers divide the courses in a self-contained classroom according to their interests in specific subject matter.

While differentiated staffing is in neophyte stages at Mr. Hess's school, it received earlier attention from John Dewey who observed:

As a result of experience, the other chief modification has been with regard to specialization on the part of teachers. It was assumed, at first, that an all-round teacher would be the best, and perhaps it would be advisable to have one teacher teach the children in several branches. This theory, however, has been abandoned, and it has been thought well to secure teachers who are specialists by taste and training—experts along different lines. One of the reasons for this modification of the original plan was the difficulty of getting scientific facts presented that were facts and truths. It has been assumed that any phenomenon that interested a child was good enough, and that if he were aroused and made alert, that was all that could be expected. It is, however, just as necessary that what he gets should be truth and should not be subordinated to anything else. The training of observation by having the child see wrong is not so desirable as sometimes it has been thought to be. The difficulty of getting scientific work presented except by those who were specialists has led to the change in regard to other subjects as well.

On the other hand, however, it has been recognized that, in the effort to avoid the serious evils of the first situation, there is a tendency to swing from one extreme to the other. That when specialists are employed the result is often that each does his work independently of the other, and the unity of the child's life is thus sacrificed to the tastes and acquisitions of a number of specialists. It seemed, however, not a question of the specialist but of the expert. When manual training, art, science, and literature are to be taught, it is a physical and mental impossibility that one person should be competent in all these lines of work. Superficial work is bound to be done in some one of them, and the child, through not having a model of expert workmanship to follow, acquires careless and imperfect methods of work. The school, accordingly, is endeavoring to put the various lines of work in charge of experts who maintain agreement and harmony through continued consultation and cooperation. When the different studies and occupations are controlled by reference to the same general principles, unity of aim and method are secured. The results obtained justify the belief that the undue separation, which often follows teaching by specialists, is a result of lack of supervision, cooperation, and control by a unified plan (Mayhew and Edwards, 1936, pp. 35–36).

TEACHER CENTERS

Teacher centers are being built to facilitate the needs of teachers like Mr. Hess and his colleagues who are now spending more time preparing materials to facilitate individual student development in a particular content area.

At their teacher center Mr. Hess and other staff members meet to discuss their teaching methods in light of current views of content and the nature of student learning. As in most centers, the following five components are characteristic of teacher centers:

1. *Centrality of teachers*—the teacher who is interested in expanding her own learning is the focus of the teacher center, for here she learns to prepare a curriculum that facilitates her children's learning.
2. *Voluntary participation*—persons in charge of the teacher center program realize that if they facilitate teacher interests and needs, teachers will attend.
3. *Heterogeneity of participants*—centers are open to anyone interested in teaching.
4. *Focus on curriculum content*—the intent of center programs is to aid the teacher in developing a child-centered curriculum consisting of methods and materials.
5. *Independence*—teachers are encouraged to explore, to try new ideas. Through learning about themselves, these teachers learn a great deal about their students.

If teachers can avert the pitfalls of overindividualizing that make a youngster helpless in a group and unable to deal with stress, they will have greatly improved the educative process. One real danger of a curriculum founded on individual growth is that the student will become overly independent of group processes. While realizing that mindless conformity has been universally exaggerated by schools, we can still argue that learning to work with groups is a goal not at odds with the goal of individualization. The aim is not to compel the student to behave or learn by the standards of others, but to learn how to live in a group.

A good program of individualized instruction develops students able to deal with stressful situations. Students in these programs for long periods of time are pursuing their own interests. They may need some experience and guidance when they encounter failure and helplessness. If their learning program is devoid of these problems the danger is very great that it is degenerating into routine learning. Also many children are not self-directive due to dependent personalities or immaturity. Therefore, these students may have difficulty achieving prescribed objectives, which encourage independent pursuit.

Social/Psychological Ramifications

The classroom teacher is similar to the psychologist in that both are involved with the scientific study of the mind. While mental processes are explored by both, the psychologist is primarily involved with the designing of theories about these processes. The classroom teacher is primarily interested in developing and implementing a classroom management system that will encourage these processes. Realizing their interests, let us begin by exploring the work of the psychologist and conclude with the task of the teacher. Remember that both espouse the philosophy of Mr. Hess and others interested in nurturing individuality. Cognitive processes can be described in different ways, and experts have developed whole schemas for sharing their ideas about cognition. Thinking processes may be categorized under any number of headings, but for the purposes of this book let us consider two broad headings that indicate two somewhat different mental processes. The first of these processes is *logical thinking* and deals with formal, well-structured thought processes that are used in the ordered solving of problems. The second category, dealt with in connection with cognitive process, is an informal, divergent kind of thinking that could be labeled *creative thinking*.

If the school is to nurture the individual, it most surely must concern itself with both kinds of thought processes used by students. In this section of the chapter, we will examine some of the psychological theory dealing with children's thinking and then suggest practical application for the personalized classroom.

LOGICAL THINKING

Under this broad heading a number of processes will be examined: concept formation, the generalizing process, and hypothesizing and predicting.

Concept formation. A concept is a word or phrase that identifies or classifies a group of objects or events or ideas. Given any group of objects, we are concerned with finding likenesses and differences so that the likenesses can be classified or given in a concept label. A concept may be concrete: dog or car, or it may be abstract: democracy or love. The concept may be more or less inclusive as well. Animal is more inclusive than mammal; mammal is more inclusive than dog; and dog is more inclusive than English Shepherd. Authors sometimes focus on one element rather than another and so inclusiveness may be stressed by one author, whereas abstractness may form the base for another definition.

Concept formation is a mental state or process which means, or refers to, more than one object or experience, or to one object in relation to others. Conception or concept formation denotes process, while concept denotes the product. The designation of a concept in words is called a term.

The transition from perception, or mere awareness, to conception is complex and much remains to be learned about it. In moving from perception to conception, Piaget observed that (1) the amount of redundant material decreases, (2) the amount of irrelevant information that can be tolerated without affecting the responses increases, and (3) the spatial and temporal separation over which the total information contained in the stimulus field can be integrated increases (Piaget, 1962, p. 121). As the concept forms, then, repetition becomes less essential, irrelevant information distracts less, and time and space separation can be greater without disturbing the learner.

Our investigator who has studied the complex process of concept formation in some detail is L. S. Vygotsky. (1960) It appears that during a child's early years, he associates a number of objects with a word; sometimes the association is based only on a chance impression. From this somewhat random collection of objects, the child improves the unorganized *congerie* or heap (as Vygotsky calls them) by trial-and-error methods, organization of his visual field, and reorganization of the heaps by associating elements from different heaps with a new word. This tendency continues as the child matures, but he begins to unite objects on the basis of more concrete or factual bonds. In a sense, he is beginning to determine the attributes of Aristotle's categories, although as yet the child does not distinguish between the essential and the nonessential (relevant and irrelevant) attributes. The child may associate objects on the basis of similarities, contrasts, proximity in space or time or on the basis of his own practical experiences. In this phase of concept formation, which Vygotsky refers to as thinking in complexes, the subjective associations are supplemented by more objective bonds, but the child still groups objects *in toto* with all of their attributes.

Experts in areas of specialization other than psychology are also interested in this process of identifying common attributes. In the field of mathematics, for example, the process is referred to as pattern detection. This is the process of learning the characterization of a class of inputs by detecting the common pattern of attributes. Items may belong to two or more sets of samples (groups) and in labeling these patterns one ignores, temporarily, the differences and names the similarities only.

In the final stage of concept formation, the child singles out elements and is able to consider these elements apart from the concrete experience in which they were encountered. The application of a concept to new situations that must be viewed in these terms presents an even greater difficulty. "When the process of concept formation is seen in all its complexity, it appears as a *movement* of thought within the pyramid of concepts, constantly alternating between two directions from the particular to the general and from the general to the particular." (Vygotsky, 1960, pp. 80–81)

Concept formation in its simplest form consists then of three basic steps:

(1) differentiation of properties/elements of objects/events. This involves the breaking down of global wholes into specific criteria.

(2) The second step is that of grouping or collecting these specific elements together. A careful analysis of common characteristics must be made here. Commonalities provide pattern detection.

(3) Thirdly, the individual must name or label or categorize the elements. This step may also provide for the decision about exclusion or inclusion of a new element in the category. This requires pattern recognition, that is, prime variables occur or sufficient criteria are represented to permit inclusion in the category.

As evidenced in an earlier example, José and his peers, like children in other elementary schools, are growing both mentally and physically. Therefore, they need to be given many opportunities to subject the concepts they have already developed to careful scrutiny and to be provided with experiences that will expose them to new objects, events, and ideas. Having concepts defined carefully will help the student in comprehending what he reads and in carrying out evaluative thinking procedures.

Concept attainment. Several factors affect concept attainment. The kind of concept, abstract or concrete, and the developmental age are factors in concept attainment. The number and degree of intensity of experiences the individual has will also affect the attainment of concepts. This suggests that there is time and a kind of experience that is appropriate for a child—a "teachable moment"—or the *"right kind* of experience at the *right time* for the developing organism" (Hooper, 1968, p. 423). Several of Piaget's concepts deal specifically with this idea.

Accommodation: When the individual encounters something new that does not fit his existing structure, he accommodates the new by modifying or reorganizing the present structure.

Assimilation: When the individual internalizes the change so that he can handle the new experience with ease as a part of his own life space, he has been able to assimilate the new.

One can consider this accommodation/assimilation process by a single term—adaptation. In dealing with children some time must be allowed for the accommodation process. Ginsburg and Opper give a prime example of infant accommodation.

Suppose an infant of 4 months is presented with a rattle. He has never before had the opportunity to play with rattles or similar toys. The rattle, then, is a feature of the environment to which he needs to adapt. His subsequent behavior reveals the tendencies of assimilation and accommodation. The infant tries to grasp the rattle. In order to do this successfully he must accommodate in more ways than are immediately apparent. First, he must accommodate his visual activities to perceive the rattle correctly; then he must reach out and accommodate his movements to the distance between himself and the rattle; in grasping the rattle he must adjust his fingers to its shape; and in lifting the rattle he must accommodate his muscular exertion to its weight. In sum, the grasping of the rattle involves a series of acts of accommodation, or modifications of the infant's behavioral structures to suit the demands of the environment. (Ginsburg and Opper, 1969, p. 19)

Stages. Piaget suggests that the evolution of thought takes place in the following stages that coincide with rough age-developmental stages: (1) Sensory motor stage or the preverbal intelligence, running roughly birth to 18 months or two years. (2) Preoperational, the stage in which children group and categorize on a functional basis. For example, using pencil with paper. A child grouped a knife with a carrot and a potato because, "you peel them with it." This is common in young children two to seven or thereabouts. (3) Concrete operation or thinking with objects and concrete events from seven to 11. (4) Formal operation is the stage of conceptual or formal thought from 11 years on. At this stage the child likes to think in abstract terms and enjoys hypothesizing.

Piaget asserts repeatedly in his research and his writings that cognitive developmental changes are related to biological developmental processes. Each stage of cognitive growth (he labels four specific stages), with its concomitant changes, emerge logically and inevitably from the preceding one. The stages are not reversible nor is a stage avoidable. "According to Piaget, every child must pass through the stages of cognitive development in the same order." (Wadsworth, 1971, p. 28) The child cannot skip the concrete operations stage altogether, and he cannot go through the concrete operations stage and then the preoperational stage in reverse order. Piaget is a true developmental stage theorist and postulates that one stage builds on another, that the child accomplishes certain learning tasks before going on to more complex tasks. Thus, skipping stages and reversing stages are not possibilities.

Although these stages are identified with certain age ranges, these ranges are not precise or binding, but are only approximations. "Cognitive development flows along, but the stages are useful to the observer conceptualizing the developmental process." (Wadsworth, 1971, p. 26) The rate at which children pass through these processes is not fixed and may be affected by intelligence, general health, social conditions, and other variables.

Turn to page 181. Read the teacher/student interaction. Now see if you can determine the stage of development of the students in Mr. Hess's classroom.

TEACHING APPLICATION

Given information about the way in which children form concepts and the variables that affect concept attainment, teachers should be prepared to assist students in forming concepts at a level appropriate for them.

Here are two somewhat different ways the teacher can help students identify and clarify the parameters of a concept. In Taba's (1967) *Handbook* she suggests that the teacher provide the children with an initial broad experience, like a walk around the school, a film, or some slides. This can then be followed by organizing the many details of the experience into a workable grouping of research topics. "Task I" looks like the following:

CONCEPT FORMATION

Overt Activity	Covert Mental Operation	Eliciting Questions
1. Enumeration or listing	Differentiation	What did you see? hear? note?
2. Grouping	Identifying common properties, abstracting	What belongs together? On what criterion?
3. Labeling or Categorizing	Determining the hierarchical order of items. Super and sub-ordination	How would you call these groups? What belongs under what?

As you can see concept identification begins with lists of discrete items. After viewing a film on the Pilgrims, one group of students listed the following items:

Pilgrims	Massachusetts	furs
churches	utensils	tobacco
meeting houses	fireplaces	lumber
houses	slaves	schools
gardens	plantations	haystacks
farmers	Indians	shoes
clothing	water wheels	rock walls
maps	goats	mills
ships	canoes	ministers

In actually getting the list on the board, a number of subquestions may be necessary. Children sometimes "get stuck" on a category and name many similar items. Look at the above list for an example. The students had listed meeting houses and houses. If they had continued with sheds or houses for the cattle, it would have been a good idea to shift their thinking by saying "Did you see any other things in the film that interested you?" This will break the chain of imitative thinking that is building up.

At this point in the classroom, all students should be encouraged to participate. Everyone has seen something worth recording.

The students categorized the preceding list under the following concept heading:

people	travel, transportation
buildings	tools
industries	things to wear

The symbols $\vee$, $\sim\!\sim$, o were used to quickly group the items. For example:

Pilgrims	ships
churches	shoes

Some of the items did not fit any of these broad categories and the students then reexamined the list to determine what other labels would be needed to include these disparate items.

The second technique for developing concepts is the "question initiating" one. When this technique is used, an "opener" or introductory broad experience is provided as in the Taba process described earlier. Following this "opener" the student is asked to work in a small group or choose a partner and list all the questions that occurred to him as he watched the film or took the walk. What questions does he have for which he would like to find answers? A long list of 20 or 25 questions can be raised by brainstorming in this way. A separate slip of paper should be provided for jotting down each question when the questions have all been jotted down—a sorting and grouping into categories follows.

Utilizing either one of the techniques suggested will help students determine the specific, concrete details that are subsumed under the category label—the concepts of industries, for example.

Once the category has been formed, it will be necessary to reexamine the variation within the category so that a general statement may be developed about the concept. It will be important now for the student to gather a large fund of information about the category he has chosen so that he can organize the data and, on the basis of his organized information, develop some general statements.

GENERALIZING

Once the data have been collected and organized the students can develop some generalizations based on the data. The generalizing process produces an end product that has required differentiation and synthesis of ideas. Poincaré (1952) says,

However timid we may be, there must be interpolation. Experiment only gives us a certain number of isolated points. They must be connected by a continuous line, and this as a true generalization. . . .The curve thus traced will pass between and near the points observed; it will not pass through the points themselves. Thus, we are restricted to generalizing our experiment, we correct it . . . (Poincaré, 1952, pp. 142, 143).

"Detached facts cannot therefore satisfy us and that is why our science must be ordered, or better still, generalized" (Poincaré, 1952, p. 143). There are an incomprehensible number of facts about mankind. These must be ordered and generalized if they are to have any meaning at all for the learner. The learner himself must be the primary agent in ordering and generalizing from many items of data in order that he may find meaning from his collection of facts.

PREDICTING, HYPOTHESIZING

A review of research suggests more than isolated facts. It enables us to generalize and, on the basis of these generalizations, to predict.

The fact observed will never be repeated. All that can be affirmed is that under analogous circumstances an analogous fact will be produced. To predict we must therefore invoke the aid of analogy. (Poincaré, 1952, p. 142)

We base our prediction on as large a number of facts as possible. "However solidly founded a prediction may appear to us, we are never absolutely sure that experiment will not prove it to be baseless if we set to work to verify it" (Poincaré, 1952, p. 144). Even so it is far better to predict without complete certainty than not to hypothesize at all. It is important that students learn to hypothesize and then carry out research that will verify or negate their hypothesis.

According to Piaget, there are several indications that a child is in transition between the concrete operations level of thinking and the formal thinking stage. One such indicator is the child's ability to transcend time and space via symbolic representation, possibly verbal symbolism. He sees the hypothetical consequences of a proposed solution, and he can suggest alternate solutions. The child goes beyond the time and space barriers, and solves problems intellectually. Usually this occurs during adolescence and the youth delights in considering "that which is not." The child is engaging in what is called antecedent/consequent thinking, in predicting what will happen and on the basis of this selects the consequence that will be least hazardous and/or expensive to him.

TEACHING APPLICATION

Antecedent/consequent thinking deals with a child's ability to foresee the consequences of certain antecedents. One might also ask the child to reverse that process and determine the antecedents that would have produced certain consequences. Ralph Ojemann (1963) has termed this "causal thinking"; that is, the child looks at an event and projects backward in time to determine the cause, or causes, that might have brought about the event. Ojemann's studies of elementary school children have emphasized the idea that certain similar behaviors or events may have developed from different causal bases or a multiplicity of causal bases.

The discussion that follows shows the student engaged in hypothesizing or predicting "If this happens *then* this will follow." The students are demonstrating clearly that one consequence leads to and effects another consequence, they are showing you "futuristic thinking."

Student/teacher interaction sequence. Students had completed their study of the desert nomads. The class had been discussing the changes that would take place if suddenly the desert could have all the water it needed. Many "chains of change" had been developed around:

1. ways of earning a living;
2. growth of towns;
3. education, and so on.

At this point the teacher injects the idea of how people feel about change. The following sequence takes place:

MR. HESS. With all these changes in the desert, what would happen to the old ways of life?

JOSÉ. They would be forgotten and they wouldn't use them any more.

WONG. They probably would use them, because their ancestors had used them.

ERNESTINE. There would be quite a lot of changes.

MR. HESS. What kind of changes?

ERNESTINE. Their jobs.

MR. HESS. What do you mean?

CAROLE. They wouldn't like it very well because they would probably want to stick to the work of their ancestors.

FELICIA. It would probably be strange to them.

MR. HESS. Strange in what way?

JOSÉ. They would feel sort of funny, like they were just being born and all that.

MARIA. I don't think the old people would like it very well because they would think their way was better.

MR. HESS. Why?

MARIA. Because they were taught it, and they would want their sons to do the same thing. Anyway, they would grouch.

JOSÉ. In a couple of years they would start changing and year by year, pretty soon, they would be modern.

MR. HESS. What do you think the children would think about this?

MARK. They would probably think that they had a new world.

JOSÉ. They wouldn't think it was so important. But their parents would think it was more important, because they have been that way more years than the children have.

The ability of these students to predict and show causative rationale behind their predictions is apparent. By using questions that suggest the need for rationale and refocusing when the discussion bogged down, the teacher sharpens the thinking process.

Creative thinking. As suggested throughout this chapter, "the mission of education is to persuade each child that he is a richer source of ideas than he suspects and to enable him to experience the exhilaration that is inherent in the creative use of mind." (Kagan, 1971, p. 47) As the mission of education it becomes at least partly the teacher's responsibility.

The teacher might best encourage the creative use of mind by demonstrating his own interest in novel situations and curiosity about different or unique ideas. In a memorial to Robert Kennedy, Frank Mankiewicz said, "He was one of those rare men whose education continues after adulthood. He was learning all the time: from books, from his staff, his friends, the press, and from joyous participation in the public life of his country" (1968, p. 52). Kennedy's delight in learning was obvious to many. The teacher must clearly show an interest in learning to the children in the classroom. Having shown this interest and delight in learning to a child, it is important, then, that one provide the child with the opportunity to develop and pursue his interests in learning about novel situations that fascinate him. Some experts refer to this as discovery learning.

There are several advantages to discovery learning:

1. It enables the child to identify problems.
2. It develops the learner's self-confidence and attitudes toward alternative solutions.
3. It encourages the student to discover broad principles and larger connections between different bodies of knowledge.

There may also be some disadvantages involved in the process of discovery learning

1. It is not suitable for use in a classical curriculum since it does not lend itself readily to a structured approach.
2. There is a need for highly skilled teacher guidance in discovery processes.
3. There can be an "arbitrary nature" about the ideas or knowledge gained this way. A sense of ownership emerges about the conclusions; that is, "Since I discovered it, it must be right." Thus, continuous self-evaluation of one's ideas may be difficult.

Sometimes discovery is considered as though it were a completely creative thing. Others point out that the function of discovery is specialized and limited, and that there are certain kinds of discovery within the realms of possibility in certain content areas. One of the requisites for discovery is skill and/or knowledge in a broad content area. Recently, the author conducted a rough survey of the creative discoveries made by several graduate classes of experienced teachers. The range of talent and interests was tremendous and fascinating, indeed. One man discovered how to produce fancy hats for children's operettas and someone else had pooled all the resources and materials he could muster in order to produce a new curricular structure for his high school department. Still another person created beautiful hand-tooled jewelry. In these and other samples of the items that were suggested we saw a person's unique discovery that combined a number of elements in a new and different way.

1. In each of these, however, the person stated clearly that *skill* was necessary—that part of the skill that was required to produce this item could be learned by other people. Pribram says, "Discoverers make their discoveries through what they already know: They match the unfamiliar against a thoroughly incorporated body of fact." And goes on to add "Novelty rises out of variations on the familiar." (Pribram, 1964, p. 107). This means that a person does not create on a completely knowledgeless basis, but that he has probably already done considerable work in a field of endeavor if he is to make a truly creative discovery in that field.

2. A second requirement for creative thinking is the *unique combination of a given person's talents and background which is probably not reproduceable.* Some skills and information are necessary in order to be able to produce in a given field but they will not guarantee a unique discovery in a field. "We need a balance between overinformation and freedom, a point between lack of information and the fettering of imagination by too much of it." (Peel, 1960, p. 171). The person who is truly creative seems to have been able to detect that delicate balance and combine it with elements from his own unique life space to produce a new product.

3. A third element mentioned by most of the group sampled but referred to in different ways was "mindset." Some persons said that they had to be highly motivated, others said they were determined, and still others that the job they set out to do required a great deal of persistence. These qualities one might call "mind set." It would seem obvious that the carrying out of the task involved in the discovery usually does take some degree of determination. The idea for the piece of jewelry or for the new curricular design may come to the person's mind rather quickly but to carry this through so that it is a product others can share seems to be time-consuming.

4. There is evidence of *emotional involvement* in the creative act. Persons indicate an unusual degree of satisfaction with a creative accomplishment because they have been highly involved emotionally in the production of the idea and/or product.

W. J. J. Gordon discusses "mental states" that may help a person be more able to discover new relationships. He is interested in the area of scientific discovery and uses the term "synetics," which means "the joining together of different and apparently irrelevant elements." Gordon delineates the "mental states" that are beneficial to the synetic process as follows:

1. Detachment—involvement remove a problem from its familiar setting, see it differently—then become involved in order to produce a new insight.
2. Deferment—resist the first solution that comes along.
3. Speculation—permitting the mind to run free to search for solutions.
4. Autonomy of the object—crystallization of ideas into some kind of solution.

Gordon talks about some ways in which persons may achieve these mental states. For example, he says that the use of a *personal analogy* is one way in which one can help the student to be more productive in the solution of a problem. In role-playing sessions, when we ask the child to assume the role of another, and then ask "How did you feel when you were Tommy?," we are using personal analogy.

A second device that a person can use to achieve problem-solving mental states is the *direct analogy*. We use a direct analogy when we compare and contrast or use parallel facts, knowledge, or technology. We say, for instance, "You need to know how the people in the Fiji Islands solve their housing problem. Let's think about how the people in the Arctic solved theirs." You have studied the way baboons get along in groups. Can we find similar areas of behavior in human group behavior?"

The third stage is that of *symbolic analogy*. One might use impersonal and objective objects to solve a problem. When utilizing this thinking style, we are trying to discover how something we know about compares to something we do not really know a great deal about.

A fourth means of achieving these mental states is the use of the *fantasy analogy*. Gordon talks about the wild ideas that one thinks about. We say, "Wait a minute about saying, 'that is irrelevant,' let's look at the apparent irrelevancies—let's examine this idea again to see whether it does, in some situations, make sense."

Other persons have also been concerned about the processes involved in original thinking. J. J. Gallagher suggests some steps as being useful to productive thinking:

1. Preparation—"This is the stage in which the problem is investigated from all directions and is primarily a problem of identification and fact gathering period" (1964, p. 359).
2. Incubation—person does not consciously think about the problem. There is, perhaps, some kind of internal process of association of new information with past information and some internal reorganization of the information.
3. Illumination—"Aha phenomenon"—in this stage the creator finds the solution to the problem.
4. Verification—put the idea to test to determine validity.

DISCOVERY IDEAS COMPARED?

Synectics	Productive Thinking
W. J. J. Gordon	J. J. Gallagher
detachment—involvement	preparation
deferment	incubation
	illumination
	verification

These two persons dealing with the topics listed above show some genuine similarities. Both of these deal with the ill-defined, hard-to-grasp topic broadly defined here as "creative thinking." In order to evoke a creative response, some choices must be left open to the student. This can be done easily in the classroom. The student who tries to produce a different kind of response may feel some doubt about selecting a mode of response that differs from the one chosen by the rest of the group. The teacher must actively encourage unusual responses and this may help students dare to respond in different ways. Students may feel great insecurity about their products. It may be difficult for a very divergent response to meet a suggested standard criterion (1000 words). Because of this, the teacher may wish to provide guidelines, but suggest that they are only guides and that some products may differ from these guidelines. Ultimately, teachers should propose activities that have no guidelines.

It is a precision balancing act for a master teacher to determine when to support and encourage, and when to leave the creator alone with his own thoughts. No gimmick can be given to you that will allow complete success with this task. Real human sensitivity is necessary, and that is a quality not easily described or taught.

If one wishes to nurture individuality, careful assistance in the development of logical thinking would be an imperative. Acceptance and encouragement of divergent thinking and the creative student is equally important.

Sometimes the requirement of a grade or for coverage of certain content and ideas may place constraints on the teacher. Administrative policies, parental pressure, and sometimes fellow teachers may cause a teacher to conform or make the teacher afraid to try new ideas. These variables will each have to be carefully assessed by each teacher who wishes to implement some aspects of creativity in his "model of teaching."

TRANSFER OF LEARNING

In deemphasizing the content of learning and emphasizing the overall learning process teachers came to grips with the heart of education—the transferability of what is learned. It is comparatively easy to teach people exactly what they need to know in a precisely stated situation. This comes under the broad rubric of training. Teaching people broad concepts, generalizations, and attitudes that will enable them to successfully resolve future and undefinable problems is not as easy.

Many teachers today hold onto the remains of faculty psychology principles that governed the perennialist model. Though those early educators did not see themselves exactly as trainers, they did believe that the mind was like a muscle in that exercise would improve its ability to learn in future situations. The emphasis on recitation stems from this belief. Also they accepted propositions such as: Studying geometry teaches one to think logically. All psychoeducational research has demonstrated no transferability from any of those subject areas believed to develop intellectual discipline.

William James called this whole theory into doubt with his tests at the end of the nineteenth century. He argued that memory and transferability of learning are enhanced most if the general topic is broadly understood. Learning a lot about postwar Reconstruction improves the memorization of the Reconstruction Acts. It does not improve one's general ability to memorize and/or learn anything else. Furthermore, James argued, general comprehension of the time period is the only thing that can improve lasting learning.

But he still was defining learning in terms of assimilation of a mass of information. Those who began to urge various adaptations of the personalized model began to urge that the criteria of being educated should involve the ability to solve problems. This means that transfer is not a result of a strengthened mind, but of a mind more equipped with general abilities and attitudes that aid the student in unfamiliar settings.

These characteristics of a learning situation enhance transfer. First, the learner must be aware of the broader explanation of why a phenomenon occurs. Knowledge that a particular weed killer effectively destroys dandelions is less likely to transfer than the knowledge that the solution will destroy any and only broad leaf plants because the weed killer needs a broad surface for its fatal chemical action. Second, the learner's attitude toward new situations must be considered. One is not likely to do well resolving a difficulty if he believes he can only do so by trial and error; that is, that he must fumble continuously until he happens on the right solution. If he believes that he can do better by stopping to respond logically to the specific symptoms of the problem he will do better. The third factor is related to this ability to pause before resolving a problem. Transferability depends, too, on one's self-image. The learner develops the ability to take a chance on a partially reasoned solution to see if it works. Transfer occurs most readily for the youngster who, if he fails, is able to use that failure and connect it with his previous learning to construct a new alternative.

Personalized educators worked steadily toward the development of learning environments that produced these three traits. To them transfer of problem-solving ability was a very high priority. Of course, transferability has by now become a feature of most educational models to one degree or another, but it was the progressive educators who gave it its modern form and urged it upon teachers.

SOCIAL PROGRESSIVE EDUCATION IN AMERICA
A Capsule Summary Of Its Background Philosophy

WORLD-VIEW   A changing, material world which progressively evolves into a higher order. Our present "scientific-democratic" order finds its truth and values pragmatically through cooperative group dynamics.

IMAGE OF MAN   Contemporary, pragmatic man is an active, cooperative worker seeking a better, reformed social order. He sees himself as a "whole man,"—intelligent, emotional, social—a single, material organism.

THEORY OF   An inductive, "scientific" thinker, man learns by
KNOWLEDGE   problem solving via trial and error. Based on his experience, his learning is a process of "reconstruction" in which he reflects on each experience to put it into his overall mental perception, giving it meaning, and thereby gaining control over it for his future life.

VALUES   Established pragmatically through trial and error. Holds priority for scientific and democratic processes and cooperative efforts to build a better society.

THEORY OF   Sees the schools as the epitome of society through
EDUCATION   which he can critically examine society's tenets, processes, and values, and thereby socially reconstruct it into a reformed, social order of the future.

MAN AND   Man works through society in a democratic fash-
SOCIETY   ion to achieve his goals. Society must be entirely open so that all can participate in the continued progress of the community.

ROMANTIC EDUCATION IN AMERICA
A Capsule Summary Of Its Background Philosophy

WORLD-VIEW	Sees the individual being corrupted by social institutions that foster competition, authoritarian power, and greed. Seeks to create a new social order by creating free, creative individuals.
IMAGE OF MAN	A healthy organism, substantially good and, if he submits to his own inner conscience, capable of growing into a free personality. However, he can also be corrupted into a competitive, selfish individual by the larger corrupt social order, should it be allowed to intrude into his formation.
THEORY OF KNOWLEDGE	Man learns naturally through his experience of his environment. He has an inner entelechy which leads him to retrace in his own learning growth, all the accomplishments of civilization.
VALUES	Values are formed in his own conscience—a voice to which he must submit totally. He values freedom, creativity, individuality, and self-determination.
THEORY OF EDUCATION	Allow the child free access to the world of experience, undisturbed by social institutions, including the active teacher, and he will be a natural, successful learner. Learning is active and personally involving, and the lessons learned affect the student's entire personality.
MAN AND SOCIETY	Man and society are very much at odds. Man developing in a state of nature, without the constraints of society, is happy and fulfilled. Only society corrupts and prevents man from achieving happiness.

REFERENCES

ALLEN, R. V. "Grouping Through Learning Centers." *Childhood Education* (Dec. 1968), pp. 200–203.

BARMAN, ALICEROSE AND LISA COHEN. "The Troubled Child." *The New York Times Magazine,* Nov. 8, 1971, pp. 19–108.

BARRO, STEPHEN M. "An Approach to Developing Accountability Measures for the Public Schools." *Phi Delta Kappan,* 52 (Dec. 1970), 196–205.

BELL, TERREE. "The Means and Ends of Accountability." *Proceedings of the Conferences on Educational Accountability.* Princeton, N.J.: Educational Testing Service, 1971.

BINET, ALFRED, AND THERESA SIMON. *The Development of Intelligence in Children.* tr. Elizabeth S. Kite. Baltimore: The Williams and Wilkins Co., 1916.

BOSSONE, RICHARD. "Disadvantaged Teachers in Disadvantaged Schools." *Contemporary Education,* 41, No. 4 (Feb. 1970), 183–185.

BOYER, J. B. "Materials for Black Learners." *Educational Leadership,* 28 (Nov. 1970), 191–193.

BROUDY, H. S. *The Real World of the Public Schools.* New York: Harcourt Brace Jovanovich, Inc., 1972.

BRUNER, JEROME. *The Process of Education.* New York: Vintage, 1961.

––––––––. "The Process of Education Revisited." *Kappan,* 53, (Sept. 1971), 18–21.

BUMSTEAD, R. A. "Texarkana, The First Accounting." *Educate,* 3 (March 1970), p. 00.

BUROS, OSCAR K. *The Sixth Mental Measurement Yearbook.* Highland Park, N.J.: The Gryphon Press, 1965.

CARLSON, K. "Equalizing Educational Opportunity." *Review of Educational Research,* 42 (Fall, 1972), 453–475.

THE BRITISH GLOWDEN COMMITTEE REPORT. *Children and the Primary: A Report to the Central School Advisory Council for Education,* Her Majesty Stationery Office, Volume I, 1967. British Information Services, 845 Third Ave. New York, N.Y.

CLEGG, A. A. "The Teacher as Manager of the Curriculum?" *Educational Leadership,* 30 (Jan. 1973), 307–310.

COLLINS, B. M. "Beyond Sesame Street: TV and Preschoolers." *Educational Leadership,* 28 (Nov. 1970), 143–147.

CREMIN, LAWRENCE. *The Transformation of the School.* New York: Vintage, 1961.

CRONBACK, LEE J. "Presentation vs. Discovery of Generalizations." In *Educational Psychology.* New York: Harcourt Brace Jovanovich, Inc., 1963.

CUNNINGHAM, LAVERN L. "Our Accountability Problems." In *Emerging Patterns of Administrative Accountability,* edited by Lesley H. Hrawder, Jr. Berkeley, Calif.: McCutchan Publishing Corp., 1971.

DELONE, RICHARD H. AND SUSAN T. "John Dewey Is Alive and Well in New England." *Saturday Review,* 53 (Nov. 21, 1970), 69.

DEWEY, JOHN. *Democracy and Education.* New York: Macmillan Publishing Co., Inc., 1916.

––––––. *Experience and Education.* New York: Macmillan Publishing Co., In., 1938.

––––––––. *The Child and the Curriculum* and *The School and Society.* Chicago: University of Chicago Press, 1956.

DYER, HENRY S. "Statewide Evaluation—What Are the Priorities?" *Phi Delta Kappan,* **51**, No. 10 (June 1970), 558–569.

FEATHERSTONE, JOSEPH. "An English Lesson for America." *The New York Times Magazine,* Section 7, September 20, 1970, pp. 10, 12, 14, 16.

————. "Kentucky Fried Children." *The New Republic,* **163** (Sept. 5–12, 1970), 12–16.

————. "Primary School Revolution in Britain." *The New Republic* (August 10, 1967), 17, 19, 21.

FOOTLICK, J. K. "Inequality in America: A Problem Too Vast For The Schools To Overcome?" *Carnegie Quarterly,* **20** (Fall, 1972), 1–7.

FRENCH, R. L. "Individualizing Classroom Communication." *Educational Leadership,* **28** (Nov. 1970), 193–197.

GALLUP, GEORGE. "The Public's Attitude Toward the Public Schools." *Phi Delta Kappan,* **52** (Oct. 1970), 100.

GALLAGHER, JAMES J. "Productive Thinking." In *Review of Child Development Research,* edited by Martin L. Hoffman and Lois Waldis Hoffman. Vol. **I,** New York: Russel Sage Foundations, 1964.

GINSBERG, HERBERT, AND SYLVIA OPPER. *Piaget's Theory of Intellectual Development.* Englewood Cliffs, N.J.: Prentice Hall, Inc., 1969.

GOODLAD, JOHN. "Individual Differences and Vertical Organization of the School." *Individualizing Instruction: 1962 NSSE Yearbook,* 1962.

GORDON, W. J. J. *Synectics—The Development of Creative Capacity.* New York: Harper and Row, 1961.

GRIEDER, CALVIN. "Education Parks May Replace the Neighborhood School." *Nation's Schools,* **76** (Dec. 1965), 14.

HART, HAROLD H. (ED.), *Summerhill For and Against.* New York: Hart Publishing Co., 1970.

HARMES, H. M. "Specifying Objectives for Performance Contracts." *Educational Technology,* **II** (Jan. 1971), 52–56.

HOLT, JOHN. *How Children Fail.* New York: Delta, 1964.

————. *How Children Learn.* New York: Dell, 1967.

HOOPER, I. H. "Piagetian Research and Children." In *Logical Thinking in Children,* edited by I. E. Sigel and F. H. Hooper. New York: Holt, Rinehart, & Winston, 1968.

JACKSON, J. J. AND V. E. JACKSON. "Needed: Personalized Models of Learning." *Educational Leadership,* **30** (Oct. 1972), 20–23.

JENCKS, CHRISTOPHER. "Education Vouchers." *The New Republic,* July 4, 1970.

————, ET. AL. *Inequality: A Reassessment of the Effect of Family* and *Schooling in America.* New York: Basic Books, Inc., 1972.

JENKINS, MARION (ED.). "Here's to Success in Reading Self Selection Helps." *Childhood Education,* **32** (Nov. 1955), 124–131.

KAGAN, JEROME. *Understanding Children—Behavior, Motives, and Thoughts.* New York: Harcourt Brace Jovanovich, Inc., 1971.

KILPATRICK, WILLIAM H. "An Effort at Appraisal." *The Twenty-Fourth of the National Society for the Study of Education,* Bloomington, Ill.: Public School Publishing Co., 1925.

KOHL, HERBERT. *The Open Classroom.* New York: Vintage, 1969.

LAMBERT, P. "Notes on the Use of Flanders Interaction Analysis." *Journal of Educational Research,* **58** (Jan. 1965), 222–224.

LARSON, RICHARD M. "The School Curriculum and the Urban Disadvantaged: A Historical Review and Some Thoughts About Tomorrow." *Journal of Negro Education,* **38** (Fall, 1969), 351–360.

LEVINE, DANIEL. "Integration in Metropolitan Schools: Issues and Prospects." *Phi Delta Kappan,* **54** (June 1973), 651–657.

LONGSTREET, W. S. *Beyond Jencks: The Myth of Equal Schooling.* Washington, D.C.: Association for Supervision and Curriculum Development, 1973.

MANKIEWICZ, FRANK. "Two Tributes." *Look Magazine Tribute to Robert F. Kennedy,* Special Issue (1968).

MARIN, PETER. "Children of the Apocalypse." *Saturday Review,* **53,** (Sept. 19, 1970), 71–73.

MARLAND, S. P. "The School's Role in Career Development." *Educational Leadership,* **30** (Dec. 1972), 203–213.

MATLIN, ARNOLD H. AND FRANCES A. MENDELSOHN. "The Relationship Between Personality and Achievement Variables in the Elementary School." *The Journal of Educational Research,* **58** (July-Aug. 1965), 457–459.

MAYHEW, KATHERINE C., AND ANNA C. EDWARDS. *The Dewey School.* Appleton-Century-Crofts, 1936.

McDONALD, FREDERICK. *Educational Psychology,* 2nd Ed. Belmont, Calif.: Wadsworth Publishing Co., Inc., 1968.

McGEE, J. C. "What About the Comprehensive High School?" *Educational Leadership,* **29** (Jan. 1972), 363–365.

MEEHAN, M. L. "What About Team Teaching?" *Educational Leadership,* **30** (May 1973), 717–720.

METZNER, SEYMOUR. "The Urban Teacher: Saint, Sinner or Sucker?" *Phi Delta Kappan,* **51** (May 1970), 489–492.

MILLER, H. G. AND J. W. "Individualized Instruction through Diagnosis and Evaluation," *Childhood Education,* **46** (May 1970), 417–421.

MILLS, P. "A Philosophical Base for Curriculum Decisions." *Educational Leadership,* **29** (April 1972), 631–637.

MORGENSTERN, ANNA. *Grouping in the Elementary School.* Pitman Publishing Corp., 1966.

MOSSER, GLORIA. "Movement Education The Why and Hows." *Grade Teacher,* **88** (Dec. 1970), 60–64.

OJEMANN, RALPH, H. "The Significance of a Causal Orientation in Human Development." *Keeping Abreast of the Revolution in Education.* A Report of the Twenty-Eighth Educational Conference sponsored by American Council of Education, 1963.

OLSEN, E. G. "Enlivening the Community School Curriculum." *Phi Delta Kappan,* **54** (Nov. 1972), 176–179.

PEDDIWELL, J. ABNER. *The Saber-Tooth Curriculum.* McGraw-Hill Paperbacks, 1939.

PEEL, E. E. *The Pupil's Thinking*. London: Oldbourne, 1960.

PIAGET, JEAN. *Plays, Dreams, and Imitation in Childhood*. New York: W. W. Norton, 1962.

PILCHER, P. S. "Open Education: In Britain and the USA." *Educational Leadership*, **30** (Nov. 1972), 137–141.

PINES, MAYA. "Infants are Sometimes Smarter than Everyone Thinks." *The New York Times Magazine*, November 28, 1970, pp. 32–33.

POINCARÉ, HENRY. *Science and Hypothesis*. New York: Dover Publications, Inc., 1952.

POSTMAN, NEIL AND CHARLES WEINGARTNER. *Teaching as a Subversive Activity*. New York: Delacorte Press, 1969.

PRIBRAM, KARL H. "Neurological Notes in the Art of Educating." In *Theories of Learning and Instruction*, National Society for the Study of Education. Chicago: University of Chicago Press, 1964.

RITCHIE, C. C. "The Eight-Year Study: Can We Afford To Ignore It." *Educational Leadership*, **28** (Feb. 1971), 484–486.

ROGERS, CARL. *Freedom to Learn*. Columbus, Ohio: Charles E. Merrill Publishers, 1969.

————. "Can Schools Grow Persons." *Educational Leadership*, **29,** No. 3 (Dec. 1971), 215–225.

ROUSSEAU, JEAN-JACQUES. *Émile, Julie, and Other Writings*. New York: Barrow's Educational Services, 1964.

SAXE, R. W. *Opening The Schools: Alternative Way of Learning*. Berkeley, Calif.: McCutchon, 1972.

SILBERMAN, CHARLES. *Crisis in the Classroom*. New York: Random House, 1970.

SMITH, NILA BANTON. *Reading Instruction for Today's Children*. Englewood Cliffs, N.J.: Prentice-Hall, Inc., 1963.

STANFORD, G. "Sensitivity Education and The Curriculum." *Educational Leadership*, **28** (Dec. 1970), 245–250.

TABA, HILDA, ET AL. *Teacher's Handbook for Elementary School Studies*, Educational Series, Reading, Mass.: Addison-Wesley Publishing Co. Inc., 1967.

TANNER, D. "Inequality Misconstrued?" *Educational Leadership*, **30** (May 1973), 703–705.

TENENBAUM, S. "The Insufferable Lot of the American Middle Class Child." *Educational Leadership*, **27** (Dec. 1969), 277–281.

VYGOTSKY, L. S. *Thought and Language*. Cambridge, Mass.: Massachusetts Institute of Technology Press, 1960.

WADSWORTH, BARRY J. *Piaget's Theory of Cognitive Development*. New York: David McKay Co., Inc., 1971.

WASHBURNE, CARLETON. *Child Development and the Curriculum*, Part I. Thirty-eighth Yearbook of the National Society for the Study of Education. Chicago: University of Chicago Press, 1939.

WOELFEL, NORMAN. *Molders of the American Mind*. New York: Columbia University Press, 1933.

CHAPTER 5
Education : Interactional

Philosophical/Social Commentary

BEFORE delving into our discussion of the social and intellectual background of interactional education, discussion specifying the exact nature of this model will follow. Unlike the three previous models, which most of us recognize and most have experienced, this educational style is elusive by the very nature of its noninstitutional make-up.

Many proponents endorse Bruce Joyce's description as an interactional model. Other advocates identify it as "radical," or "humanistic." However, it might help to look briefly at the intended meanings of these two terms. "Radical," from its Latin base, refers to the *roots* of the educational process. Followers of this model wish to delve beneath the surface questions of techniques and content to the "what" of education. They wish, also, to grapple with the root questions of processes, goals, and values; the "why" of education. Charles Silberman charges that, if in the past, teachers have butchered education,

. . . it is because it simply never occurs to more than a handful to ask *why* they are doing what they are doing, to think seriously or deeply about the purposes or consequences of education. (Silberman, 1970, p. 11)

Silberman sees this "mindlessness" not only as the core problem of education, but as a problem extending "throughout the entire society." So it is that the interactional model sees these root "why" questions of education tightly entwined with the "why" questions about the society.

"Humanistic" underlines the model's pivotal focus: *man,* a social being who fulfills his potential only in interdependency with his fellow man and the viable context of a human community. This predominant social concern leads us to select the descriptive term, interactional, for in the eyes of this model, learning results from the interaction *between the teacher and the student,* between student and his content, and between his thought and his life.

The essentialists and technologists see education passing from teacher to student, in a single-directioned process. Progressives and romantics reversed the flow to move from student to teacher, but still see it largely as a single direction. The interactionists, however, see a "dialogue" taking place between the teacher and the student, and learning unfolding from the interchange of that conversation.

In the interactional model, learning is more than fact-gathering; it is having some experiential understanding of those facts, seeing them interpreted into a whole and understood in the context of our lives. Each student and each teacher has his own set of experiences and his own unique perspective. Learning occurs when several look, together, at a particular problem from their own various points of view, and then listen and "teach" each other out of these various experiences. The resulting insight offers something more than the mere sum total of each contribution. Certainly the teacher's experiences are broader and his thoughts more articulate than those of his students, but the difference is one of degree, not of exclusion. Every interactional teacher is also a "student" in his class; every student also a "teacher."

Most describe this as the Socratic method. It cannot be the case if Socrates is seen smugly probing his student for the "right" answer, already secure in his own mind. But it would definitely be so if Socrates is seen as being engaged in an uncontrived conversation, uncovering problems and searching for solutions neither he nor his student were aware of at the outset. And definitely so if both Socrates and his student intend to incorporate their newly discovered truths into their lives.

In another sense, this model is interactional *between the student and his content*. As noted, his content interests go beyond the informative "what" of facts or the operative "how" of skills and lead him into the inquiring "why" of purpose and meaning. He is both socially conscious and self-conscious. "How can I understand all the goings-on of my world? Where is it going? Who am I and what is my place in the world? What are my values?" In a phrase, his concerns are *meaning and identity*.

Content is an immediate aspect of the learner's environment. He sees himself neither as totally determining nor as totally determined by his environment, but as involved in a reciprocal relationship with it. His views and demands on life influence its shape and patterns while its forces and limitations extract accommodations from him.

Life is to be engaged, as a conversation, with a listening sensitivity and a social responsibility.

This brings us to the final characteristic: learning is interactional *between thought and life.* A new-found truth can never be considered as "authentic" until it is tried in the student's day-to-day life. There alone, living according to its demands and limitations, can he perceive the dividing line between reality and imagination. Once he has tested it, the student can then bring his new experience back to the learning dialogue and revise his thoughts according to his new perceptions.

"Interactional," then, will be the model used to discuss "education for change," interactional between teacher and student, between student and his content, and between the student's ideas and his daily actions. The *between* is the focus of the interactionist's view of learning. A schematic drawing of its dynamics might take the shape shown in Figure 5-1.

FIGURE 5–1.

This educational process is not limited to the typical classroom. Wherever two or more people, people critically concerned with their social environment, of any age, gather together for social interaction, you have interactional education. Call it, if you will, the "consciousness raising" of Women's Liberation, a college dorm rap session, a sixth-grade political science class, or one of Paulo Freire's adult literacy groups—the range of settings of announced purposes are of a wide variety. It is the process of learning, not the environment alone, which distinguishes this model from the others.

SOCIAL-HISTORICAL SETTING FOR THE INTERACTIONAL MODEL

Have you not heard of the madman who lit a lamp in broad daylight and ran up and down the market place shouting incessantly, "I'm looking for God! I'm looking for God!"

"Where is God?" he shouted. "I'll tell you! We have killed him—you and I. We are all his murderers! . . . Do we hear nothing of the noise of the gravediggers who are burying God? God is dead! God is dead! And we have killed him!" (Nietzsche, *The Gay Science,* as translated in *The Grave of God* by Robert Adolf, 1967, pp. 13–14)

This message, first announced by Nietzsche's imaginary madman in 1886, was rumored about among small circles of intellectuals and scientists until proclaimed from the cover of *Time Magazine* in 1966, "God is Dead!"

As the interactionists view all social histories as interpretations, their own interpretation is tersely stated in this shocking proclamation. Nietzsche refers to the platonic "God," this one word that sums up the entire motif of Western culture. Our overarching "meaning of life" which holds all the little pieces together, our mental umbrella, has collapsed and we are left running from one social crisis to another until a new umbrella can be constructed in its place. To more fully appreciate this interpretation, we might first look at it from the larger "Western civilization" point of view, then review it in more detail from the more specific American experience.

Man and his world, thought Plato, possess two dimensions, the material and the spiritual. Of the two, it is the spiritual that makes the difference for here we have the realm of God, ideas, free will, creativity, human potential, and cultural meaning.

But for a variety of reasons, Western man's attention gradually dropped from the spiritual to the material realm and the former began to fade from view. In place of divine right kings and czars, we established democracies and socialistic states. Where once theology and the humanities reigned, our culture enthroned science and technology. Where we once wrote divine creation, we now write cosmic evolution, and for God's providence we substitute behavioral determinism.

Until our present century, the process seemed to be a path of "enlightenment," a breaking out of centuries of darkness. Man and his material world was far more realistic and satisfying than the abstractions of a spiritual order that stood beyond observation and experimentation; the harmony and beauty of nature, more unifying than a God who was indescribable.

Only with the twentieth century did this promising material world begin to crack and break apart. Harmonious nature revealed herself to be blood red in tooth and claws as two World Wars tore Europe asunder. Value-free science produced a hydrogen bomb, and an "enlightened" people liquidated six million members of another race. But our basic tragedy was the emerging realization that our Western cultural "map of life," which distinguished right from wrong and truth from error, the map which inserted direction and purpose into our lives, was no longer available.

While classicists such as Hutchins and Dawson (Cf. Ch. 2), urged educators to restore the old map, there was no going back. With our faith in a spiritual order rejected and our trust in nature proven misguided, we had nowhere to turn and fell into cynicism. Life's purpose now appears much like Camus' *Myth of Sisyphus* or Sartre's comment that it makes no difference whether one is the President of France or a barroom lush—both careers being equally inconsequential. Man is alone in his world and lives his life without purpose or consequence. "God" is dead!

But we Americans have little time for this European pessimism. Our belief system, though less deeply rooted, is still well intact. The American dream of material prosperity for all seems to be ever climbing and ever showering its benefits. American technology comfortably outfits the average middle class family with television sets and automobiles, air conditioners and dishwashers, and a whole assortment of convenience appliances fast becoming necessities. The United States enjoys a higher standard of living than any other nation on the earth and, like Jack's magic beanstalk, which extended beyond the clouds, we never doubt that we will always be able to climb even higher.

This is not to say that we have sold our principles and values for electric can openers. There is a strong belief system supporting our progress: the Puritan ideology with its Calvinistic ethic. Our growth, we believe, is both sign and consequence of our ingenuity, our hard work, and the rightness of our ways. Delivered from the bondage of monarchical Europe, we were brought to this promised land as God's chosen people to undertake the noble experiment of a free government. We have since remained faithful to this high calling and our work prospers accordingly. No doubt, if and when others see the light of our example and choose to follow in our footsteps, they too will share in these same rewards of a better life.

The bigger and better of material progress is continually guided by our pragmatic ingenuity and urged onward by the "hard work will be rewarded" ethic. So long as the "proof" of its promise is maintained, the faith of its adherents will be firm. But recently the interactionists have felt a shaking at the foundations of this "proof." The quality of our "better" life is being challenged.

Never was this faith so high as in the early 1960s. As Harvey Cox demonstrates in *The Secular City*, President John Kennedy epitomized the pragmatic man, particularly as he rehearsed the American belief theme in his Inaugural Address. (Cox, 1966, p. 52) Consequently, much of our ability to believe seems to have been assassinated with him. One by one, we became disillusioned with the programs of Camelot. The poverty program failed; racial discrimination and segregation remain; the Peace Corps fell into disrepute, and the lengthy Vietnam war shattered the myth of our invincibility and nobility of purpose. "Progress" itself proved to be on a collision course with a polluted environment and our unlimited resources began to reach extinction.

But the greatest threat to our American Dream appears to be in the quality of life itself. Progress and technology are spinning off unforeseen and unwanted side effects, particularly in an uprootedness of our families and an estrangement from the personal dimensions of life.

The average American family has become unbelievably mobile, packing up and moving to a new home every three or four years. Lifelong neighbors are almost unheard of; "dutch uncles" and maiden aunts no longer live down the street. They are visited, at best, once a year and forever remain strangers to our children. Seldom do you find a home in which grandparents live with their children. Except in a few ethnic communities, the family has become uprooted and isolated by modern life.

Further estrangement is taking place within the family. The father commutes greater distances to work and now spends, on the average, one-half of an hour per day with his children. Those wonderful conveniences that freed his wife from her homemaking chores, have also forced her out of the house to acquire a second income to pay for this liberating higher standard of living. Children, now two to a family rather than the four or five of previous generations, have their time well-organized into programs and institutionalized into day care centers and schools. In many instances our modern home has become a convenience for eating and sleeping.

This depersonalization is even extended to the family's community relationships. The first-name milkman and breadman are a memory. The corner grocery store has long since become the anonymous supermarket and the neighborhood school is transformed into the consolidated system. The family lawyer of yesterday is now a law firm and the family doctor is being replaced by a computerized health plan. Complexity and specialization make personal relationships near-impossible. In a television interview following a recent air tragedy, a hospital psychiatrist explained in bland monotones how he and his staff were distributing sympathy and support to the distraught relatives of the victims according to predesigned and tested psychiatric procedures.

The advances of modern technological life have pulled our roots up out of the old community, shorn us of our personal contacts, and left us isolated, not only in our nuclear families, but even one member from another within those families.

In sum, the interactionists see a crisis of faith dawning on America. The belief system that promised continuing progress and the better life is beginning to be questioned. Purpose and motivation, the stuff that makes it all go, is being critically challenged. Our American "God," they suspect, may be dying as well.

We are in a dilemma. To continue on, trusting that technology and material advancement will automatically resolve our life-quality crisis, as the essentialists and technologists seem to suggest, is to abdicate our human responsibility before the mindless machine. On the other hand, to step out of modern technological life and "return to the ways of nature," as the romantics and counterculture advocates urge, is naive and impossible. Peter Berger dramatizes this dilemma in the following anecdote.

A few months ago my friend was in an airplane, thirty thousand feet over the Middle West somewhere. He wanted to sleep. Next to him was a young man in full counter-culture regalia who wanted to talk. My friend (otherwise a very pacific type) became hostile. "You know," he said to the young man, "this is really a swinging airline. I was talking to the pilot before we took off, in the bar. He told me really mindblowing things about this airplane. They really hang loose, you know. Like none of this bit about not drinking when they're flying. In fact, they smoke pot right on the plane, most of them. They even screw the stewardesses right there in the cockpit." And so on. Please remember that this conversation took place at about thirty thousand feet over, like, Indiana. Not surprisingly, the young man became very nervous indeed. As a matter of fact, to coin a phrase, he became positively uptight. (Berger (ed.), 1973, pp. 217, 248)

Whatever his own lifestyle, the young man wanted his pilot to be as technologically straight as they come, at least as long as he was handling the plane on which he was flying. We cannot chuck our advanced technological life, and yet we cannot long survive so estranged from our human sources of life. What can we do?

If the precise solution to our dilemma is presently obscure, at least the path is obvious to the interactionists. The task is fundamentally educational. We must accept responsibility and "humanize" our technological lives. We must discover within ourselves that human potential and world-meaning which is both compatible with, and creative of, this, our late twentieth century. In the pattern described above, we must initiate the dialogue, mutually analyze and criticize our present social order, then formulate and implement new, culturally humane orders. What they are looking for is, at base, a new cultural umbrella, an overarching "meaning of life" to pull our world together and again give us direction and purpose, values, and a life to be lived. That cannot be invented, but only discovered out of a communal conversation.

MIND-SET OF THE INTERACTIONISTS

Image of Man. Man is the pivotal figure in the interactionist's mind . . . man, not in an isolated individuality, but in interrelationship with his fellow man and with the world about him.

Man is born in interrelationship. Who is he? Who is he capable of becoming? What meaning and purpose will he attribute to life? All these fundamental questions will be resolved into answers through his interrelationships with his parents, his family, and his approximate community. Not simply answers, but his very being, physical and psychological, comes out of these interrelationships. It would be impossible to conceive of his growth, his personality development, his formation of a self-concept, his education, or of any other essential step in his human formation without this context of a community of other persons. And to the degree that this primal community of persons is truncated or uprooted, to that degree is his personality formation threatened.

But for children and adolescents, it is indispensable to have a coherent, fairly simple and viable society to grow up into; otherwise they are confused, and some are squeezed out. Tradition has been broken, yet there is no new standard to affirm. Culture becomes eclectic, sensational and phoney. (Our present culture is all three.) . . . It is precisely for the young that the geographical and historical community and its patriotism are the important environment. (Goodman, 1956, p. 217)

There is much about our modern life that stifles this human interaction. The face-to-face community is continually being replaced by anonymous institutions. Men come to find themselves members of "lonely crowds," living shoulder to shoulder, but impersonally, like co-passengers on an elevator or on public transit. While operating under the rubric of "individualism," our competitive world actually levels us into mass identity. We strive to wear the same style of clothing, talk about the same topics in the same way, drive look-alike cars, and live in rows of identical homes. We are unwittingly being boxed into a collective society and the essential community that fosters personality is being extinguished.

If the trend toward collectivization minimizes individual choices and human identity, the interactionists counterstrive for the restoration of community back into our society, not the pseudocommunity of the suburban land developers, but genuine community.

A community is genuine, not by being soft enough to be established by easy sentiment, but by being hard enough to meet the severe tests of the following three criteria: (1) Its members are independent ends, not dependent means or cogs in a machine. (2) Its avenues of communication, dissent, honesty and mutual esteem are clear. (3) Its differentiation of roles and offices is fair. (Novak, 1969, p. 45).

For only in such a humanizing environment can man continue to unfold his potentiality.

"No evolutionary future awaits man except in association with other men," observes Teilhard de Chardin (1959, p. 240). This is the age of the Noosphere, the evolutionary unfolding of man's reflective consciousness. The Geosphere phase, the evolution of inorganic matter, and the Biosphere phase, the physical evolution of living matter, have converged into completion and a new phase of diversification now bursts outward to unfold the thinking awareness and free choice dimensions of mankind. Man, as reflective consciousness, is evolving toward yet undefined horizons in his path of "hominization." "Hominization" is Teilhard's word—it requires this distinct spelling. Of all the beings of reality, he alone is yet incomplete; he is the focal point and deciding force of the world's future.

World View. Of all creation, only man has a "world," a conceptual image of his environment "out there," an image which he not only knows, but lives in as well.

Only man can collect all the multitudinous pieces of his experience and perceive of them as a single totality. This holistic image embraces not only his experiences, but elements he has not experienced but only imagined as possible, and not only the present, but a future as well. What he sees is not a sum total of parts, but a unified, interpreted image, a "world," separate from himself, standing out there facing him.

While such an image is synthesized within each individual, it emerges out of his conversation with his community, and even out of the larger conversation of the community of mankind. And while it is unique to the specific experiences of each man, it bears a basic identity with the larger common world-view shared by the entire culture. Each individual voice contributes to the formation of this cultural world-view, as it develops maturity over several generations.

At the same time, the individual is born into and lives his life within that same cultural "home." He forms and is formed by his cultural world-view. On the one hand, it gives him strength, purpose, identity, his place to stand on the surface of the earth, and on the other, it places limits on what he considers possible, valid, or valuable. It circumscribes his world. One can easily understand this if one imagines a conversation between an American capitalist with his world-view and a Russian communist with his, or between a Western scientist and an Oriental mystic.

While spanning many generations, world-views rise and fall in rhythmic patterns, now gaining in strength and consensus, now falling into ritual lip service and transition. Martin Buber describes periods of clear definition when "man lives in the world as in a house, as in a home," and periods of transition and alienation when "man lives in the world as in an open field and at times does not even have four pegs with which to set up a tent. (Buber, 1965, p. 126)

In the minds of the interactionists, this latter experience, homelessness, describes our present age. Victor Frankl, the Viennese psychiatrist, calls it an "existential vacuum."

Every age has its own collective neurosis . . . The existential vacuum that is the mass neurosis of the present time can be described as a private and personal form of nihilism, for nihilism can be defined as the contention that being has no meaning. (Frankl, 1963, p. 204)

Such a world-view is not an appendage to man's life, a cultural luxury, but a base necessity for survival. "Men do not do without a system of 'meanings' that everybody believes and puts his hope in . . . " asserts Paul Goodman (Goodman, 1970, p. 6) and only by renewing the communal conversation can we break loose the ritualized fragments of our presently defunct world-view and begin the gestation and birth process of a new, humanized view. This ponderous task is properly defined as the process of education.

Theory of Knowledge. The interactionists see truth as an unfolding process of becoming, rather than as the setting down of objective facts verified by rational or scientific methods. Certainly the principles of contradiction and laws of science have their validity, but it is a validity overshadowed by the immediate experiences of reality by the individual.

Experiential knowledge is the involved knowing of one's life, a knowing from the inside.

> You do not attain to knowledge by remaining on the shore and watching the foaming waves, you must make the venture and cast yourself in, you must swim with all your force, and in no other way do you reach anthropological insight. (Buber, 1965, p. 124)

It goes beyond details or even the sum of details and perceives the inner "whole." It searches out and "knows," for example, Rembrandt's "Self Portrait," or Beethoven's "Leonora Overture," or that person "John" in a way that may be inclusive of, yet move far beyond, all the certain facts that science and logic can reveal. This truth can never be written off as mere "subjectivism." I do not know merely me at the expense of "John," but "John" himself in his personality as I have met him. In this sense, experiential knowledge imposes an even heavier discipline than that of objective knowledge.

While penetrating, my experiential knowledge can never be comprehensive. My knowing of "John" is certainly limited to my experience. Your insight of "John" would also be limited, yet hold a uniquely different perspective from mine. And so, by considering together that which comes out of each of our authentic perspectives, we would arrive at a truer, deeper understanding of "John." This method of seeking together a fuller perspective of truth is called "dialogue."

The search for truth recognizes and utilizes objective evidence as its presupposition. Yet it is fundamentally experiential and conducted through interdependent dialogue. Out of this ongoing process, man reaches closer and closer to the yet undisclosed absolute truth.

Values. The interactionist comes to the value question with two points of view: his method of selecting values and his own characteristic set of values.

On the one hand, the very nature of his "community of differences" requires that he respect and encourage a variety of value positions within the community, just as he accepts various perspectives on truth. He may never impose his unique set of norms on others. Moreover, he respects the norms of others, listens to them attentively, and searches out his own position in his conversation with them. Without conversing with this "community of differences," he could never come to determine his own set of values.

Ultimately, each individual must act on his own personal decision. If he lives in a strong cultural tradition with which he identifies, he may be guided by its norms. He consults with the wisdom of his community and its life experiences. But for all their guidance and support, he alone can take the final step and respond with his personal "yes" or "no."

Yet, on the other hand, interactionists do support a distinctive set of values of their own. They recognize the essential importance of power, order, and structure. They also accept the validity of institutions, political processes, and the technologies of our age. But this recognition and acceptance is given only so long as these elements in society serve and support the further humanization of man. Above them stand the values of love, trust, cooperation, freedom, and responsibility.

Freedom and responsibility are high values in most modern mind sets. Here, nearly all vestiges of determinism are rejected, and the virtue of responsible, individual freedom is supported to a near absolute degree. Man remains at all times both free and obliged to respond with his own voice. Even out of his experience in the German concentration camps, Frankl writes, "Man *can* preserve a vestige of spiritual freedom, of independence of mind, even in such terrible conditions of psychic and physical stress." (Frankl, 1963, p. 164)

Yet freedom is not to be exalted into an end in itself as the romantics have done. Freedom is a "footbridge, not a dwelling place," crossing us over into personal responsibility. (Buber, 1965, p. 92) Responsibility refers not to the heavy "ought" of the finger-shaking parent, but to the open response one makes to the person or situation before him. One's ability to respond forms the basis of both community and dialogue.

The mind set of the interactionist places the highest value on the internal progress of man. Interactionists see this progress as deeply threatened, but not without hope. To emerge, this new era requires the fostering of richer community environments, social and intellectual interdependence, and a sharpened consciousness that sweeps away our present, contradictory cultural reality and creates a new sense of yet untested possibilities.

THEORY OF EDUCATION

Relying on an interactionist's definition of education: " . . . Becoming critically aware of one's reality in a manner that leads to effective action upon it," we recognize that a review of this argument must begin by first examining and criticizing our present educational approach. Then we must recreate a new approach out of the needs and possibilities that have been uncovered. (Paulo Freire, from *School is Dead,* by Everett Reimer, 1972, p. 121)

Critique. Like the church of the middle ages, which claimed an exclusive monopoly on salvation, so many schools today claim exclusive control over man's earthly life. But the power of this claim holds only so long as the myth of "schooling" goes unanalyzed and unchallenged. "Schooling" must be demythologized.

Certainly schools have existed from the earliest times, yet our schools of today are an entirely new social phenomenon and deserve the special designation, "schooling." In 1900, observes Paul Goodman, only 6 per cent of our youth finished high school and less than 1 per cent went to college. (Goodman, 1962, p. 17) This is radically different from our present wall-to-wall educational age, just three generations later, when more than 90 per cent finish high school and more than 50 per cent attend college. Prior to the Industrial Revolution, schools were a private, noncompulsory affair, attended by a small minority, an exception to the social pattern. Today schools are compulsory for all from the ages of six to 18. Embracing the entire society, they are governmentally controlled and funded and fit tightly into our social system.

Modern society promotes the following myths about the purposes and benefits of schools: They offer free education to all; through education all have access to higher standards of living; education will bring equality to our society; and they offer their clients critical minds and increased individuality.

Much contradictory evidence exists. Through the exclusive monopoly of public funds acquired through taxation, the schools require attendance. Through the unequal distribution of those funds and several other social factors, schools stratify their students on the social ladder, enabling only a few to enjoy a higher standard of living but condemning most to an inferior social level. In this way the client himself is made to feel that his "failure" is his own doing. Rather than promoting equality, our schools are widening and hardening the gap between the haves and the have nots. Finally, they promote not individuality and critical minds, but social conformity and indoctrination.

These inequities and misuses of education cannot be corrected and the state of American education cannot be improved until the above myths are "demythologized" and a more honest portrait of present education is revealed.

The problem, however, does not apply to all schools, but, rather, to all of society. Schooling plays a hand-maiden role to our social system. It is the exclusive certifier for job competence and therefore the single gateway into adult society; the student must either enter by this gate or remain on the fringe of society for the rest of his life. The initial choice is not difficult to make since schools are compulsory by law. When sociologists study the school functionally, they usually have only two other parallel institutions with which to compare it, prisons and insane asylums!

Schools are not only the gatekeepers for society, but the *de facto* social stratifiers as well. In the primary grades, schools begin the sorting process. Those who will attend college are distinguished from those who will not; those who will enter scientific, intellectual professions are divided from those who will follow humanistic, social service occupations. Students advance to the upper middle class or retire to the lower class by the grace of the American school system.

An important task of schooling in a mass society is vocational training. This training, too, is often specialized; that is, a student is soon prevented from an alternative route to prepare himself for occupations. His competence and extent of knowledge will be measured, not primarily by his ability, but by the number of years he has spent in school: 12 is minimal and 16 is good. Seldom is serious learning received outside school.

In this capacity of job trainer, the schools form a reservoir for the labor market, not only providing the numbers and the particular specialities as needed, but maintaining the necessary flow. In periods of need, schooling is abbreviated; in periods of high unemployment, the number of years required for certification increases. Over the years, our schools have generally experienced a certain "inflationary" erosion; the number of years increases while the quality of education per year declines considerably.

Schooling as a vocational encounter is being implemented in many elementary schools. Curricula similar to the *World of Work* program, designed for kindergarten through grade six, stresses that all work is good, all work is honorable.

Curricular emphasis is on developing a positive attitude toward work. Children are taken on numerous field trips to observe "workers," not with the intent that the children should make a career choice, but that they should be exposed early in life to a number of job opportunities.

Many teacher training institutions are initiating programs for prospective elementary teachers regarding the role of career or vocational training in the elementary school. But it is very difficult to include a work-oriented program in schools that are not unwittingly socializing the youngsters.

Another important task of schooling is social indoctrination. During their school years children develop all the characteristics required for their working society: promptness, cleanliness, hard working diligence, cooperation, and a docile dependency on the parent institution. These items of the school's "hidden curriculum" are even more effectively taught than the skills and facts of the formal curriculum.

In all, contemporary schooling represents the interests and needs of its sponsor, the industrial society, rather than those of its students. And there is little in the present social context either among industrialists or professional educators, who would desire to disturb this convenient arrangement.

I keep resorting to the metaphor, school monks: the administrators, professors, academic sociologists and licensees with diplomas who have proliferated into an invested intellectual class worse than anything since the time

of Henry the Eighth. Yet I am convinced as they get their grants and build-
ings and State laws that give them sole competence—that the monks are
sincere in this blind faith in the school . . .

The schools offer very little evidence of their unique ability to perform any
of these [stated goals]—there is plenty of evidence to the contrary—but they
do not need to offer evidence, since nobody opposes them or proposes
alternatives. (Goodman, 1962, pp. 7–8)

Proposal. "Men *are* because they *are in* a situation," Paulo
Freire tells us. "And they *will be more* the more they not only critically reflect upon their existence but critically act upon it." (Freire,
1970, p. 100) Demythologizing the present schooling situation is only
the first step in the creation of a new education. Now the interactionists must discover what "untested feasibility" lies beyond the
present situation. Insisting that they do not constitute a new propa-
ganda system to replace the old, they do not have answers to impose
upon their students, but only a method—a "way"—by which to help
their students find a new society with a new form of education.
Their concern, then, is to restore a more humane climate in which
the educational dialogue can take place.

The first aspect of the more humane climate to be restored is
community. If man can only realize his potentiality in a communal
relationship, then he certainly cannot be educated except in community. Yet, as Friedenberg observes, our modern trend is away
from community toward atomization and institutionalization. All
man's social needs—health, politics, religion, education—are being
organized for mass efficiency, with the personal interchange reduced
to near extinction. Somehow this trend must be reversed.

Leonard Woodcock, head of the United Auto Workers, proposed
replacing the depersonalizing efficiency of the assembly line with
groups of workers who cooperatively assemble the entire automobile. Similarly, education must replace our school plants of
hundreds or thousands with personalized units, sufficiently small for
each student to know the other and for all to work together in a
climate of trust and interdependent cooperation. Paul Goodman has
proposed the use of minischools, each with ten teachers and 100
students. The one-way indoctrination of traditional classes and the
individualistic style of the open classroom must be replaced by social
interchange.

Teachers must come to know and trust each other, respecting the
experiences and abilities that each represents. This argument can be

made with any model of teaching. Interactionists, however, go one step beyond merely acknowledging and tolerating individuality among teachers. They urge an open interchange of varying beliefs in the presence of students so that students can model themselves on persons who express and modify their beliefs and conclusions. The teacher is not simply the authority who teaches but also a student who learns through the unique experiences and insights of his students. He is a teacher-student just as his students are student-teachers. Their dialogue depends upon this interchange of roles and mutual respect, without which there can be no true education. "No one teaches another, nor is anyone self-taught. Men teach each other." (Freire, 1970, p. 67)

Within the educational community stands the *dialogue*, a phenomenon somewhat difficult to define, even though it has become a common expression among educators. Dialogue is a disciplined conversation that can only take place in the trusting environment of a community. Its participants concentrate on the object of their concern, each contributing out of experiential knowledge, and all intent on fully uncovering the object's meaning. They proceed without the defenses or pretensions required in an atmosphere of competition, personality jostling, argumentation, propagandizing, or personal manipulation. Participants proceed from the assumption that a truth is obtainable and that each of the participants is sufficiently intelligent and capable of contributing to the identification of that truth. Interactionists are fully cognizant of the relativism of truth and the importance of establishing the presuppositions and value implications involved in arriving at any conclusion.

For Freire, "Dialogue is the encounter between men, mediated by the world, in order to name the world." (Freire, 1970, p. 76) To "name" the world means to correctly and critically identify the object under examination, and to disclose its full import for all to understand. But to so reveal and identify an object, you thereby allow it to be transformed into that which it is potentially capable of becoming. Dialogue is both reflective and active.

If men, by naming the world, transform it, dialogue imposes itself as the way by which men achieve significance as men. Dialogue is thus an existential necessity. (Freire, 1970, p. 77)

A second climate condition to be restored to the educational process is the *situation*. Learning must be located in its actual context.

Contemporary schools represent "alienated knowledge," knowledge cut off from its source, uprooted and packaged into tight little books to be opened and distributed far from its origin and environment. Learning occurs *in* the professions and trades and in all real life encounters. It is a process of becoming conscious of the uniqueness of the life situation, with all its circumstances, and being permitted to act upon that situation. This essential requirement is called by Freire, *praxis*: reflection and action on the world order.

> The [student] must confront reality critically, simultaneously objectifying and acting upon that reality. A mere perception of reality not followed by this critical intervention will not lead to a transformation of objective reality. (Freire, 1970, p. 37)

Such learning is not possible if one is removed from the order's environment.

The third condition necessary for interactional education is the development of a *critical consciousness,* a clear penetrating insight into our social process with an eagerness to go beyond its present limits into its as yet untried possibilities.

At present, our schools are more like mental blenders, in Edgar Friedenberg's estimation.

> What comes out, when it is functioning effectively, is not merely uniform but bland and creamy; by its very nature inimical to clarity, yet retaining in a form difficult to detect, all the hostile or toxic ingredients present in the original mixture. (Friedenberg, 1962, p. 78)

It is not that our students are presently given a biased, albeit clear picture of American society, but that they are given a murky, vague impression that makes it nearly impossible to critically evaluate. If education is the process of defining oneself through interaction with his society, the outlines of this society must be clearly drawn.

In addition to these clearly defined terms and limits of the social milieu, the student must be made free to explore beyond these limits into the realm of possibility. If restricted to the immediate situation, the student must either accept the present order and his own social stratification within it, or he can become restive and struggle to achieve the "ideal man" image within the present order. In either case, he is held captive to the uncritical blinders of the existing social system. Only if he ventures beyond the sphere of indoctrination and stands outside it, will he critically discover both the myth that he lives by and his ability to move beyond this myth into a new actualization of his human potential. The goal of interactional education is to help him make this leap and thereby achieve a critical consciousness of his cultural reality.

Teachers and students (leaders and people), co-intent on reality, are both subjects, not only in the task of unveiling that reality, and thereby coming to know it critically, but in the task of re-creating that knowledge. As they attain this knowledge of reality through common reflection and action, they discover themselves as the permanent re-creation. (Freire, 1970, p. 56)

DOONESBURY by Garry Trudeau

(Copyright, 1972, G. B. Trudeau. Distributed by Universal Press Syndicate.)

Cultural Revolution. School and society are so linked in the interactionists' minds that they cannot conceive of a reform of the one without a total modification of the other. Schools cannot be humanized unless society is humanized. But to reform all of society is to speak of revolution. Interactionists recognize this, but quickly clarify it by pointing out that revolution comes in various forms: violent, political, economic, and cultural. It is this latter form, a cultural revolution, which they propose, that is, they propose the transformation of both public and personal mental outlooks.

Man's present vision of reality is based on habits formed out of years of economic consumerism.

. . . the cultural revolution believes that these habits have radically distorted our view of what human beings can have and want. He questions the reality that others take for granted, a reality that, in his view, is the artificial by-product of contemporary institutions, created and reinforced by them in pursuit of their short-term ends. (Illich, 1971, p. 173)

The cultural revolutionary believes that new habits and a new mental outlook can take advantage of the achievements of twentieth-century technology, yet use them for the enhancement of our humanity rather than subjugating our humanity to their seductive accomplishments.

A new world is being forged on the foundation of rapid technological growth. Man need not be the victim of this subsequent change, but can be its initiator and director. Only through education can this be possible. It demands an active interdisciplinary search for a new, humanized world-view.

But one thing is certain: man must decide or the decision will be made for him. The future will not wait. "No one will live all his life in the world in which he was born, and no one will die in the world in which he worked in his maturity," warns Margaret Mead. (Gross and Gross, 1969, p. 271) As educators, interactionists serve as the cultural midwives, lending assistance to a culture attending to the growth of a new view of man.

I call this new style *prefigurative*, because in this new culture it will be the child—and not the parent and grandparent that represents what is to come. Instead of the erect, white-haired elder who, in postfigurative cultures, stood for the past and the future in all their grandeur and continuity, the unborn child, already conceived but still in the womb, must become the symbol of what life will be like. This is a child whose sex and appearance and capabilities are unknown. This is a child who is a genius or suffers from some deep impairment, who will need imaginative, innovative and dedicated adult care far beyond any we give today.

Now, as I see it, the development of prefigurational cultures will depend on the existence of a continuing dialogue in which the young, free to act on their own initiative, can lead their elders in the direction of the unknown. (Mead, 1970, p. 87–88, 94)

Advocates of the classical, technological, and personalized models often criticize the interactionists for the absence of specific teaching skills. While the goals of the interactional model are amply expressed by theoreticians such as Freire, Friedenberg, and Illich, practitioners have difficulty with implementation since the day-by-day learning for the elementary school-age child is never discussed. This can be explained, in part, by the newness of the interactionist's critique. The fact remains, however, that the student will certainly have difficulty venturing beyond the sphere of alleged indoctrination if he cannot read, write, or engage in problem-solving pursuits. Unfortunately, such important theoretical tasks as deep and thorough cultural reform have failed to include implementation strategies for younger learners.

Interactionists allude to a pedagogical integration of the process-centered aspects of learning (how a child thinks) and the content-centered setting (how much information is known) in an attempt to foster freedom as a way of thought and life. While the actuality of such an integration has not yet materialized, theoreticians do encourage the practitioners, both learner and planner, to view intellectual freedom as the long-range curricular objective. Thus, the role of the practitioner is one of designing for himself appropriate learning environments and processes.

This hope of intellectual and personal freedom being realized, one begins to contemplate the next stage. This radical idealistic goal cannot be accomplished by simply reorganizing environments. If this time-consuming task of liberating teaching styles is to be used, teachers and learners must become more than ideological instruments if theoreticians are to be able to effectuate, realistically, the needed educational changes they espouse. The overhaul proposed is substantial. Interactionists are not intending to reform an existing practice; to put a grin on a corpse, as some describe it. They urge a complete restructuring of the aims and activities of both the school and the society.

Curriculum Implementation

FIGURE 5-2.

The generic characteristics of this model are:

1. STUDENT Learns in his dialogical relationship with others; learning is an interdependent effort. He shares his perceptions of reality, listens intently to the perceptions of others, then revises his world-view from his learnings.

2. TEACHER Creates a "community" atmosphere of interdependence and trustful dialogue. Recognizing his broad experiences, the teacher nevertheless shares and listens in the same manner as each of his students.

3. CONTENT   Focuses on aspects of the contemporary sociocul-
                    tural world. After realizing cultural purposes and
                    values the student critically evaluates them in
                    light of man's human dignity. This effort is fol-
                    lowed by reordering one's life according to her
                    new perceptions. One's further experiences, then,
                    will either confirm new perceptions, or lead one to
                    further reevaluation.

If one were to view a school community espousing this philosophy, he might witness the following interaction.

As Molly, Shannon, Denise, Paul, Bev, and Bob piled into the school
station wagon to begin their trip to the Science Museum Planetarium, Molly
thought that she was glad to be part of this new alternative community-
based school which allowed the student responsibility for her actions. Her
thoughts, however, were interrupted by Shannon who chided, "Maybe I'll
be able to understand myself better after a visit with the planets." "I'm going
to book myself a trip to Mars," added Paul. "Great, and I'll come and visit
you at Christmas," laughed Denise.
     "Wow, school is fun," thought Molly, who had been a member of this
alternative school plan for only six weeks. Molly liked school because of the
communication that existed between resource instructors and students. She
also felt that she was learning more because she planned her own classes and
was therefore extremely interested in the content. Through the experience of
planning her own curriculum Molly was becoming more aware of herself as a
person (for example: What were her interests? Was she interested in pursuing a topic of study? What "turned her on?" What did she want to do in later
life?)
     Harold DeLeo, the resource instructor, entered the car and the trip began.
The students had gotten involved with astrology when Harold had been
invited by Bob to visit the school and discuss astrology charting. As interest
grew, Sally suggested a visit to the planetarium.

Molly's personal reflection is greatly encouraged in this model.
None of the other models deemphasize cognitive learning enough to
allow for intellectual meandering. Interactionists depend heavily on
the kind of argument Carl Rogers sets forth.

     . . . we frequently fail to recognize that much of the material presented to
students in the classroom has, for the student, the perplexing, meaningless
quality that learning a list of nonsense syllables has for us. This is especially
true for the underprivileged child whose background provides no context for
the material with which he is confronted. Thus, education becomes the futile
attempt to learn material which has no personal meaning.

Such learning involves the mind only. It is learning which takes place "from the neck up." It does not involve feelings or personal meanings; it has no relevance for the whole person. (Rogers, 1969, pp. 3–4)

Trips, resource instructors, community involvement, and student-faculty government were familiar sounding phrases at Molly's school, which was housed in the basement of a church. This school, while publicly funded, had been created as a result of the dreams of several concerned public-school teachers who believed that an alternative to classical public-school learning, which so often destroyed the dreams and desires of many children, was needed.

While the ideas of field trips and guest speakers are not unique to the interactionist model, the manner of their origin (occurring because of a felt student interest) is indeed unique. The curriculum of this model is planned by and for the learner, with the long-range goal of developing a constructive social critic. While this goal cannot obviously be realized by age eight, the foundations of this continuous social process are often established very early in the intellectual growth of a child.

Many interactionists accept the fact that reading, writing, math, and science are important to the social process. However, they accept no prescribed plan for acquiring such knowledge. The pursuit of such learning is personal and will thus be planned by the learner with the aid of someone already fully informed of the learner's desires.

It is not possible to spend any prolonged period visiting public schools without being appalled by the mutilation visible everywhere: mutilation of spontaneity, of joy in learning, of pleasure in creating, of sense of self. The public schools, those "killers of the dream," to appropriate a phrase of Lillian Smith's, are the kind of institutions one cannot really dislike until one gets to know them well. Because adults take the schools so much for granted, they fail to appreciate what grim, joyless places most American schools are, how oppressive and petty are the rules by which they are governed, how intellectually sterile and aesthetically barren the atmosphere, what an appalling lack of civility obtains on the part of teachers and principals, what contempt they unconsciously display for children as children. (Silberman, 1970, p. 83)

The founding philosophy of Molly's school was that students must play the major role in developing their own curriculum that would, therefore, be based on their interests. The students may then select a resource instructor from his existing school system, other local educational institutions, the local community, or local business. Thus, the community becomes the educational environment and the student becomes the initiator of his own learning.

The major goals or purposes Molly's teachers had for formulating such a school were: (a) to involve all participants in the decision-making process, (b) to encourage acceptance of responsibility for learning and the learning environments by *all* members of the educational community, (c) to ensure individual rights, majority rule, and equal opportunity to *all* participants in *all* activities. These goals serve as the central focus of many schools espousing interactional values.

An example of a school practicing this philosophy is Sudbury Valley.

The idea of Individual Rights is that every person is endowed with certain "inalienable rights," rights that belong to him as his own, as his inherent possession—not granted as a gift by some benevolent ruler, not given as a privilege by an all-powerful state, but belonging to him, without qualification, as his rights. They cannot be removed, or explained away; nor can they be violated by any person, government, or power, as long as law and order prevail.

The idea of Majority Rule is that all decisions governing the community are decided by the community in a politically democratic way. The first root idea, of Individual Rights, covers those actions in a person's life that primarily affect himself, and for which he is individually responsible. The second root idea, of Majority Rule, covers those actions that primarily affect other people, and for which the community is responsible.

The idea of Equal Opportunity is that every person has an equal chance to obtain any goal. There is no privilege—a condition stressed even in our written Constitution. People are born equal, and they start out with equal chances in life.

This basic right is violated by any and every imposed curriculum, new or old. It makes no difference whether or not there are a lot of electives; what matters is whether or not students have to choose anything at all. It makes no difference whether naked force or moral persuasion or simple seduction is used as a technique to "motivate" students to learn something; what matters is whether someone on the outside does the "motivating," or whether the student—exclusively, and by right—motivates himself. The distinction here is not a fine line at all, but rather an easily recognizable boundary that differentiates between an educational system that has the power somehow to impress its will on students, and one that leaves the power of decision with the student, where it belongs. (Sudbury Valley School Press, 1971, pp. 12–13)

Since Molly's school focused primary attention on the student and his learning desires, the basement school building served merely as a learning base dependent upon the surrounding community to facilitate learning experiences through real-life situations. The learning base serves the student as his contact-making center.

Frequently, the learner needs contact only with the learning site: he goes there directly, and uses only its resources. This is the case with the majority of learning experiences in the adult world. However, often the learner can use additional facilities for a variety of reasons: he may need a place to think and study; he may need a place where he can collect himself between different learning experiences, or where he can simply spend time deciding on what he would like to do; he may want contact with others in the same situation as he is in, and need a place which is institutionally set up to serve his and their needs; he may need assistance, advice, or special instruction, and need a place that is staffed to provide these or to provide access to these. Such a place, fulfilling these and other needs, is a base for learning. (Sudbury Valley School Press, 1971, pp. 15–16)

Compared to the other three models of schooling the interactional model is comparatively new. As such it remains rather diffuse, but two general forms can be discerned. One group follows the direction laid out in Theodore Brameld's social reconstructionists' philosophy. The second group, adapting some of the Rogers' arguments, contends that schools should ignore society as much as possible and concentrate on the mental health and happiness of the students. Two persistent problems in investigating interactional school reforms are sorting through the variety of alternatives and sorting through the glib assault they have leveled on the traditional, the technological, and progressive models. It is important to recall that the interactional model began before 1968 and that a great deal of serious thought has gone into it.

Advocates of the interactional model claim that it was the first educational reform that circumvented the questions of how to make education more efficient. They argue that they are not interested in making the whole routine better, but are questioning whether it should be done at all. Though both types of interactionist educators have this negative impetus they do have positive recommendations to make.

TEAM TEACHING
Team teaching is one of the least radical tactics utilized by both personalized and interactionist educators. We have somewhat arbi-

trarily included it in the interactionist model. It could almost as easily be categorized as personalized because one of its central features is increasing teacher-to-student contact. It decreases the likelihood that a student will be involved in a situation that has severe personality conflicts. But it has other qualities that fit more with the interactionist model.

Most significantly, team teaching is a daily display to learners that integrating cooperation and specialization is both possible and profitable. A great deal of planning is required for this reform. There is a high risk that it will become an administrative overlay upon the matter of the sterile and dull traditional "teach-at-em" style. A good deal of bad teaching has been bootlegged under the alleged reform of bad teaching.

Like nearly any reform it demands, first of all, leadership throughout the school. Many reforms fail because they were conceived (or plagiarized) during the summer vacation. They become a reality during August and both teachers and students return around Labor Day to find an unexpected, new arrangement. Though intended to solve a problem of a segmented education in which curriculum had become "what happens when each teacher closes their door," the new scheme is doomed. Even though many may be committed to its success, the pressure of day-to-day teaching precludes any real reflection upon all the implications of the new idea.

Team teaching particularly and abruptly exposes teachers who have become accustomed to doing exactly as they alone please. One of the underlying purposes must be a utilization of topical specialities. That is, one teacher may be inclined toward science, another toward language arts, a third toward social studies, and so on. The pitfall is obvious. The teaching will follow university academic specializations in which each teacher was forced to select a major field of study. A great deal of effort must be devoted to identifying the long-range goals of the team and of the school. Only in this way can the hazard of a transparent administrative patchwork be averted.

The promise of team teaching is that it will loosen up relationships between teachers and between teachers and students. If the students and teachers are in constant interaction, and if the leadership has carefully attended to the problems of group dynamics and school-wide goals, the likelihood that students will confront more new ideas, in a situation in which they can feel free to compare them with others, is increased. In that active comparing and choice-making do we find the most enduring learning. The danger is that it is easy to mistake movement for progress. It is easy to conceal much genuine stagnation in a flurry of activity.

RECONSTRUCTING THE SCHOOLS

To the reconstructionist the educated man is one who can effect changes that will carry out his beliefs in society. No longer are schools charged with the responsibility of developing a generation aware of the main features of our culture or a generation able to analyze dispassionately the swirling conflicts in our society. To the interactionist educator the schools must develop citizens able to effect needed changes in our society. In many instances this requires an active intervention into the beliefs and activities of young people. This intervention violates a long pedagogical tradition in America which holds that schools must teach objectively and avoid the inculcation of values in any way. The reconstructionist replies that it is impossible to teach independent of values and that we are much more honorable getting our value judgment out in the open. The basic task for a decent reconstructionist is to open up the schools, avoid the pitfalls of Dewey's scientism, and still not take over the students with a particular ideology.

Brameld typifies the reconstructionist paradox by stating:

The reconstructionist teacher, governed though he is by utopian values and therefore critical of many existing practices and future plans, would not impose his convictions upon anyone. He directs this initiating period of study chiefly by making sure that students penetrate deeply enough to discover the actual rather than the merely ideological, picture of the community. He lets the picture speak for itself. (Brameld, 1956, p. 23)

Not very deeply buried in that proposition is the belief that students will "see the light" about their existing condition and come to agree with the teacher. It is a very short step to say that the schools, operating on the doctrine of majority rule, should begin to take positions and affect policy on socioeconomic matters. Rather than becoming an open forum through which a variety of solutions are paraded and given equal respect by the school, the school begins to develop attitudes in youngsters that accord with the general consensus. The reconstructionist has made a major pedagogical contribution in revealing that schools have not been dispassionate. It would be difficult to classify the many teachers who have generated a passive patriotism as anything other than agents of cultural policy. They have perpetuated a value system every bit as much as the ill-disguised subversive who tries to convince kids to "join the revolution." The issue becomes, then, is it possible for a reconstructionist teacher to urge social change without taking over the direction of that change. If he does, is he still a reconstructionist?

Part of the answer to this delicate matter probably lies in the concept of the teacher as a subversive. If the teacher sees himself as deeply at odds with the sociopolitical values of his community, but he persists in challenging those values and in manipulating students to support his view, he will no doubt soon be expelled from the system. In order that our students develop skills in evaluating points of view and political ideologies it may, instead, be more effective for the teachers to be encouraged to challenge the existing, prevalent community attitudes. This form of reconstructionism has in mind not the manipulation of students and the creation of a cadre of fellow-believers, but rather the development of perspective in young people so that they will know what their argument looks like from the outside. This represents one important means by which the teacher can open up the schools without having his intentions degenerate into a palace revolution. This requires the greatest respect for the loneliest and "weirdest" points of view. The aim of the school is to examine the possibilities and predict the outcome of certain propositions. One of the most common errors made by sociocultural school reformers is the mistaking of majority favor for thoughtful analysis. Emphasis on thoughtful analysis does not preclude acting on one's conclusions. But emphasis on majority rule can often interrupt a thoughtful analysis.

A meaningful school operating on the principles of reconstructionism, then, might well have the whole range of political opinion among its faculty and its students. They may or may not be working for the same ends in terms of a utopia, but, more importantly, they are dealing with each other in an atmosphere that is intent on bringing clarity to their thought. One of the gravest errors of the reconstructionist model is its tendency to exaggerate the importance of consensus in goals. This exaggeration also leads to a false belief in consensus of goals leading inexorably to consensus of means. As a result, often worthwhile radical teaching is brought down and students emerge sorely confused.

Another of the grave errors of the reconstructionist model is the tendency to overemphasize the public dimension of the youngster's personality. Often the person's whole identity is achieved in terms of his ability to respond to public policy issues. Many were led by a sense of impotence in the face of enormous social injustices to live their lives in the solution of serious problems. They began to seem like one-dimensional people. This overpoliticized atmosphere led many others to applaud the observation of television personality Dick Cavett, "Politics bores my ass." Though many school people agreed because troublesome controversial public issues had disturbed the smooth functioning of the schools, more thoughtful educators were trying to stress that other aspects of the human experience were being ignored by the new trend. This trend by no means approached gaining control of schools, but if it had persisted unrestrained it would have diminished the scientific domain of education as well as the humanities and the fine arts. The former could well have experienced some challenge to the hegemony it achieved in the early 1960s, but the humanities and fine arts did not need yet another group of educators asserting that they are a frill. The pure reconstructionist often represented an obstacle to the tendency of the humanities to integrate the styles of learning from all the facets of human experience.

The pure reconstructionist could well afford to take counsel from those desiring to integrate the student's formal education. It would be easy to avoid both the long-range view and the intricate value systems involved if a student were urged merely to solve a public problem. One of the more persistent faults of the hasty reconstructionists is a tendency to see problems as solvable with some tinkering. Many important issues can be resolved by some minor adjustments, but many others involve substantial changes in attitudes and philosophies. Correspondingly, there is a tendency among reconstructionists to meld conflicting beliefs into one. A greater respect for pluralism in American society might help a reconstructionist to solve the conflicts more than his hurrying to find a solution. Often it is only a matter of generating some tolerance rather than trying to see to it that everyone agrees.

Dissatisfaction with society in general, and schools in particular, has also spawned a different radical departure from ongoing practices. A large number of educators favor reordering curriculum and methodology in such a way as to improve mental health. Instead of achieving their identity in terms of their struggle against the status quo these people favor generally ignoring, or acquiescing to, the ongoing society. They contend that the development of self-actualized and autonomous individuals is all that is necessary to cure the ills of society. As evidenced by Molly's attitude, the school is not assigned an activist role in effecting changes in society but is seen as a haven in which the healthy growth of young people can be nurtured. The intent is to make them as independent of society as possible. The teacher is seen as a fellow learner who is continuously growing and fortifying his independence. The subject matter is completely overhauled. There are virtually no required courses and there is no sequence to one's learning. Whereas there is little free choice in the curriculum of the traditional school and the students in the progressive school select from a predetermined set of subjects, these students have absolute freedom in the definition of their interests. In fact, in many instances they are encouraged to select the unusual and nontraditional activity. Instead of finding their happiness in relation to other individuals or to groups of individuals, this philosophy holds that each person has within himself the essence of his own happiness. The task of the educator is to develop an open and supportive environment without any coercion. In this way the inner potential can reach its fullest fruition. Presumably man's social affairs will be more felicitous after all members of the society are stable and self-actualized. Thus, the theme of Molly's school is one of student-initiated learning.

Certainly this is not a new theme since many years ago George Washington said, "I have even laid it down as an established maxim to believe that every person is—most certainly ought to be—the best judge of what relates to their own interests and concerns."

Student-teacher roles fluctuate since both are ascribed to by choice. "Instruction," says Illich, "is the choice of circumstances which facilitate learning. Roles are assigned by setting a curriculum of conditions which the candidate must meet if he is to make the grade. School links instruction—but not learning—to these roles." (1970, p. 63)

Many visitors to Molly's school are concerned about evaluation. How are students graded? Are these students prepared for college? How are alternative schools meeting state requirements for public-schools? How are they utilizing the community?

The following answers to such questions are often offered. There are no formal tests, grades, or external evaluations. Each person determines the worth of each experience he pursues. If the student is self-motivated, he will master his pursuit or become disinterested and begin another project. Successful mastery of a project will be all the motivation needed to encourage a student to experiment, to create, to perceive, to inquire, to continue learning.

If the student is self-directed, he will be completely able to plan his future learning experiences or to request aid from persons able to offer suggestions. When a person foresees that future learning experiences include college, he will initiate the learning encounters he may need in order to fulfill the selected college entrance criteria.

Most state boards of education require students to have yearly learning experiences in physical education and history. Since students at Molly's school share equally in formulating school governing policies, they provide situations to meet such certification requirements. For example, walking to school, riding one's bicycle, or having a basketball game may fulfill the physical education requirement, while studying one's ancestry, or working in a social-political movement may be sufficient to fulfill state history requirements.

Since students within the school are part of the community, the school attempts to grow through utilizing community facilities. Apprentice programs provide students with the opportunity to become acquainted with community trades, crafts, professions, museums, rivers, parks, and so on. Education, thus, is a community enterprise.

Schools like Molly's are beginning to appear by larger numbers each year since more and more educators are becoming cognizant of Toffler's *Future Shock*, which emphasizes that yesterday is gone, and today will be gone tomorrow. Our world changes rapidly. We are a mobile people daily producing overloads of information. Therefore, in such a transitory environment:

students need to learn far more than the basic skills. Children who have just started school may still be in the labor force in the year 2030. For them, nothing could be more wildly impractical than an education designed to prepare them for specific vocations or professions or to facilitate their adjustment to the world as it is. To be practical, an education should prepare a man for work that doesn't yet exist and whose nature cannot even be imagined. This can be done only by teaching people how to learn, by giving them the kind of intellectual discipline that will enable them to apply man's accumulated wisdom to new problems as they arise, the kind of wisdom that will enable them to *recognize* new problems as they arise. (Silberman, 1970, pp. 83–84)

Aware of cultural reality, some schools are beginning to base education on a democratic ethos—faith in man, and faith in the workings of man. Schools are reassigning to the individual his own life responsibility. While doing so the school also becomes the responsibility of the total group involved with the learning process.

While these may be new schools for a new era, the

. . . underlying assumptions are as old as recorded philosophy: that good character is born out of responsibility and trust; that excellence is born out of personal commitment; that self-discipline is born out of freedom; that creativity is born out of leisure; and that the good life is all of these, embedded in an atmosphere of patience and good faith. (Sudbury Valley School Press, 1971, p. 47)

The primary difficulty with this version of the interactionist school model is its tendency to put all its eggs in one basket. It has effectively severed the growing youngsters from the ongoing affairs of society. His ability to cope with a social system that is, by definition, significantly inhumane is left largely to chance. It can easily represent a retreat from reality and, in so doing, ultimately do a great disservice to the student. This is not to say that the model is without redeeming value, however.

There can be little doubt that schools have not been geared toward allowing—let alone encouraging—individual uniqueness. Neither have they been accustomed to varying the definitions of a mentally healthy person. It must be realized that one can be at odds with the status quo and still be stable and that one can be indifferent to the status quo and remain a well-integrated individual, but for the school to carefully devise a cocoon in which one matures apart from reality and then emerges full blown to carry on as an adult is to unjustly prejudge the interests of youngsters. This is sometimes an extension *ad absurdum* of the romantic criticism of the schools, but this absurdity serves us well in defining the strengths and the limitations of the mental health model.

HUMANIZING THE SCHOOLS

A radical departure from the three basic models—traditional, technological, and progressive—proceeds from Ivan Illich's proposition for deschooling society. He contends that we have created a monstrous and paralyzing force in our system: schools. So deep has been the negative influence upon our culture that he recommends radical and abrupt surgery. The schools have become a sacred cow to the extent that schools are no longer even questioned. And they have disseminated biased notions of learning, of society, and of progress. Illich charges schools with becoming recruiters and omnipotent "channelers" of people for a consumptive society. In effect he is arguing that society is an overly technologized cesspool and that schools are witless perpetrators of an essentially antihuman system. Again a review of social injustices often makes it difficult to disagree with his analysis of the status quo, though he may be a bit shrill at times. But a serious loophole exists in his suggested reform.

At the root of his attitude is a sense of conspiracy. He believes that the vast majority of the population are essentially decent and pro-human beings. He must believe this because his model calls for entrusting the acculturation of youth to the masses of society. The sources of society's problems are the power brokers. Among these are school people who have let the society grow to its apparently unhappy state and have not only resisted those trends, but have continued to feed young people into the system. Most significantly it has prepared these young people without generating in them a questioning attitude. Though this critique may be overdrawn at times, it does afford a markedly different approach to schooling. His recommended solution however could easily turn out to be nonrevolutionary.

There are two basic themes in his model deschooled society. On the one hand there is nothing resembling compulsory schooling and there are strict laws prohibiting discrimination on the basis of one's prior schooling. He rejects the contemporary school system as an unjust monopoly with alarming selective powers to determine who will do well in society. He sees these powers as arbitrary and capricious. Only by breaking the monopoly will we regain the free choice we had before mass schools. On the other hand, he sees the creation of a skills bank through which people can voluntarily learn whatever skills they desire. They will be gaining a skill from someone expert in that skill instead of from someone once removed from the practice of that skill as existed in the old school. At this point we could well find that these recommendations turn out to be strikingly nonradical.

In the first place this plan largely, but intentionally, ignores the informal education of the learner through which he develops his general attitudes, his philosophy, and his style of life. Illich favors the pluralism that will result from this approach. However, since the old system has worked its woe on people for so long they have become hapless partners in this "global degradation and modernized misery" that Illich refers to as man's present condition. The street academies and independent schools have often confronted this problem of sending their youth to be skill-trained by someone who is receptive to the idea of finding a niche in the system. The street academies who aim at broadside reform as Illich hopes for also intervene into the students' informal education much as the social reconstructionists urge. Determining how much they are going to behave as social reconstructionists versus how much restrained freedom they will allow (to the point of not intervening if the youngster chooses wrongly) is a fundamental problem of the deschooled society.

If the leaders of the independent schools conclude that a sick system cannot entirely cure itself, they raise another moral issue with the skills bank. In actual practice it can easily work out that the teachers at the independent school are inculcating ideas in a manner not wholly different from those older-fashioned perpetrators of mindless patriotism. Of course, the new values they are pushing are directly at odds with those older beliefs. Yet at the same time they are using as skills teachers people who may not agree with the philosophy of the reconstructed school. Unless these schools incorporate the independent skills of teachers working outside the schools into the whole picture of the school, they will leave themselves open to the charge of exploiting. One explanation, unsaid, but often inescapable, is that the school has given up on the older generation and is devoting itself to the liberation of the younger, purer generation. Usually, this paradox is not lost on that younger generation and an ethical crisis results. A more responsible alternative is to, in fact, incorporate the older people into the affairs of the schools. This does not have a lot of appeal because it slows the progress to the newer society, but it does enable students to get a more honest picture of the conflicts they are about to meet as young adults.

Because it is so new, the interactionist model is not as clearly defined as the other three. However, the fact that it is such a swirling mass of paradoxes and uncertainties does not make it any less significant. By no means does that mean that we as educators should wait and see how it works itself out before giving it formal consideration. The problems of the other three models and the urgency for solution compel us to attend to every detail of the radical critique and the radical recommendations. We must do so immediately and without prejudice in order to help clarify what we do in schools and what is possible in schools.

Social/Psychological Ramifications

The psychological elements of interactional education that are of most relevance for the teacher are: self-concept, group and teacher/pupil interaction, and attitudes and values. Although the topics will be dealt with separately there is a clear interrelationship among them. Again it must be stressed that while these topics may be of concern to some teachers within any of the models, they are certainly held in highest esteem by the interactionist.

Self-Concept. It is evident that one who engages in interaction with others as a means of bringing about change will need to be a confident, positive, individual. Listen to this first grader: "See what I can do. I can run and jump. I look good. I feel good. There is nothing wrong with me." One would assume that this first grader has a positive self-concept. The self-concept is the impression one has of his physical self, his mental self, his emotional self, and his social self. It is the way in which the individual views himself. Jersild says,

> The self includes, among other things, a system of ideas, attitudes, values, and commitments. The self is a person's total subjective environment; it is the distinctive center of experience and significance. The self constitutes a person's inner world as distinguished from the outer world consisting of all other people and things. (Jersild, 1952, p. 8)

Thus, the interactionist emphasizes more than the other models the importance of self-image in one's cognitive and affective learning. Teacher self-concept is as relevant to the success of the teaching act as is the child's self-concept. Rogers states,

> Learning will be facilitated, it would seem, if the teacher is congruent. This involves the teacher's being the person that he is, and being openly aware of the attitudes he holds. It means that he feels acceptant toward his own real feelings. Thus he becomes a real person in the relationships with his students. (C. R. Rogers, *On Becoming A Person*, 1961, p. 287)

Failure to measure up to cultural expectations seems to produce low self-esteem. A high school dropout says, "I really haven't done anything, but I would be somebody anyway if I had finished high school." Another one says, "I am seventeen and in the tenth grade, and I still don't read good. And when you can't read, you soon get discouraged." (Bowman, 1966, pp. 83–84)

There is nothing inherently wrong with not finishing high school; thousands of people, down through the centuries and in other parts of the world today, have not finished high school and could not, or cannot, read. But this boy feels personally inadequate because of his failure—"I haven't done anything." In the cultural setting in which he lives, these demonstrations of skill are deemed important. Because he cannot provide this demonstration of knowledge and skill, the student feels less than adequate as a person.

Unfortunately, the example cited is not an isolated one. Many people feel inadequate because of academic failure and many others feel inadequate socially or in terms of physical appearance or accomplishment. The base for inadequacy is the comparison between the cultural standard that surrounds the individual and his own estimate of how well he measures up. It is clear that either the cultural standard or the individual's estimate could be changed to bring about a more positive self-concept. It also seems evident that the individual estimate might be easier to change on a short-range basis whereas the cultural standard of a large group would shift more slowly. Let us examine one specific instance in which a researcher tried to deal with the negative self-concept of a minority group.

TEACHING APPLICATION
In his study of the Passamaquoddy Indian children, Pecoraro reports,

Substantial evidence exists concerning the attitudes and personalities of school-age youngsters living on the Pleasant Point and Peter Dana Point Indian Reservations (Maine). This evidence indicates a high incidence of a negative self-image and anticipated rejection and failure on the part of the Passamaquoddy youngsters. (Pecoraro, 1971, p. 5)

Because of this evidence, Pecoraro decided to do a study that would hopefully improve the self-concept of the Indian child and present information to the white youngsters with whom they associated that would lessen their prejudice. He was really trying to deal with the two variables mentioned earlier: the cultural setting and the individual's assessment of himself. Pecoraro compared fourth, fifth, and sixth grades of Indian and non-Indian groups and had experimental and control groups of both groups at all three levels. The experimental treatment consisted of a series of specially prepared lessons on Indian history and culture. The concepts around which the lessons were built were the following: Arts and Crafts, The Reservation, Children, History and Culture, Employment, Successful Indians.

The major influence in deciding what areas to concentrate upon in the developing of lessons was the concern for the negative self-image of the Indians. Various Indians on the two reservations at Peter Dana Point and Pleasant Point were consulted to see which areas they felt should be emphasized in the lessons. In addition, the Indian Governors and the tribal council gave advice to the direction of the special lessons (Pecoraro, 1971, p. 27). Slide/tapes and 8 m.m. sound films were the primary teaching tools. The description of the film dealing with the processing of an ash tree might be of interest. Ash Pounding: This ancient skill is well described in this film. The hours of work needed to obtain the thin layers of ash necessary for making baskets is graphically depicted. Also shown is the new machine developed by the extension division of the University of Maine, which eliminates much of the backbreaking work and encourages an expansion of the art of basket making (Pecoraro, 1971, p. 30).

Overall the attitudes of the Indians and non-Indians in the experimental groups did become more positive. The Indian community also reacted positively to this educational effort.

Developing materials of this kind is needed, but it requires much more than wishful thinking or half-hearted effort. The fact is that the development of the materials referred to here required nearly a year of work for two men and involved driving many miles, often at night, over the Maine winter roads. The pictures and tapes were all developed by Pecoraro with the assistance of Edward DiCenso, an art consultant in the Maine State Department of Education. The tapes and slides had to be synchronized and organized in such a way that many teachers could use them with ease. The tapes required direct work with Indian groups, because they participated in the recordings. Helping students develop a positive self-image requires commitment to the individuals with whom you work and a sensitivity to their feelings.

In the classroom, teachers need group assessment tools that will give them some notion of the students' self-concept. In order to find out how children felt about themselves, a "Smiling Faces" test was used. The students who took the test were pre-first, first, and second-grade children. The children had only to mark the face with a crayon while the teacher read the word. Examples were done on the board before the individual children marked their tests. The self-image test was used before and after a summer program that involved sports such as swimming, health-care training, reading, and language arts, including many oral presentations by the children. Many field trips and direct experiences in the community were also a part of the emphasis on a positive self-concept. It was interesting to see the self-image improve as a result of attention to all details. The students did show significant improvement in self-concept as a result of this special treatment. Do you think Molly and her peers were in a classroom situation that would foster the development of a positive self-concept?

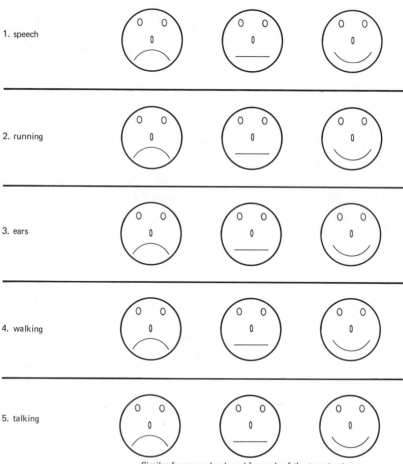

Similar faces are developed for each of the twenty stems.

FIGURE 5–3. (Copyright 1972 by Martha Tyler John)

HOW I FEEL ABOUT MYSELF AND MY BODY

(☹) I don't like it at all and I wish it could be changed.

(😐) I have no special feelings about it one way or the other.

(🙂) I am completely satisfied and I would not change it if I could.

1. speech	11. health
2. running	12. eating
3. ears	13. myself
4. walking	14. how I say things
5. talking	15. my skills at sports
6. looks	16. how I do things
7. height	17. how other people like me
8. arms	18. my memory
9. eyes	19. how I work
10. legs	20. my work in school

GROUP INTERACTION

If one is to be an agent of change, he must be able to interact effectively with other people. Most of us like to work with others and share our ideas, at least part of the time.

Here are some ideas that will improve social-interaction within your class.

1. Each person should be involved in the planning process.
2. Groups are more successful if they reach decisions by consensus rather than "voting down" the minority.
3. It will greatly facilitate the planning if members "listen to" each other carefully.
4. Each member should support the group decisions and the project will be accomplished much more readily.

Rogers suggests that interaction will facilitate inner freedom if the following conditions are part of the setting:

A. confrontation with a real problem,
B. trust in the human organism,
C. genuineness in the teacher,

D. acceptance,

E. empathy,

F. resources.

(Rogers, 1969, p. 32)

Regarding these factors, teachers should consider the links between variables that contribute to student social interaction (Figure 5–4).

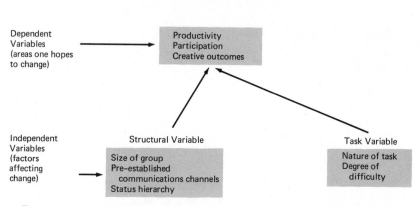

FIGURE 5–4. (Adaptation of a design by Krech, Crutchfield, and Ballachey, *Individual in Society*, 1963)

The dependent variable is the area one wishes to change (usually increase or improve) and the independent variables are the manipulatable items that may affect the dependent variable. In considering the structural variable (1) the size of the group can be varied. Usually small groups of between five and seven can communicate more readily than large groups. (2) By using a sociometric measure, the preexisting status hierarchy and communication channels can be determined. A knowledge of the hierarchy will enable the teacher (a) to form subgroups that will be compatible, (b) to locate isolated students in order to plan assistance for the loners so that they may achieve some degree of recognition and a feeling of belonging.

Consider the task variable. It is essential that the teacher understand the nature of the task and the problem demands in terms of the time requirements and talents. Heterogeneous grouping is usually advised for tapping different capabilities. It is also important that the teacher know how difficult the task is. Any skills or new concepts needed should be provided for in a systematic fashion. Multiple resources, books, media, and direct experiences should be designed to provide an imput of information on the problem.

FORMING GROUPS IN THE CLASSROOM

In an initial assessment raise the following questions:

1. Has the class had previous group work experience?
2. Do the students have good expressive skills [verbal, (following instructions, oral reporting), writing (note taking, report writing)]?
3. Are the students individually self-directive?

You can gather information that will give you directions for beginning group work in your classroom by observing the students carefully in a variety of settings and by looking at their classwork individually before placing them in groups.

For very young children the teacher should begin with the total class involvement in planning a project. Dramatization, construction, and sequencing the events in a story, or making a bulletin board together will provide a focus for group planning. Making choices can be a part of the student's learned social skills. Selecting pictures that best represent a concept like cooperation will require the exercise of choice. The students can suggest picture captions, decide on jobs to be done, and choose questions to ask in an interview. These are other examples of making choices as a group to solve a particular problem. The children can also learn to *contribute* to a class project. They can bring in materials, share in making a mural, suggest ideas and resource people. Total class training sessions organized to practice group planning, making choices and contributing to a large scale project will provide the basic for small group behavior that follows.

TIPS FOR THE TEACHER

1. Begin with one small group. Start with one group that works well together. Let them arrange their desks in a small circle and proceed to plan and make choices about their project. It would be a good idea for them to elect a chairman and to carry out their ideas. In this way they will have a full range of group work experience and will have encountered several of the problems in working together that will crop up again and again.

2. Use the "seed" group as leaders for other groups. Once the initial group has completed a project, the separate individuals from that group can then serve effectively as helping persons in new groups who have no experience.

3. Set some well-defined, accomplishable tasks that provide early reinforcement. If the group is getting the job done, the students will be more satisfied with the group and with their participation in it.

4. Work with each group specifically in turn. This should be done so that the students are aware of your attention and feel comfortable in knowing that your time is theirs. Sit down with them and systematically explore the "state of the project" with each group member.

5. Provide resource materials of several kinds. Media will help the intake of information sessions to be more understandable to all group members. Materials for making media aids for the group report should also be provided.

6. Discuss reporting with the students and develop suggestions for a brief, lively information sharing session.

GROUP DISCUSSION

The schools can help students understand other people better by providing opportunities for interaction in the classroom. "To the extent that our schools are instruments of a democratic society," state Postman and Weingartner (*Teaching as a Subversive Activity*, p. 1), "they must develop in the young not only an awareness of this freedom but a will to exercise it, and the intellectual power and perspective to do so effectively." Genuinely open discussions are, at times, resisted by school leaders because they threaten the belief that only teachers know the right conclusions, or because they are allegedly inefficient, and too often lead to discussion of controversial and taboo topics.

A small group discussion will be one place where students will be able to express their feelings. "In an age of increasing specialization, the social studies is perhaps the last refuge for free, open-ended discussion in which children can become aware of the ideas and feelings of others from differing backgrounds and abilities" (Levi-Strauss, 1966, p. 214). Discussions of the type Levi-Strauss speaks of would be considered nondirected or partially-directed. If there is direction it will be in terms of the process that makes the discussion most meaningful to the participants. In a discussion it is important that the participants:

1. Listen to each other's ideas and build on them.
2. Try to clearly paraphrase previously expressed ideas.
   Example:

"Well—ah—it seems to me that-the-ah, what was it he said? Oh yes, that about the temples—well, we could maybe do something like that. What I mean is—maybe we could make one-ah-a sort of temple that is."   *Poor*

"Tommy suggested that we make a temple. Maybe we could make a model of one."   *Better*

3. Try to reach agreement on important decisions. This means that all people in the group participate in discussions and "iron out" their differences.
   Example:

"We voted you down, George," would have very different results from "Why did you want to do it this way, George?"

In one discussion group of sixth-grade boys and girls, the solutions the students provided to open-ended problem stories were many and varied. One boy, Brad, kept bringing the group back to reality. Here is an example: The discussion was based on the Shaftel and Shaftel (1967) story "Finders Keepers" in which three boys wreck a boat and need to repair it. They find a wallet in the bus station. One student suggested, "He's rich—after all he's got a check for $292.00 in his wallet. He'll give us a twenty dollar reward." (They needed $19.00 to pay for damage.) Brad answered, "I don't think the man is rich; my mother's paycheck is more than that, and we are not rich." Back to the drawing board. The youngsters then tried to think of another more realistic solution to their problem. The discussion allowed the students to profit from Brad's more practical experiences and opened up many possibilities that might otherwise have remained dormant. Discussions allow children to learn from each other. They also provide the teacher with insights into the needs and interests of children.

GLASSER'S CLASSROOM MEETING

A special kind of discussion has been suggested by William Glasser (1969); it is the classroom meeting. He feels that, "To begin to be successful, children must receive at school what they lack: a good relationship with other people, both children and adults (Glasser, 1969, p. 16). A teaching strategy was designed to reduce loneliness and promote positive human interaction. There are six elements in his suggested strategy.

1. Development of a warm, positive *involvement* within the classroom group, sometimes identified as classroom climate.
2. Group must concern itself with *present behavior.*
3. The student must make a *value judgment* on his own behavior.
4. The child must *select a better course of action* from among alternatives.
5. He must make a *commitment* to put his choice in action.
6. It is important that the teacher be honest and face *nonperformance without excuse.*

In connection with the last four criteria, Glasser says:

They [the students] need teachers who will encourage them to make a value judgment of their behavior rather than preach or dictate; teachers who will help them plan behavior and who will expect a commitment from the students that they will do what they have planned. They need teachers who will not excuse them when they fail in their commitments, but who will work with them again and again as they commit and recommit until they finally learn to fulfill a commitment" (Glasser, 1969, pp. 23–24).

And what of the person who must perform this task? How can she/he continually work toward these ends? Who is this teacher?

The teacher described by Glasser and Leonard realizes that there are three kinds of classroom meetings: social-problem-solving meeting, open-ended meeting, and the educational-diagnostic meeting. The kinds of social problems one might consider include "being left out," "the individual versus the group," and "organizing for survival." (Glasser, 1969, pp. 23, 24) Some of the same social problems are dealt with in *Role Playing for Social Values* by Shaftel and Shaftel (1967). In the open-ended meeting the search for multiple solutions to students' interests is encouraged. The teacher assumes a nonjudgmental stance in these discussions. The educational-diagnostic sessions evolve directly from the content being studied. It becomes clear to the teacher or students that they are not sure of the concept or facts they are attempting to deal with. Class sharing after students have sought out information will help in an informal circle in the classroom. It is a fine place to learn to listen to the ideas of others and define and clarify your own as well. Some classrooms have been a place for informal discussion in the past. The problem has been one of balance. At one end of a continuum teachers provided information and no opportunity to reflect on—or exchange—ideas. At the other end of the continuum, the class was one long bull session, with no input of new ideas or information and no real effort to resolve issues, even on a personal basis. Glasser's classroom meeting seems to be a middle ground between these two extremes. A basic structure and the opportunity to explore other students' ideas are both incorporated in the model. Such class discussions help develop the social skills the student needs to become an effective problem solver. In adapting the classroom meeting model to the interactionist model it is important to remember that the interactionist views the world as the classroom; thus the skills suggested by Glasser must be seen as applicable to social adaptation.

ATTITUDES AND VALUES

Attitudes are learned, emotionally toned predispositions to react in a consistent way, favorable or unfavorable, toward persons, objects, situations, or ideas. An individual's attitudes are inferred and cannot be measured as directly as skills, facts and concepts. (Klausmeier and Ripple, 1971, p. 518)

Values are the standard held by individuals and groups. They help each individual "define what he believes is best for him by providing guides by which judgments of worth are made." (Douglass, 1967, p. 121) "Our values show what we tend to do with our limited time and energy." (Raths, Harmin, Simon, 1966, p. 27) Both attitudes and values are defined as having emotional overtones and as having cognitive and action components. Klausmeier and Ripple differentiate between tastes, attitudes, and values in an interesting way. Tastes are specific, temporary, external and objective; whereas values are general, permanent, and internal. For example, one might have a taste for John Denver's music, a positive attitude toward modern music, and value music as an important part of his life. Several years from now, he may have a taste for another performer and have experienced some shift in his attitude toward modern music; perhaps he now likes it less and likes folk music more. In all probability, he will still value music.

Attitudes change as society changes and values change also, albeit more slowly. It is generally recognized that schools have the responsibility of developing prosocial values, but there is no general agreement on what these values are nor how they should be taught. Should the school teach the attitudes and values of the present day or try to anticipate those of the future?

VALUE CLARIFICATION

If you are interested in helping students clarify their present values, you will need to examine your own values carefully.

It is only when teachers get their own values straightened out that they will be able to help their students sort out the confusion and conflicts that surround all of us. The clarification of values contributes deeply to a person's sense of identity and self-worth." (Simon, 1972, p. 651)*

This is readily stated, but not so readily achieved because values have one foot in the past and the other in the present, and it is sometimes very difficult to sort out the whys and the wherefores of your own value system. There seems to be an inverse relationship between the number of items you value and the amount of value or commitment one ascribes to the item. For example, there are very few items for which you would demonstrate full commitment by giving your life. There are many things you would choose or prefer. Sorting out degree of commitment is a typical value clarification procedure. Rank order preference is one of the techniques suggested by Simon. You can design any number of exercises for your class that will promote an examination of priorities.

Try a simple exercise yourself. Draw a time line and let each mark represent four years. Then, fill in the important events from your life. Now extend your time line for two more sections. What would you place on your future time line? What events would you most like to record there?

Go back over the time line you have made and analyze the recordings. Do most of your marks deal with the category of education, family events, travel, illnesses, personal accomplishments, or tragedies? You will undoubtedly accent those things that are of value to you. You will mention quantitatively more of one category than another. This will provide beginning indicators of your values.

* For information about current Values Clarification materials or nationwide training workshops, contact Values Associates, Box 43, Amherst, Massachusetts 01002.

ROLE PLAYING

To prepare students so that they can anticipate the future, a more active involvement seems in order. Role playing is dynamic and open-ended and " . . . is an inquiry process; it is practice in decision making." (Shaftel and Shaftel, 1967, p. 14) It is really practice in making decisions that involve other people, and in interacting with other people's ideas and feelings.

There is no way to remake or cultivate attitudes in one grandiose stroke; but teachers can help students to study them by providing opportunities for actually playing out their implications and effects in classroom situations. ("Introductions," Gordon, Kaplan, 1970)

The use of role-playing in the classroom has long been advocated by educators because it is one technique that allows the student to become involved in the examination of his own values and in negotiations and compromise. These are social skills that seem worth developing, indeed they seem to be sadly neglected skills.

Role playing a problem situation provides the class with a direct, immediate sample of human interaction, and develops a common experiential base for the examination of the interaction process. Together the students enact several solutions to a problem, and then can discuss, "What happened here?" The students can see the impact of their emotions on the problem solutions they have just worked out.

A complete description of role playing is provided in *Role Playing for Social Values* by Shaftel and Shaftel (1967). The role-playing methodology is carefully described, and the kinds of questions that arise in role-playing sessions are considered. It seems obvious from even the brief discussion given here that the teacher must make several decisions in conducting a role-playing session. While a game or a role-playing situation is posed as essentially value free, many values may be brought to the fore in the solutions that are suggested. In some instances this is one of the purposes of the role-playing session. Because of this, some real skill is necessary for handling complex, value-laden issues.

"When properly used, role-playing permits the kind of 'discovery' learning which occurs when individuals in groups face up to the ways they tend to solve their problems of interpersonal relations, and which occurs when, under skillful guidance, young people become conscious of their personal value system. As a result, young people are helped to develop a sensitivity to the feelings and welfare of others and to clarify their own values in terms of ethical behavior." (Shaftel and Shaftel, 1967, p. 9)

ANTICIPATING CHANGE

It is no longer sufficient for Johnny to understand the past. It is not even enough for him to understand the present, for the here and now environment will soon vanish. Johnny must learn to anticipate the directions and range of change. (Toffler, 1971, p. 403)

Role playing not only helps the student see many possible solutions to a given interpersonal problem, but it helps students to predict the consequences of a given solution. It allows the student to practice many antecedent/consequent sequences in a miniature, nonthreatening situation.

People vary widely in the amount of thought they devote to the future, as distinct from past and present . . . They also vary in how far they tend to project. Some habitually think in terms of the "deep future." (Toffler, 1971, p. 419)

The more rapid the pace of change, the more the student needs to be able to think in "long-range" terms.

As children reach the formal-operations level of thinking, they become more able to anticipate the consequences of their behavior. One way to classify consequences is in terms of the time involved in the development of the consequences: for example, (1) short-range immediate effects of an antecedent and (2) long-range consequences. A child's ability to determine the long-range consequences of an act might be termed "futuristic thinking."

In addition to looking at short- and long-range thinking, students' responses were also classified in terms of concrete or abstract responses. The examples that follow will illustrate the different response categories.

Short-Range Responses
    Concrete: "He will fall over a log."
    Abstract: "He will get hurt."
Long-Range Responses
    Concrete: "He will fall over a log and he might break a leg."
    Abstract: "He will get hurt and have to stay alone all night, and he
               will be scared."
Studies by John (1967) have considered two possibilities:
1. If children participate in role playing, they will give signifi-

cantly more long-range responses than will children who do not participate in role-playing sessions.

2. If children participate in role-playing sessions, they will give significantly more abstract responses than will children who do not participate in role-playing sessions.

The results showed that students who participated in role-playing sessions did show significantly more futuristic thinking. The children became more long range in their thinking, but they did not show a similar transition from concrete to abstract thinking.

One might infer from the findings of this research that a child is more apt to be able to solve complex problems in which one act may provide the stimulus for a chain reaction. He is also more likely to see these possibilities in advance if he actively participates in solving hypothetical problems. Since this seems to be a desirable skill, it suggests that the social studies curriculum provide more opportunities for hypothetical deductive thinking and more situations in which the child could be actively involved in such problem solving. Role playing clearly provides an opportunity for such thinking and involvement.

To be most useful, it seems that several solutions might be enacted in which one builds on the consequences of the preceding solution. This would provide the best opportunity for practice in long-range thinking. A schema that represents this idea is shown in Figure 5–5.

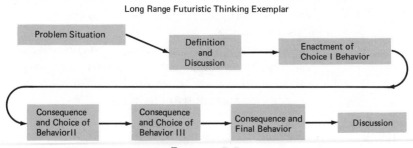

Long Range Futuristic Thinking Exemplar

FIGURE 5–5.

Utilizing the consequent build-up idea will force an extension of ideas and promote futuristic thinking. Having practiced solutions in mock situation in school, the child will then be more able to transfer this skill to real-life problem situations. "Even more important than any specific bits of advance information, however, is the habit of anticipation. This conditioned ability to look ahead plays a key role in adaptation" (Toffler, 1971, p. 419). It is certain that children must be able to adapt in a rapidly changing world. It is the responsibility of the school to help students develop the futuristic thinking processes that will make such adaptation possible.

INTERACTIONAL EDUCATION IN AMERICA
A Capsule Summary of Its Background Philosophy

WORLD-VIEW	Man not only possesses a "world-view;" he lives in it. Western and American views of life have reached a point of crisis. Present analysis exposes them as absurd, oppressive, and alienating. So uprooted, man must create an entirely new cultural home.
IMAGE OF MAN	Man grows to maturity through his relationships. While he needs the support of material goods and institutional structures, he has a greater human need for human community, self-identity, a meaning of life, and cultural roots. He is now suffering in homeless isolation.
THEORY OF KNOWLEDGE	Man "knows" experientially and dialogically. The person formulates an interpretation of his experience of reality which is as faithful to the evidence as he can make it. Truth matures through interpersonal exchanges of these interpretations— dialogue. Truth is not subjective but transjective—"between" man and his experience. It is made authentic only by living it.
VALUES	Values are: community founded on unity of differences, not uniformity; responsibility to the other; the courage to trust and enter interdependent relationships. Power and structure are not rejected but must subserve the more human values, not dominate them.
THEORY OF EDUCATION	Education, as distinct from "schooling," occurs only in genuine community and through authentic dialogue. Secondarily, its goal is the student's

self-identity. Primarily, it enables him to see beyond his present cultural limits, to reevaluate and devise better modes of life. Learning occurs only in the context of life and is complete only with its implementation into life actions.

MAN AND SOCIETY   Individuals and society are in a continuous and constantly enriching mutual interaction. Education is not confined to schools, but is a life-long experience of interacting constructively with society.

REFERENCES

ABT, CLARK C. "How To Compare Curriculum Materials." *Nation's Schools*, **86,** No. 1, (July, 1970), 21–28.

ADOLF, ROBERT. *The Grave of God.* Translated by N. D. Smith. London: Oates, 1967.

ALEXANDER, WILLIAM M. "The Junior High School: A Positive View." *NASSP Bulletin,* **49** (March, 1965), 276–285.

AMIDON, E. "Interaction Analysis Applied to Teaching." *National Association of Secondary School Principals Bulletin,* **50:** (Dec. 1966), 93–7.

ANDERSON, ROBERT H. "The Nongraded School: An Overview." *The National Elementary Principal,* **47** (Nov. 1967), 4–10.

AUSTIN, CLAIRE E. "The Relationship of Role-Playing and Futuristic Thinking with Ninth Graders." *Boston University Journal of Education,* **152,** No. 4 (April 1970).

BAHNER, JOHN M., "Grouping Within a School." *Childhood Education,* **36** (April 1960), 354–356.

BERGER, PETER, ET. AL. *The Homeless Mind.* New York: Random House, Inc., 1973.

BOWMAN, P. H. "Improving the Pupil Self-Concept." In *The Inner-City Classroom: Teacher Behavior,* edited by R. D. Strom. Columbus, Ohio: Merrill Publishing Ed., 1966.

BRAMELD, THEODORE. *Toward a Reconstructed Philosophy of Education.* New York: Holt, Rinehart, & Winston, Inc., 1956.

BROUDY, H. S., *The Real World of the Public Schools.* New York: Harcourt Brace Jovanovich, Inc., 1972.

BUBER, MARTIN, *Between Man and Man.* New York: Macmillan Publishing Co., Inc., 1965.

CULLUM, ALBERT, *Push Back The Desks.* New York: Citation Press, Inc., 1966.

COX, HARVEY. *The Secular City.* New York: Macmillan Publishing Co., Inc., 1966.

DOUGLAS, MALCOLM P. *Social Studies from Theory to Practice.* Philadelphia: J. B. Lippincott Co., 1967.

ELSILA, D., "Unionization: A Labor View." Educational Leadership, **29** (Dec. 1971), 222–49.

FRANKL, VIKTOR E. *Man's Search for Meaning.* New York: Washington Square Press, 1963.

FREIRE, PAULO. *Cultural Action for Freedom.* Cambridge, Mass., Harvard Educational Review, 1970.

————. *Pedagogy of the Oppressed.* New York: Herder and Herder, 1970.

FRIEDENBERG, EDGAR, CARL NORDSTROMAND, AND HILARY GOLD. *Society's Children: a Study of Resentment in the Secondary Schools.* New York: Random House, Inc., 1967.

FRIEDENBERG, EDGAR. *The Vanishing Adolescent.* New York: Dell Publishing Co., 1962.

FURTH, HANS G. *Piaget for Teachers.* Englewood Cliffs, N.J.: Prentice-Hall, Inc., 1970.

GETZ, H., "From Traditional to Competency—Based Teacher Education." *Phi Delta Kappa,* **54** (Jan. 1973), 300–303.

GLASSER, WILLIAM. *Schools Without Failure.* New York: Harper and Row, Publishers, 1969.

GOODMAN, PAUL. *Compulsory Mis-education and the Community of Scholars.* New York: Vintage Press, 1962.

————. *Growing Up Absurd.* New York: Random House, 1956.

————. *New Reformation: Notes of a Neolithic Conservative.* New York: Random House, 1970.

GORDON, ALICE KAPLAN. *Games for Growth.* Palo Alto, Calif.: Science Research Associates, Inc., 1970.

GREER, C. *The Great School Legend! A Revisionist Interpretation of American Public School.* New York: Basic Books, Inc., 1972.

GROSS, BEATRICE AND RONALD, (EDS.). *Radical School Reform.* New York: Simon & Schuster, 1969.

HARE, A. P., AND SLATER, P. E. (as reported in *Individual in Society,* David Krech, Richard S. Cruthfield, and Egerton L. Ballachey, eds.) New York: McGraw Hill Book Company, Inc., 1962.

ILLICH, IVAN D. *Celebration of Awareness: A call for Institutional Revolution.* New York: Anchor Books, 1971.

————. *Deschooling Society.* New York: Harper and Row, Publishers, 1970.

JERSILD, ARTHUR THOMAS. *In Search of Self: An Exploration of the Role of the School in Promoting Self-Understanding.* New York: Columbia University Press, 1952.

JOHN, MARTHA A. "The Relationship of Imitation to Children's Ideational Fluency." *Boston University Journal of Education,* **152,** No. 4 (April, 1970).

JOYCE, BRUCE, *Models of Teaching.* Englewood Cliffs, N.J. Prentice-Hall, Inc., 1972.

KARMEL, LOUIS J. "Sex Education No! Sex Information Yes!" *Phi Delta Kappan,* **52** (Oct. 1970), 95–97.

KLAUSMEIER, HERBERT J. AND RICHARD E. RIPPLE. *Learning and Human Abilities and Educational Psychology,* 3rd Ed. New York: Harper and Row, Publishers, 1971.

KOHL, HERBERT. *The Open Classroom.* New York: Random House, Inc., 1970.

KRECH, D., R. S. CRUTCHFIELD, AND E. L. BALLACHEY. *Individual in Society.* New York: McGraw-Hill Book Company, Inc., 1963.

LEFKOWITZ, L. J. "Paraprofessionals: An Administration/School Board Conspiracy?" *Phi Delta Kappan,* **54** (April, 1973), 546–548.

LEONARD, GEORGE. *Education and Ecstacy.* New York: Delta, 1968.

LÉVI-STRAUSS, CLAUDE. *The Savage Mind.* Chicago: University of Chicago Press, 1966.

MEAD, MARGARET. *Culture and Commitment: A Study in the Generational Gap.* New York: Doubleday and Company, Inc., 1970.

NOVAK, MICHAEL. *A Theology for Radical Politics.* New York; Herder & Herder, 1969.

PECORARO, JOSEPH. *The Effect of a Series of Special Lessons on Indian History and Culture Upon the Attitudes of Indian and Non-Indian Students.* Unpublished doctoral thesis. Boston University, 1971.

POSTMAN, NEIL AND CHARLES WEINGARTER. *Teaching as a Subversive Activity.* New York: Delacorte, 1969.

RATHS, LOUIS E., MERRIL HARMEN, AND SIDNEY B. SIMON. *Values and Teaching.* Columbus, Ohio: Charles E. Merrill Publishing Co., 1966.

REGAN, K., ED. *Don't Smile Until Christmas: Accounts of the First Year of Teaching.* Chicago: University of Chicago Press, 1970.

REIMER, EVERETT. *School is Dead: Alternatives in Education.* New York: Anchor Books, 1972.

ROGERS, CARL. *On Becoming A Person.* Boston: Houghton Mifflin Company, 1961.

————. *Freedom to Learn.* Columbus, Ohio: Charles E. Merrill Publishing Co., 1969.

SHAFTEL, FANNIE R. AND GEORGE SHAFTEL. *Role-playing for Social Values.* Englewood Cliffs, N.J.: Prentice-Hall, Inc., 1967.

———— AND MARTHA JOHN. "Role Playing Pilot Study." Washington, D.C.: Department of Health, Education, and Welfare, Office of Education, *Report to Stanford Research and Development Office,* 1969.

SILBERMAN, CHARLES. *Crisis in the Classroom.* Random House, Inc., 1971.

SIMON, SIDNEY. "The Teacher Education in Value Development." *Phi Delta Kappan,* **53** (June 1972), pp. 649–651.

————, LELAND HOWE, AND HOWARD KIRSCHENBAUM. *Values Clarification, A Handbook of Practical Strategies for Teachers and Students.* New York: Hart Publishing Co., 1972.

SPADY, W. G. "Authority, Conflict, and Teacher Effectiveness." *Educational Researcher* **2** (Jan. 1973), 4–11.

SUDBURY VALLEY SCHOOL. "About the Sudbury Valley School." *The Sudbury Valley School Press,* 1971.

TEIHARD DE CHARDIN, PIEIRE. *The Phenomenon of Man.* New York: Harper & Row, Publishers, 1959.

TOFFLER, ALVIN. *Future Shock*. New York: Bantam Books, 1970.

WELLS, C. E. "Will Vocational Education Survive?" *Phi Delta Kappan*, **54** (Fall, 1973), 369–370.

WOODRING, PAUL. *A Fourth of a Nation*. New York: McGraw-Hill Book Company, Inc., 1957.

CHAPTER 6
Summary

THIS text has attempted to expose you to four models of education with emphasis on the philosophical, curricular, and sociopsychological dimension of each. Historical, educational, social, and methodological examples have been utilized to illustrate, compare, and contrast each of the models from the points of view of the content, teacher, and student. Your quest as a teacher or prospective teacher is to pinpoint your philosophy of education and explore its curricular, sociopsychological ramifications.

Have you accomplished your task? Can you discuss your view of the world and the purpose of education in it? Although students learn in a variety of ways, how do you think they learn best? What do 'to learn' and 'to teach' mean to you? What values, which you hold rather high, will you be transmitting to children? If you will encourage your students to become a certain kind of person, what 'image of man' are you proposing? As suggested, throughout your reading of this text, your answers to these questions are very personal since they reflect your personality, beliefs, values, and educational identity.

Mr. & Mrs. George Smith, *The Smith Family*. Copyright Washington Star Syndicate, Inc. Reprinted by permission.

The task at hand is not to select one of these models and conform yourself to it, much like selecting a suit off the Robert Hall racks and making do, but rather to visit your private tailor and carefully select your preferred material, discuss that style and its adaptations to fit your personality and tastes, and gradually work with the tailor through a series of fittings until you have a suit made for you and you alone. This task calls for time, patience, and thoughtful choices on your part. It especially calls for a profound trust in your own intuition, your ability to follow that inner "knowing" wherever it may lead until proven different.

Needless to say, what you end up with will not be a once-and-for-all answer to your quest for a teaching style, but only an answer for today, ready and open for tomorrow's revision. You will also discover that the quest, the process, is far more valuable to you, the professional teacher, than is the answer.

COULD WE NOT HAVE A PERMANENT PHILOSOPHY OF EDUCATION?

Before sending you out on this quest, let me speak to one major complaint rumbling around inside you. Why is all this effort necessary; couldn't our educational world be made a lot simpler? Why does American education have to be such a differentiated process?

Suppose, for a moment, you were a teacher in the Soviet Union. How would you then proceed on this quest? At first glance, you may well prefer the Soviet model, for there, the heart of our problem, an articulated philosophy of education, is clearly and permanently settled.

The official philosophy of the U.S.S.R. is dialectical materialism. Unlike the United States where philosophy is a peripheral and a pluralistic topic, Russia holds its philosophy in central, national importance. All college students, for example, are required to take several courses in the theory of dialectical materialism before learning to apply its principles to their individual professions. The entire Soviet system, all political, economic, social, cultural, and educational endeavors are built upon these philosophical principles. The task of educators, then, is to develop a psychology of education and a curriculum which will apply, in an optimum manner, the theory of dialectical materialism and thereby form the "Soviet Man."

To give a comparative example, the Russian educator is not engaged, as we are, in a lengthy debate on hereditary versus environmental factors influencing intelligence. Russia's philosophy is almost totally oriented toward an environmental view of the world and therefore rules out the hereditary argument as incompatible with its basic principles. Following this lead, psychologists seriously consider only the environmental factors in their research.

Not only are there not several alternative philosophies for the Russian citizen to study and entertain, but the orthodoxy of dialectical materialism, both theoretical and applied, is carefully and continually reviewed by a central government agency. The U.S.S.R. is a huge territory, three times the size of the United States, and embraces approximately 100 different "nations" and languages. It is its philosophy, and its careful transmission through the educational system, which enables this vast land to adhere as a unit and to grow and develop. Thus its central importance!

Do not believe that there are no educational debates in Russia since, quite to the contrary, there certainly may be. However, Russia has one philosophy of reality and one philosophy of education. The range of psychological and curriculum decisions left to the teacher is quite narrow and stable when compared to our system.

In many ways this comparative example may appear highly attractive to you; it certainly was to our students when discussed in class. This single-mindedness leads to much clarity, security, and well-channelled energy in Soviet education. They do not experience the continual pendulum swing from classical to interactional and back again every decade or so.

However, you need to determine if you want to be relieved of the responsibility of choosing your own teaching style. Do you want to be free of the creativity and the pluralism of our educational programs, all in the name of simplicity and efficiency? Would you really prefer to place the good of the state above the identity of the individual (seeing yourself as one of these individuals) and capitulate the decision of what you will do in your classroom to some office in the Department of Health, Education and Welfare (HEW)? Democracy, as we have often been told, requires a heavy burden of individual involvement and responsibility. And at best, it is never neat, clear, and singular.

Becoming a person, becoming your own man or woman, is never proposed as an effortless decision, to be accomplished in an afternoon. It is granted that many of us never achieve personhood, and some never even choose to seek it as an ideal. Yet for all of this, most prefer our pluralism and our individual responsibility.

The quest we propose in this book is not unrelated to these major tasks in life—becoming a free, mature adult—since it is the road to becoming a powerful, effective teacher in the classroom as well.

THE QUEST—HOW TO PROCEED

Where to begin? Your quest need not appear overwhelming if you can be offered some practical, step-by-step guidance and assistance. Once the path has been outlined, the journey will not only seem less awesome, but your own imagination will suggest several interesting side trips over and above what we have thought of here.

LEARN TO ANALYZE THE EDUCATIONAL SETTINGS OF OTHER TEACHERS

As a first step, and as a way of encouraging your own perceptions, develop the habit of analyzing the classroom settings of other teachers you might be observing or working with. Begin with the immediate classroom as it presents itself to you. Look around and take in all that you can.

CURRICULUM PROCESS

1. In this setting, what is the role of the teacher? Who is she to the students? Can you think of a metaphor or a descriptive word such as we have used in this text to describe her function and relationship to the class: facilitator, expert, resource person, co-equal confronter, and so on?

2. What is the role of the student? What are the expectations and limits the teacher sets for them? Can you pick out a parallel metaphor or descriptive word that will describe their function and relationship to the teacher: receivers of the word, creators, individualists, technicians, obedient children, and so on?

3. How do the teacher and students interact with each other? Is the basic flow one-way or two-way . . . open ended or planned and determined? Where does the content find its source: in books, in the teacher, in the student's curiosity, in the syllabus, and so on. Once having entered the class, what patterns or "flow" does the content have and how is it finally disposed of?

4. Does the class have any interesting and significant rituals or symbols that tell you something of their educational setting? How do the students come in and go out? How does a student go about the task of going to the bathroom or visiting the library? How does he greet the teacher, principal, visitors? How is the day begun and closed? Is a ritual involved for such things as pencil sharpening, and if so, what does it tell you about the basic roles, patterns, and purposes in this classroom?

5. How would you describe the learning climate of this class? Is it

quiet, active, friendly, individually oriented, teacher dominated, task oriented, almost unstructured, enthusiastic, altering in tempo, even paced, and so on? Would you describe the atmosphere as friendly, fearful, respectful, "hard at work," personal-growth oriented, and so on?

These, and other questions you can develop on your own, will lead you to a rather insightful picture of the curriculum process of the class you are observing. Certainly, it will occur to you that much of what teacher "X" is doing, you would not do, nor even approve of in your classroom. This is to be expected, just as teacher "X" would not follow or even approve of many of the procedures you will adapt for your classroom. Each of you are your own unique persons and have your own unique approaches to education. In this light, it is important to engage your observations, not on an "approval" or "condemn" basis, but on an "understanding the other: what and why" basis. On another occasion, you may want to debate; the present objective is to learn from others. Such competitive, hostile attitudes will only cloud your observational powers.

When you have this ground picture of teacher "X's" curriculum process established, move on to the next level of analysis: the theoretical design behind the curriculum. We will treat these areas in more detail when we design your task of developing your own psychology and philosophy. For the effort of analyzing another's classroom you can only infer what teacher "X's" psychological and philosophical designs might be. If you have the opportunity to sit down and talk with this teacher, it would be invaluable. The kind of questions you might want to discuss with her (or observe and infer on your own) would be:

EDUCATIONAL PSYCHOLOGY

1. What is your theory of learning: How do children "learn" and what do you see as your function in "teaching" them?
2. How do you motivate your students to learn? Does your motivational source come from within the student, or does the class (or entire school system) have a reward system? What is it? How does it work? Does it distort the learning process at all, or insert noneducational values into the educational process?
3. How do you discipline your class? What is your standard method of "preventive discipline" in which you keep the class

coordinated as a group? How do you handle small individual problems? Major problems? Does your method of class control produce any side, educationally distracting results?

4. How is the student's work evaluated? Does the student have a clear picture of his progress? How clear a picture of his progress do you, his teacher, have? Do you experience limitations in what your method of evaluation or your evaluation data produces? Are there less desirable side effects to this system of evaluation?

PHILOSOPHY OF EDUCATION

1. What is your world view, that is, in what terms do you interpret the world and what picture of the world do you give your students?

2. What is your image of man, that is, how do you picture the ideal, mature human being, the perfect product of your educational efforts? What part does day-to-day work in the classroom play in helping your students achieve that mature status? What coordinative relationship does it have with the home, church, and other parallel institutions in developing this mature personality?

3. What is your theory of knowledge? If you and your students are basically dealing with truths, how would you define what a "truth" is and what process do you teach them to follow to arrive at this "truth"?

4. What is your value system? What values do you consider paramount, especially for your students? How do you teach these values to them? Do you teach them a process for finding or choosing their own values?

5. What, overall, would you say is the purpose or goal of education in this, your classroom? In the end, what are you trying to accomplish?

This is an outline you might use since our intentions are not to impose, or unconditionally recommend, the above observational outline, but only to "prime the pump" as you develop your own grid. Some of these questions may seem heavy and overburdensome for such an observation; others, which you will want to add, have probably been overlooked. The particular grid you develop for your analysis is important in terms of its ability to help *you* penetrate beneath the surface of your visiting observational site. We recommend the activity as a whole, both because these analyses will help you develop a facility for the process of formulating a full, integral, and practical teaching style, and because each analysis will tell you as much about your own ideas as it will of those of teacher "X."

MR. BELLUS'S CLASS:
A SHORT TEST OF THE ANALYSIS PROCESS

As a way of testing the analysis process, read through and analyze the educational style of each of these students and the educational style of Mr. Bellus himself, using the brief clues given in the dialogue. Because of the brevity of the clues, refer to our four models for "fill-in" support.

MR. BELLUS (teacher). Beginning tomorrow you will determine what you want to learn and how you will accomplish your learning. You will also determine how you are to be evaluated. Any plans you make will be fine with me as long as they do not infringe on the rights of those around you.

RONNIE. Does that mean that we can do whatever we want all day long?

MR. BELLUS. Yes, as long as you believe that you are learning from the experience.

TOM. Mr. Bellus, I need some suggestions because I'd like to learn a lot of things.

JOYCE. Well, I'll just play my guitar all day because I'm really into music and besides I need some practice.

ELIZABETH. Mr. Bellus, would it be OK if I go to gym all day because I'd like to practice my hook shots? I just made the basketball team.

MR. BELLUS. If you believe that shooting basketballs is a learning experience you need, and you are not interfering with the gym schedules of other students, you certainly may proceed.

ANDY. Well, I'm going to stay right in this classroom and continue to study the same texts that we have been studying because I want to go to college and I need a 'good' education.

BERNIE. I eventually want to work with my Dad's construction company, so I'd like to begin now by becoming an apprentice.

KAREN. I really enjoy working with technology, so I'm going to visit the media lab and set up a math, reading program with them.

RANDY. I don't like school at all, so I'm going to stay home. Is that OK, Mr. Bellus??

This example suggests the diversity of interests and goals exhibited by a group of students who have been housed together because of age. Such classrooms are in existence throughout our country. As suggested in Chapter 2, while other grouping methods are often implemented, a wide diversity of interest and learning modality is still evidenced by members of the group.

Which children would do well in *classical* experience that encourages the following interaction?

Content. Subject matter is first in importance. Consisting mostly of practical information and skill training, it is scientific and vocational in nature.

Students. Again, passive receivers. For them, education is hard work with a press to achieve in a highly competitive atmosphere. School prepares them for their adult vocational lives, but is not concerned with their emotional growth or social adjustment.

World-View. Classicists view education as the work of preparing today's students for today's world (here in the United States) both by forming in him its values and by training him for a specific occupation. In time-line interest, the essentialist is very 'now' oriented.

Which of the children would be interested in pursuing the *technological* transmission of education that encourages the following interaction?

Content. The exciting world of technology continually develops both content and methodology out of its advancing discoveries and further needs. Content is aimed at objective data and behavioral skills leading to vocational competencies.

Student. The student is technology's trainee who absorbs vast amounts of complex material and behavioral patterns, efficiently and in an unreflective manner. His new skills will be useful to the larger society in his immediate future.

World-View. The agricultural world is ancient history and the industrial world is steadily fading. The technological world is unfolding so rapidly that we are suffering from 'future shock,' yet hardly able to grasp its wonders and promises already being realized. Technological education is highly future oriented, yet a future is already present and escalating geometrically.

What kind of youngster, in what kind of situations would be most suitable for this *personalized* curriculum?

Student. Seen as a whole person, his emotional growth and social adjustment are as essential to his learning as is his intellectual development. Learning is growth.

Content. Experience is the natural teacher of the child. Subject matter arises out of the student's experiences. These are not educational in themselves, but provide the essential basis on which the student reflects, comes to understand, and thereby acquires control over them for his future advantage. Content grows organically, not logically.

World-View. To progressives, the world progresses in an evolutionary process, unfolding according to an inner pattern with each generation standing on the shoulders of the previous and enjoying a broader, more penetrating vision of reality. The present sums up the past and looks into an even better future. Each generation learns 'scientifically' by examining the evidence afresh rather than by digesting patiently the principles and conclusions of his forefathers.

Describe the child and the situation in which you would find the following *interactional* curriculum most appropriate.

Student. The student learns in his dialogical relationship with others; learning is an interdependent effort. He shares with others his perceptions of reality and listens intently as they explain their perceptions to him. Then he revises his own world-view out of what he has learned.

Content. After focusing on some aspect of our contemporary sociocultural world, the student attempts to uncover its inherent purposes and values. He critically evaluates them in the light of man's human dignity, then reorders his life according to his new perceptions. His further experiences, then, will either confirm his new perception, or lead him to further reevaluation.

World-View. The interactional educator is appreciative of history and of man's past accomplishments. Nevertheless, he feels the present impotency of man's past cultural 'homes' and sees a critical need to search and build a new cultural 'home' with new values and purposes of life. He sees education as the only sane door in this period of revolution.

But what about Mr. Bellus himself? If you were to again review the four basic models in which would you classify him?

Classical Teacher. The instructor is the *expert* who delivers this information or skill. His task is to transmit the content to the student without imposing values or opinions—just the facts! He delivers the content and trains the student to absorb it.

Technological Teacher. The human teacher steps into the background. Since the machine, the real teacher, has proven itself far more efficient and accurate in this complex task, the human teacher is "now free" to relate to the student's noneducational needs.

Personalized Teacher. He is an educational midwife, a psychologist, a methodology expert, a facilitator, and a resource person. He provides an educational environment for his student, and then serves as a resource agent.

Interactional Teacher. Carries the responsibility of creating a "community" environment for learning that has an atmosphere of interdependence and trustful dialogue. Recognizing that his experiences are more unique and his thoughts more mature, the teacher nevertheless shares and listens in the same manner as each of his students.

EXERCISES LEADING TO A FORMULATION
OF YOUR OWN EDUCATIONAL STYLE

Analyzing the teaching styles of other educators produces helpful "feedback" for you from which to gather material for your own formulation. There are other suggestions we want to offer that will also support your drawing together of this teaching style.

A. You may wish to keep an educational *journal* during your course and field experiences. This is simply a continuing commentary or educational "diary" in which you note significant ideas from class discussions, your readings and field experiences, along with your personal reactions and responses to them. If you will keep the focal question at the front of your mind: "What is my style of teaching?", fragments of your answer-preferences for this practice, reactions against that position, interest in an observed technique will continue to occur. If you keep a record of these responses as they strike you, and then reread your thoughts as they continue to develop over the months, you will find that these fragments and your reevaluations will gradually coalesce and grow in your mind, forming at least the outline of your style and philosophy of education. The *journal* is intended as a scrap book of ideas; but more than this, as a continuing dialogue with your experiences and your own responses to those experiences.

B. A series of varied field observations has proven an invaluable aid to the theory collected in this or any other book. We encourage you not only to observe all levels of education, nursery through secondary, but to sample the best of each style of education from the most regimented traditional school to the most unstructured romantic school in your area. Try to select those schools that consciously follow a particular philosophy and are fully committed to its practice. Not surprisingly, these schools will welcome visits and will even be willing to take time to talk with you and answer your questions before or after your tour. Only when the various alternative models can be seen in actual operation, can you validly evaluate both the model and your own responses toward it.

C. Another type of field experience is to serve as a teaching assistant. Different from the previous suggestion, we also encourage you to volunteer in a local school and serve on a weekly, continuing basis. While one day a week is all that can be reasonably asked, many of you will want to volunteer to assist twice a week. You will come to know your students personally and be able to develop educational roles and relationships within the teacher's program. This in-depth, continuing experience will give you many insights about your own preferred approach to teaching that will not be apparent after a single, two-hour observation.

D. Read authors who present their highly committed views of a particular style of education first-hand. Most of these books are 100 pages or less and available in paperback. Through these readings, you can analyze the author's approach to teaching in a manner very similar to analyzing another teacher's classroom style. Moreover, by comparing one author to another, you can more keenly distinguish one position from another. Since these authors write in a style that is more persuasive than objectively descriptive, you must learn to evade their persuasive influence and emotional, cloudy terms ("democracy," "freedom," "creativity," and so on) and learn to "psyche" out their basic positions. Again, our first objective in making this suggestion is to provide a forum in which you can sense your own reactions to your confrontation with each author.

The following are six books we find especially representative and appropriate:

Robert Hutchins *Higher Learning in America* (perennial)
James Conant *The American High School Today* (essentialist)
B. F. Skinner *Technology of Teaching* (technological)
John Holt *How Children Learn* (romantic)
John Dewey *Experience and Education* (social progressive)
Paulo Freire *Pedagogy of the Oppressed* (interactional)

E. The most difficult part of formulating your teaching style will be at the philosophical level. We are convinced that, although this is the most influential and critical part of a teacher's theory of education, it is also the most difficult and the last to be formulated. You will achieve your formulation of this difficult area more accurately and effectively if you first firmly anchor your sights on your particular curriculum process and technique, and then move upward toward your psychology and your philosophy. To this concern, we ask you, early in your course, to draw a schematic picture of your own idealized teacher-learner setting.

Use *T* to represent the teacher, *S* to represent each of the students, and *C* to localize the source of the content. The size of the letters will indicate their relative importance to the whole. Arrows can be used to indicate the flow of interaction through the class. You are encouraged to use your imagination, add "interest areas" or other classroom facilities you envision, and even set up a series of "phases" if you so desire. Your schematic drawing may be more elaborate versions of the ones shown in Figure 6–1.

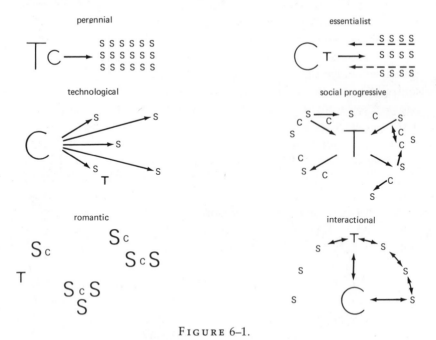

FIGURE 6–1.

Once you have completed your design, comment on the details that you could not communicate in their schematic forms, and,

further, on some of the psychological implications of your model. This task is simple enough, but it will require reflection and will significantly enlighten you on the pattern of your ideas. (Instructors are also encouraged to submit their schematic diagrams and to allow the students to compare the differences between the "ideal" and the "real" which they experience in their classrooms.)

F. Group dynamic exercises in class may help you with your formulation. Here is one example of the type of exercise we have used and do suggest.

Each of our students was first asked to take a piece of paper, blank on both sides, and to write the word "teacher" in the left-hand column. On the right-hand column, he was asked to list ten adjectives that he thought described his ideal teacher personality. Then he turned the paper over, wrote "student" on the left-hand column and again, his ten adjectives on the right side of the paper.

Next the students divided themselves into pairs. Within the pair, student "A" was to communicate to "B" his ten adjectives and the fundamental ideal of the "teacher" (and later "student") that underlay these ten words. Student "B" was to serve as an active, helpful listener, who would listen, question, clarify, probe, or summarize as he thought best, helping "A" to go beneath his ten words and into their underlying, synthetic idea. "B" was not to go into his own thought while listening to "A" but to concentrate on "A's" description and to try to fully understand it. Eye contact was considered very important. At the end of approximately ten minutes the two reversed their roles.

After "A" (and "B") clarified his fundamental picture of the ideal teacher and student, he was then encouraged to probe further within his own thoughts and to uncover the picture of the ideal human being implied by his student and teacher images. What is the "image of man" he holds in his mind and which gives hidden but powerful direction and modeling power in his style of teaching? Through this enactment, the student can move from the particular to his basic philosophical anthropology.

THE FORMULATION OF THE TEACHING STYLE

Begin with the principles of your philosophy, then work back through the psychology and finally apply these principles in the curriculum process and content, following the pattern used in the book's presentation. You may find the inductive process (from application to theory) more suitable, retracing your own steps from the curriculum design, to the supportive psychology, and concluding by revealing the underlying philosophy of life which gives an integrative and purposeful intent to the first two areas.

You may wish to begin with your schematic design and continue by asking yourself questions similar to those that you used to analyze the teaching style of other teachers, student role, and learning environment. Since we have enumerated them earlier we will not repeat them here.

Next you should move on to work out of this classroom image and begin to formulate the psychological principles and theories you will employ to achieve this classroom interaction.

What learning theory will you adopt? What is to be the design of motivation with its reward system in your class? How is discipline and how are class decisions to be implemented? Will there be a technique of group process employed and what will be the psychological patterns of interaction between you as teacher and your students as personalities? What will its limits be? To what degree does personal development and maturation enter into your responsibility within the classroom and the design of your teaching style? To that degree, what theory of growth and development is to be followed?

Once you have arrived at your base philosophy, it would be better for you to describe your outlook, principles, and values in your own terms. These are usually too personal to be contained in a preset outline and such a straight-jacketed form usually does more to hinder communication than to assist it. But if you were to ask for some guidelines or springboards on which to develop your formulation, the following outline and groups of questions might be of assistance.

A. Your ontology or world-view: Is the teacher, in your style, basically liberal or conservative in his outlook on life? In what sense? Is he inclined toward the practical or the academic, to the democratic or the authoritarian attitude, to be competitive or cooperative, socially minded or individually minded in the main? Is his basic attitude toward life aggressive, benign, materialistic, success-oriented, idealistic, disciplined, personalistic, and so on? What does "success" mean to him? What relationship does he see needed and what is his "utopian" vision? What is his goal in life? To what extent does he see himself communicating this view of life to his students?

B. Your philosophical anthropology or image of man: How would you describe an "educated man?" What kind of human being are you intending to create in your students? Do you see yourself as a model of this idealized or mature personality or will you hold historic or nationally prominent figures up before the class as models? What are the student's duties, degrees of freedom, responsibilities, privileges in your classroom? (Refer back to the "ten adjectives" for "teacher" and "student" exercise for further leads to this image of man.)

C. Your epistemology or theory of knowledge: What characteristic body of knowledge makes up "truth" for you: scientific facts, philosophical concepts, intuitional perceptions, religious beliefs, and so on? How does one arrive at truth: through experimentation, argumentation and reason, intuition, or in what manner and process? How does a good student "think?" Does the content of your classroom favor any one area over others: science, humanities, social sciences? Where does it stand in its preference between content and process?

D. Your value theory: Do you think children should go to school? What values are of primary importance to you? What type of behavior would you consider optimum in your class? What attitudes would you foster in your students? What behavior would you reward and what behavior would you punish or ignore? What kind of student is characterized as "good?" Do values have an open place in the curriculum? Are they legitimate topics for discussion? In your mind, are there absolute values or are all values subjective and/or relative? How does one find his values? What are the relative rights of parents, school, and state in forming values in the child?

These questions are not intended to be answered or even approached one by one, but are only provided as some of the questions you might deal with as you seek to uncover the underlying principles and life views that give body and integrity to your classroom teaching styles and thereby make up your philosophy of education. In the final analysis, you should be able to say what you think is the purpose and the goal of a good education for the child; the end to which you feel all the forces of education—teachers, institutions, texts, supportive staff—should be oriented. Of course, recognizing the multiplicity of professionals with the multiplicity of goals, the question is hypothetical. We will never have a singular purpose of education, but it is a recognition of the purpose of *this one teacher, clearly formulated and intended!*

PROBLEMS IN THE POSSESSION
OF A FORMULATED TEACHING STYLE

Of the several problems that can be encountered in this quest, three are briefly commented upon: the problems of *permanence, compromise,* and *integrity.*

Permanence. Many students may suspect that the formulation of a philosophy of education is threatening if not counterproductive to good teaching. A teaching style as a classroom strategy is inviting, and the tentative selection of suitable psychological theories to support these various strategies is tolerable. But the definition of a "philosophy" sounds terribly permanent and overbearing. The student may feel he is locking himself into a creed or categorizing himself for life. Rather than become static, he prefers to shy away from the entire project, at least for now.

This reaction stems from our American tendency to prefer action and dynamics to theory and static permanence, yet such a dichotomy need not exist at all. A more valid view is to see it as a growth pattern, a dialectic between thought and action, reflection which leads to future, intended, and calculated action, lending itself to a more penetrating reflection, continuing back and forth. The more one reflects and "intends" his actions, the more effective and powerful his actions will be. The more he implements and acts upon his reflections, sensing their power, and weaknesses, accuracy and inefficiency, the more realistically is he able to review and reflect upon their improvement.

We are not suggesting a permanent, once-and-for-all statement about the student's theoretical principles of teaching, to be set down in an historic permanence and adhered to from this day forth. Quite the contrary, we are encouraging the first step in what will be a continuing conversation within the teacher between his practice and his intentional theory, the one continually modifying and developing the other. Hopefully, the conversation will never end, but as it continues, the power and effectiveness of the teacher as "teacher" should increase geometrically over the years with his profession.

So have no fear that this present formulation is "locking you in" to a commitment; on the contrary, we hope it is unlocking you and opening you to a variety of alternatives in both theory and practice.

Compromise. A second problem is suggested by the earlier classroom conversation with Mr. Bellus. We are concentrating on the teaching style of one teacher. But within his classroom there will be a variety of needs and "styles" called for. An inner-city school will have an entirely different need-system from that of an upper-middle income suburb or a private school for the wealthy. A biology class will call for a different approach from that of a creative composition course. A special education class will differ from the regular class, and so on. More than this, no two classes will be alike even within the same system; if students have unique personalities, so do entire classes. Does this factor not call for a compromise of principles on the part of the teacher?

Another side to this problem presents this question: I'm an "open classroom" oriented teacher, yet my entire school is traditional. What am I to do? Should I "compromise" my principles?

If we have successfully described a teaching style as an orientation rather than as a locked-in-stance, and if, as a result of these discussions the teacher is rather confident of her own "teacher" identity, the above circumstances need not present a problem. The teacher must meet the class where it is and in terms of its outlook and needs. To some degree, she may organize and draw them closer to her persuasion as a learning process; to some degree, she will recognize and take advantage of their orientation toward learning. She as a person and as "teacher" will sense all the parameters of the situation and relate to them as persons and as "students." The direction of the class is obviously her responsibility, at least in the first instance; she will set the climate and direction. But from there, it is up to her skill as a teacher to relate to the existing and real variables which her students bring to the class. Again, it is the embrace of theory and practice that enables the teacher to relate and respond to these factors rather than to have a preset, trained pattern that she is required to impose on all situations, willy nilly, no matter what the variables or needs may be.

The same response should be made to the variables of the larger system. If an open classroom teacher knows his mind and his preferences, he will account for them and plan from the very beginning, that is, in his interviews for the teaching position. An interview is a two-sided affair, a "courting" between the teacher and the institution. There the teacher communicates her style and principles and learns of the style and principles of the larger school. If he finds that a cooperative and supportive relationship can be formed (not total agreement) then a "contract" can be formed. If not, it would be very unwise for both sides to enter into an agreement. Unsettling and destructive experiences can occur if a new teacher enters into a school of a distinctively foreign teaching style, for example, for an avant-garde open classroom teacher to enter a solidly classical school, and find herself a "subversive" with intent to disrupt and unhinge "the system." The thought sounds crusading and is recommended by many authors, but it is as destructive to students as it is to teachers and institutions. We can see no value and lots of disguised masochism in such crusades.

Once you enter the teaching field, you will want to think about your further development and growth as a teacher. For that reason alone, place yourself in a climate that is broadening, yet supportive, and conducive of that growth. Avoid one which will feed on your hostilities and counterproductive energies.

Integrity. One final concern or problem needs to be addressed: the "eclectic" teaching style. Do you find that some children would profit from more than one experience? Were you unable to pinpoint the *one best* environment for all children? If so do not be alarmed since relatively few children do learn well through only one educational setting. Your classroom may reflect student/teacher interactions that are drawn from all four curriculum models. Thus, your curriculum will be eclectic. Your curriculum will be as personal as was your search and reflections since it will be based on your belief and educational hypotheses as they relate to your particular classroom setting. Learning success is highly dependent on the student-teacher interaction that is determined by the personalities of each.

While there are as many teaching styles in the United States as there are teachers and educational writers, we strongly encourage the adoption of an eclectic curriculum. The eclectic curriculum will better meet the individual needs of greater numbers of children than will any one model operating exclusively of the others.

It is possible, and in many instances wise, for you to establish a curriculum that embraces each of these four models. It is, however, not feasible to combine parts of the underlying beliefs and values into a unitary and coherent philosophy. The underlying philosophies of each are often at odds with each other. The teacher's vital task is to select portions from each of the curriculum models fully cognizant of all the unseen philosophical predispositions that come with them.

Many inconsistencies in American education have resulted because of an attempt to develop an eclectic approach to both psychology and philosophy. A review of various theoretical positions might better enable you to see why it may be difficult to develop your own eclectic philosophy.

By referring to Rousseau's (1712–1778) educational plan for Émile one sees the process of education as a highly individual pursuit in which (1) the child is involved in learning as a discovery process; (2)

the child works toward tangible ends; (3) the child is to compete with no one. Immanuel Kant (1746–1827), follower of Rousseau, attempted to implement his theories.

Comenius (1592–1670) suggested an integration of subject knowledge for all. He stressed the pursuit of education for highly practical reasons. "Learning by doing," and "team teaching" were theories stressed by Comenius.

John Locke (1632–1704) stressed individual learning differences, and suggested that education should be a pleasurable experience. Thomas Hobbes (1588–1679), while stressing the belief in individuals, felt that natural laws should determine human behavior. From Benjamin Franklin (1706–1790) came the educational spirit of the middle class. He believed that education should be practical and usable. Thomas Jefferson (1743–1826) encouraged democracy through education. Horace Mann (1796–1859) and Henry Barnard (1811–1900) emphasized the need for useful study for all, and specifically education for women.

John Dewey (1859–1952) and William Kilpatrick (1871–1965) were proponents of general education for all. They coined the motto, "we learn what we live," thus suggesting that educational projects should be related to life experiences. Voluntary activity and interaction with learning were also strongly suggested by Froebel (1782–1852) who encouraged educators to make use of "play" in the learning setting. Authoritarianism and dogmatism in education were denounced by Francis Parker (1837–1902).

Educational philosphers and psychologists of contemporary society continue to debate how children learn, and what children should learn. An example of such controversy is always apparent when one mentions the topic of behavior modification. There are those of us (Skinner) who believe that schools must encourage learners to conform to societal conventions if they are to eventually function as self-fulfilling citizens, workers, and individuals. There are also those of us (Rogers) who denounce behavior modification as ludicrous and immoral. In an attempt to further explore your own thinking we invite you to read: Tyler, Conant, Greene, Bloom, and many other contemporary educators.

Your educational philosophy and psychology should be two influential factors as you attempt to develop your classroom curriculum. An example of the interrelatedness of philosophy and psychology may be seen by reviewing Frederich Perls' discussion of Gestalt psychology and Dewey's philosophical concept of education.

This concern for the totality of the child in the educational setting shows up in many contemporary curriculums.

Your role as a teacher, and the roles of your students, will begin to develop clarity as you further conceptualize your educational philosophy and psychology.

Some of you may feel that you have answered your quest. If so, we encourage you to continually explore your educational beliefs as they relate to the welfare of children.

Others of you may feel that you have only begun your pursuit. May we encourage your exploration, for the developmental lives of many children rest on your educational decisions. Perhaps the following activities will help you to continue your pursuit.

1. Interview a child; ask him/her what he learns in school, what kinds of activities he/she likes best, what he/she likes or dislikes about his teacher in terms of what she says and does, and then try to identify the teacher's dominant teaching model as described in the text.

2. Examine current textbooks in elementary and secondary education, particularly teachers' manuals in social studies, and determine which philosophy is reflected in the materials.

3. Examine activities for children (found in textbooks) to determine conflicts within models, and differences among academic subjects.

4. Cite an experience in elementary or secondary school that reflects a particular philosophical model. Identify teaching styles of college professors and try to determine which philosophical model the professor is trying to imitate. Does the teaching style differ from subject to subject; science versus literature courses. For example, does the professor impose assignments or do students select how they want to learn content, or do college students determine what it is they shall learn, etc.

5. Answer the question "What to teach?" in terms of the technological philosophy: should cognitive skills or factual knowledge be stressed for disadvantaged children? Suppose that as a beginning teacher you find yourself in a school that prides itself on having the most recent technological hardware, yet you are a firm believer in nurturing individuality: What would or should you do . . . change the orientation of the school? Apply for a transfer? What are the consequences in staying in this institution?

6. Contrast how teaching basic subjects, reading, writing, arithmetic would be taught in each of the models described in the text in terms of materials for children, behavior of children and of the teacher as well, and, finally, how the learning of these subjects would be evaluated.

As you continue to review your educational philosophy and psychology as it relates to the development, implementation, and evaluation of curriculum you will most likely realize that throughout educational history serious criticisms have been leveled against the fundamental aims and values of education.

Such concerns have been expressed throughout millions of volumes of educational literature. A pursuit of this literature has led many practitioners to evaluate existing curriculums in an attempt to develop a defensible basis for educational practice.

It is certainly obvious that attempts to closely interrelate theory and practice within a curricular setting have seen great progress in recent years. Questions such as: What is the underlying philosophy of this model? How will learning take place within this environment? are receiving a great deal of sustained attention by curriculum planners.

When given a particular educational theory or curriculum design the task of determining the inherent philosophical or psychological issues is certainly complex. To determine the interrelatedness of the model involves a great deal of time spent in reading, analyzing, evaluating, and structuring.

Philosophy of education may be pursued as philosophy of education. The same pursuit is true of educational psychology. But as they contribute to curriculum planning they must become interdependent if they are to serve as functional bases for learning.

As suggested earlier, each educator pursues such a functional base for her/himself. We have attempted to encourage and enable your pursuit. We wish you well in your continued endeavor.

REFERENCES

BARZUN, JACQUES. *Teacher in America*. Boston: Little Brown and Company, 1944.

BLOOM, BENJAMIN. *Stability and Change In Human Characteristics*. New York: John Wiley & Sons, Inc., 1964.

BROMELD, THEODORE ET AL. *Design for America.* New York: Hinds, Hayden, & Eldredge, Inc., 1945.

BRUNER, JEROME S. *The Process of Education.* Cambridge, Mass.: Harvard University Press, 1961.

BURNS, H. W. "The Logic of the Educational Implication." *Educational Theory,* **12** (Jan. 1972), 53–63.

CHARTERS, W. W. *Curriculum Construction.* New York: Macmillan Publishing Co., Inc., 1923.

COMBS, ARTHUR W. *Perceiving, Behaving, Becoming.* Washington: National Education Association, 1962.

DEWEY, JOHN. *The Child and the Curriculum.* Chicago: University of Chicago Press, 1902.

_____. *Democracy and Education.* New York: Macmillan Publishing Co., Inc. 1916.

_____. *Problems of Men.* New York: Philosophical Library, 1946.

FREUD, ANNA. *The Psychoanalytical Treatment of Children.* New York: Schocken, 1964.

GARDNER, JOHN. *Excellence: Can We Be Equal and Excellent Too?* New York: Harper and Row, Publishers, 1961.

GINZBERG, ELI. *The Negro Potential.* New York: Columbia University Press, 1956.

GOODLAD, JOHN I. *The Changing School Curriculum.* New York: Fund for the Advancement of Education, 1966.

GREENE, MAXINE. "Existential Encounters and Moral Education." In *Existential Encounters for Teachers,* edited by Maxine Greene. New York: Random House, Inc., 1967.

HANSEN, ALLEN O. *Liberalism and American Education.* New York: Macmillan Publishing Co., Inc., 1926.

KILPATRICK, WILLIAM H. "The Project Method." *Teachers College Record,* **19** (Sept. 1918), 318–334.

O'LEARY, DANIEL K. AND SUSAN G. *Classroom Management.* New York: Pergamon Press Inc., 1972.

PIAGET, JEAN. *Play, Dreams, and Imitation In Childhood.* New York: W. W. Norton & Company, Inc., 1951.

ROGERS, CARL. *Freedom To Learn.* Columbus, Ohio: Charles E. Merrill Publishers, 1969.

ROUSSEAU, JEAN-JACQUES. *Émile,* translated by Barbara Foxby. New York: E. P. Dutton & Co., Inc., 1911.

SILBERMAN, CHARLES E. "Give Slum Children a Chance: A Radical Proposal." *Harper's Magazine,* **228** (May, 1964), 37–42.

SKINNER, B. F. *The Technology of Teaching.* New York: Appleton-Century-Crofts, 1968.

_____. *Walden Two.* New York: Macmillan Publishing Co., Inc., 1948.

THAYER, V. T. *Formative Ideas In American Education.* New York: Dodd, Mead & Co., 1970.

THORNDIKE, R. L. "Pygmalion In The Classroom: A Review." *Teacher's College Record,* **70** (1969), 805–807.

TORRANCE, E. P. *Rewarding Creative Behavior: Experiments in Classroom Creativity*. Englewood Cliffs, N.J.: Prentice-Hall, Inc., 1965.

TYLER, RALPH W., ROBERT GAGNE, AND MICHAEL SCRIVEN. *Perspectives On Curriculum Evaluation*. Chicago: Rand McNally & Co., 1967.

Index